LEONARDO'S LEGACY

ALSO BY STEFAN KLEIN
The Science of Happiness
The Secret Pulse of Time

LEONARDO'S LEGACY

HOW
DA VINCI
REIMAGINED
THE WORLD

STEFAN KLEIN

TRANSLATED BY SHELLEY FRISCH

DA CAPO PRESS
A Member of the Perseus Books Group

Designed by Pauline Brown

Set in 12.5 point Arno Pro by The Perseus Books Group

Library of Congress Cataloging-in-Publication Data

Klein, Stefan, 1965–
   [Verm?chtnis, oder, Wie Leonardo die Welt neu erfand. English]
   Leonardo's legacy : how Da Vinci reimagined the world / Stefan Klein ; translated by Shelley Frisch.
      p. cm.
   Originally published: Frankfurt am Main : S. Fischer Verlag GmbH, 2008.
   Includes bibliographical references and index.
   ISBN 978-0-306-81825-7 (alk. paper)
   1. Leonardo, da Vinci, 1452–1519. 2. Artists—Italy—Biography. 3. Inventors—Italy—Biography. 4. Renaissance—Italy—Biography. I. Title. II. Title: How Da Vinci reimagined the world.
   N6923.L33K5413 2010
   709.2—dc22
   [B]

                                                                                2010000130

Published by Da Capo Press
A Member of the Perseus Books Group
www.dacapopress.com

First Da Capo Press edition 2010
First published in Germany in 2008 by S. Fischer Verlag GmbH, Frankfurt am Main

Da Capo Press books are available at special discounts for bulk purchases in the U.S. by corporations, institutions, and other organizations. For more information, please contact the Special Markets Department at the Perseus Books Group, 2300 Chestnut Street, Suite 200, Philadelphia, PA 19103, or call (800) 810-4145, ext. 5000, or e-mail special.markets@perseusbooks.com.

10 9 8 7 6 5 4 3 2 1

For Irene

CONTENTS

LEONARDO'S
LEGACY

Portrait of Leonardo

INTRODUCTION:
The Mystery of
the Ten Thousand Pages

THE YEAR WAS 1520, A young nobleman and his entourage were leaving the castle of the French king in Amboise. They crossed over the Loire, rode along the river, then headed into forests in the south. The nobleman, Francesco Melzi, had with him a piece of luggage that was not especially large, but so heavy that two men were needed to move it. Even so, Melzi did not let this chest out of his sight for a single moment during the week it took him to travel back to Italy. Once in Milan, the group headed east. After an additional day of travel, the travelers reached a plateau over the town of Vapio d'Adda at the foot of the Alps, where the young man dismounted at his family's majestic country estate. The chest was brought to an upper floor, and Melzi watched over it there for the next fifty years.

He was often visited by envoys from the ruling houses of Italy, who had heard about the unique treasure Melzi had in his possession. He sent them away. Had he served his master faithfully for more than a decade only to sell his work to the highest bidder? Leonardo da Vinci had died on May 2, 1519, at the court of François I of France, but

1

Melzi's affection for him was stronger than ever. "He was like the best of fathers to me," he had written from Amboise to Leonardo's half brothers, and vowed that "as long as I have breath in my body I will grieve for him. . . . Each of us must mourn the death of this man, because nature will never have the power to create another like him."[1]

Melzi began to sift through his inheritance. Leonardo had bequeathed him about ten thousand pages—his entire vast oeuvre apart from the paintings. The young nobleman's fortune afforded him the leisure to dedicate himself wholly to his mentor's bequest, though he soon realized that one lifetime would not be enough to put this estate in order. He hired two secretaries and tried to dictate at least some of Leonardo's ideas to them. He also painted the way the master had taught him. For guests who wanted to look rather than buy, he was happy to grant access to the inner sanctum of the villa—the room in which Leonardo had once lived and to which his creations had now returned.

Huge sheets of paper were piled up there, along with notepads smaller than the palm of the hand, notebooks bound in leather by Leonardo himself, and an immense quantity of loose papers of all sizes. These were far more than mere jottings by an extraordinary artist; they encapsulated his entire life—the unparalleled ascent of an illegitimate day laborer's son to a man courted by the rulers of Italy, who in his final years chose the friendship of the king of France, the path of a boy who had no higher education but would go down in history as the most famous painter of all time, and at the same time as a trailblazer in science. We cannot tell whether any visitor studied Melzi's collection the way it deserved to be studied; reading Leonardo's mirror writing is no easy task. But anyone who went to the effort of reading the lines from right to left, and the notebooks from back to front, could learn about Leonardo's military expeditions with the dreaded Cesare Borgia, captain general of the papal army, his adventurous escapes, and his trouble with the pope. Leonardo da Vinci had experienced successes and failures, fear for his livelihood, and boundless luxury; he had been both despised and worshiped.

His sketches offered a vision of a distant future in which people would understand the forces of nature and work with machines. There were flying machines, formidable catapults, automatons in human form, and tunneled-through mountains. Turning a single page would transport visitors to this collection to a very different, though no less fantastic, world. Leonardo used chalk and pen to draw the inside of a human heart and a fetus growing in a womb. Other drawings showed aerial views of Italian landscapes and cities—the way we might see them from an airplane today.

Melzi's collection afforded unique insights into the workings of Leonardo's mind. Ideas and dreams were laid out on paper; prophecies and a philosophy of life, theories about the origin of the world, plans for books; Leonardo had even written out shopping lists. He seems to have carried his notebooks fastened to his belt. In any case, he must have always had them with him to make sure that no idea would go unrecorded. It is rare indeed for an individual to keep such a detailed account of the dictates of his mind. Whoever understood Leonardo's notes could follow his train of thought on his flights of fancy and was privy to his doubts and contradictions. The notes document the interior monologue of a lonely man, his fear of not living up to his own expectations, and his awareness of the price of fame: "When the fig-tree stood without fruit no one looked at it. Wishing by producing this fruit to be praised by men, it was bent and broken by them."[2] The chest Melzi had brought from France offered nothing less than a glimpse inside Leonardo's brain.

But Melzi's prized possession is no longer intact. When Leonardo's star pupil died of old age in 1570, his son Orazio proved indifferent

One of the 10,000 pages: Reflections on the flight of birds to his father's passion. He let the plunderers have at the collection. The family's private tutor sent thirteen stolen volumes to the grand duke of Tuscany. A huge bundle went to a sculptor named Pompeo Leoni, who in turn tried to bring order to the chaos by attacking Leonardo's work with scissors and paste. If Leoni failed to see a connection between individual sketches on a given page, he simply cut them apart. He pasted the fragments onto sheets of paper, then bound and sold them. Leonardo's tattered and torn legacy began to sprinkle across the libraries of Europe like confetti. A large part of the legacy is gone. About half of Melzi's roughly ten thousand pages went missing. Studying the rest affords ample opportunity to admire the master's spectacular drawings, but the connections have been severed, and the spirit of Leonardo is no longer evident.

Even the plunderers did not diminish Leonardo's posthumous fame; if anything, the gaps in Leonardo's story created openings for myths. There are countless artists whose works have been preserved perfectly and are accessible to all, yet their names live on for no more than a few specialists. Leonardo, by contrast, whose works on public display number fewer than two dozen, continues to fascinate millions, half a millennium after his death.

The public is drawn to his works of art, of course, but even more to the man who created them. How could one individual fuse within himself what appeared to be knowledge of the entire world—and translate this knowledge into an unparalleled oeuvre? How was he able to create epoch-making paintings—and at the same time immerse himself in designing flying machines, robots, and all kinds of other devices and in contemplating a broad range of scientific questions? It seems miraculous that any one person could make his mark in so many areas in the course of a lifetime.

In 1550, his first biographer, the Tuscan painter and architect Giorgio Vasari, called Leonardo "divinely inspired."[3] The more time went by, the harder it was to understand how a man of the fifteenth century could have produced all these works. When the first facsimiles of Leonardo's scattered sketches were made available to the public toward the end of the nineteenth century, Leonardo's stature grew immensely, and he became the epitome of the "universal genius." Even Sigmund Freud, the father of psychoanalysis, shared the romantic sentiment that Leonardo was a man far ahead of his time: The artist, he declared, was like a man who awoke too early in the darkness, while all others were still asleep. Few admirers of the *Mona Lisa*, *The Last Supper*, and the rarely displayed drawings would disagree.

Additional documents by and about Leonardo, the son of Ser Piero from Vinci, bolstered his legendary status. His notes and the statements of contemporaries portrayed him as a highly contradictory and extravagant character. He proudly noted that in contrast to sculptors, he did not have to dirty his hands when he painted—yet he dissected dozens of decaying corpses. He upheld high moral values as a vegetarian and a pacifist—while designing weapons of mass destruction for bloodthirsty tyrants. He adopted a critical stance in matters of religion and was even called a heretic, yet his paintings suggest profound devoutness, and near the end of his life, he even joined a religious order.

While the artists of his era wore simple craftsman's garb, he dressed in a knee-length pink cloak and had jewel-studded rings on his fingers. A contemporary, Anonimo Gaddiano, reported that "his beard came down to the middle of his breast and was well-combed and curled."[4] A portrait (probably by Melzi) shows Leonardo as a man in the prime of life, with perfectly proportioned features and laugh lines at the corners of his eyes (see image at the beginning of this chapter). He was said to be extremely attractive and sophisticated, have a lovely singing voice, and play the lute. But some passages in his notes suggest that he was terribly lonely.

The fact that Leonardo made it difficult for us to understand him only heightens his allure. The more enigmatic an individual, the greater the temptation to fill in the blanks with fantasies. Leonardo leads us to indulge in dreams. Just as people who have recently fallen in love tend to see their own ideals in the object of their affections, Leonardo functions as a mirror of our own desires. We revere his greatness of mind, his success—and his immortality. In describing the lasting lure of Leonardo da Vinci, the French poet Paul Valéry wrote in 1894 that what remains of a person are the dreams we associate with his name.

But Leonardo has much more to offer us today than just a dream. The true significance of his achievements has become more fully apparent to us in recent years, now that researchers have devoted several decades to reviewing the pages and folios from Melzi's villa and reassembling the fragments of Leonardo's notebooks that were scattered throughout Europe and America. The spectacular discovery of a long-lost codex also shed new light on Leonardo's oeuvre. Leonardo is now finally taken seriously not just as an artist, but also as an explorer of our world. In recent years, experts in every conceivable field have begun to focus their interest on his sketches and writings. In the past, scholars who studied Leonardo were primarily art historians, who typically found many of his designs and ideas difficult to fathom. When heart surgeons, physicists, and engineers now look at these same projects from the perspectives of their respective fields, they are amazed at what they find.

Perspectives of these kinds form the basis for this book. It is not intended as a standard biography of a masterful artist as much as an attempt to get inside the mind of one of the most extraordinary individuals who ever lived—and to see the world through his eyes. The

unique documentation provided by his notebooks enables us to track
the development of his ideas. Nearly five hundred years after his death,
we are able for the first time to read and understand these notes as
they were conceived—and to learn from Leonardo.

His most precious legacy turns out to be neither the twenty-one
paintings nor the approximately one hundred thousand drawings and
sketches he left behind, but rather his creation of a new way of thinking,
which can serve as a source of inspiration today more than ever.

His approach enabled him to find answers in an era in which old
certainties had been thrown into question and people had to cope with
unforeseen new problems—just as we do today. Leonardo was far
more than an outstanding artist. In exploring the world around him,
he invented it anew.

THE GAZE

DARSHAN IS THE NAME INDIAN philosophy gives to visions of the divine on earth. Meeting a guru can be *darshan*, but generally it entails an encounter with an idol. Devout Hindus undertake long journeys to experience *darshan*. When they reach their destination, they wend their way through often labyrinthine temples and push past thousands of other pilgrims into a cramped, gloomy inner sanctum, where they finally see the idol with their own eyes.

I couldn't help but think of *darshan*, the destination of all pilgrimages, when I visited the Louvre to do research for this book. The trail to the *Mona Lisa* also leads through winding corridors, through the underworld. In the pyramids of the Louvre, throngs of museum visitors descend into a gigantic hall, where escalators suck in the masses and convey them back up past all manner of mezzanines and colonnades. Then they have to walk through a long gallery, past dozens of masterpieces of Italian art, each of which would merit careful examination. Even so, nearly all visitors make a beeline for their goal, guided by signs in fifteen languages.

The visage *of the* Mona Lisa

I had come to Paris because the Louvre has more paintings by Leonardo on display than anywhere else in the world. The *Mona Lisa* tempted me least of all. I felt as though I'd seen her face far too often already—on prints, posters, coffee cups, with and without a mustache. But I couldn't tear myself away from it. Out of the corner of my eye I noticed that I could have had *The Virgin of the Rocks, The Virgin and Child with St. Anne*, and *St. John the Baptist* virtually all to myself. Hardly anyone stopped to look at these important works by Leonardo.

Without giving the matter much more thought, I joined the stream of people in the center of the gallery heading into one of the largest halls of this former royal palace. It was here that Napoleon III once held his state meetings. Today a gigantic wall divides the back third of the hall; anyone who has visited a Greek Orthodox cathedral will be reminded of the ikonostasis, the flower-bedecked partition that separates the common worshipers from the sanctuary. The wall in the Louvre, though, tall and wide enough to accommodate a small apartment building, features a single display case made of bulletproof glass and an oak table about the size of an altar.

No one gets close. Upon entering the hall, people have to squeeze into a funnel-shaped cordoned area with hundreds of other visitors and hope for some of the fortunate few way up front to leave the enclosed area so that others can move up. Even when you finally make it all the way up, you are still about thirty feet from the display case, held back by two more insurmountable cordons and a row of security guards, but you can still pick out a smiling, rather full woman's face behind the glass. The second striking feature is those brightly lit hands, which the woman in the portrait holds crossed in front of her black dress. Many tourists want to capture this image with their cameras, but the guards will not hear of it. When they see flashbulbs go off, they pounce on the offenders with a cry of "No photo!" and order them to leave.

In front of the Mona Lisa

For the most part, though, the hall is absolutely silent, aside from hushed assertions in every imaginable European and Asian language that Mona Lisa is looking right at *them*, that her smile grows more intense as they stare at it. Behind me, I heard a German visitor murmur in a broad Franconian dialect that this museum was very well organized. Audio guides explain the masterpiece to tourists wearing earphones.

Awestruck visitors stand riveted in front of the display case. I suddenly had the feeling that I was experiencing something quite special as well. But why? Under normal lighting, the onlookers tend to see themselves reflected in the mirroring bulletproof glass. Only when the sun in the Parisian sky is at just the right angle over the glass ceiling can they recognize the finer points in Mona Lisa's features. A careful look reveals how painstakingly Leonardo must have calculated each individual effect in this painting. The shadow play around the eyes, for instance, is easy to discern even from a great distance, and makes the gaze of the young woman look deeply penetrating. But the elusive portrait does not yield much more even under optimal lighting conditions. The face on the painting, which is just under thirty inches high, is not even life-size, and the splendors of the landscape in the background cannot even begin to be appreciated from this distance. Even so, the *Mona Lisa* is a commanding presence in her glass case.

What makes this picture so extraordinary that it attracts more than five million visitors every year? Why did this painting, catalogued with Louvre inventory number 779, the portrait of a Florentine housewife of no more than average beauty, become the most famous artwork in the world?

The hordes in the Louvre cannot really study Leonardo's artwork; with all the pushing and shoving, they can barely catch an unhurried glimpse of it. Perhaps the effect of the pilgrimage to the *Mona Lisa* is far more direct. Anyone who has made the trip to the French capital and dealt with the escalators and the lines in the museum and finally comes face-to-face with the *Mona Lisa*, the best-known painting in the world, is witness to the fact that an original of all the *Mona Lisa*s on advertisements, postcards, and screensavers really does exist. Right there is the poplar panel that Leonardo held in his own hands. He worked on it for more than four years, then chose not to part with it for the remaining ten years of his life. The visitor to the Louvre is up close to an object that Leonardo took along on his travels from Florence to Rome, from Rome to Milan, and then to the French court. It seems beside the point that it is easier to make out the fine details of Leonardo's painting on any halfway decent print.

Darshan is not an aesthetic treat: the holy statues, which devout Hindus endure days of train travel to see, are often little more than roughly hewn stones. The Greek Orthodox never gain a full view of their miracle-working icons; a covering of hammered silver conceals the bodies of Jesus and Mary. But precisely because the devout cannot describe why the image is so compelling, it seems infinitely worthy of reverence. *Darshan* is an encounter with mystery.

The *Mona Lisa* is an attraction *because* it is the *Mona Lisa*. We are incapable of viewing this painting as just a picture. Everyone in the Louvre has heard about this lady's inscrutable smile. She sometimes looks as though she is peering down at the whole business somewhat mockingly. And the longer you gaze at her, the more you wonder why she is smiling—if she is—where she is sitting, and, above all, who she is. So many myths have sprung up around each individual enigma that the legends about the *Mona Lisa* have come to seem even more remarkable than the painting itself.

But how did the *Mona Lisa* become *the Mona Lisa*? Immersing yourself in the literature about this painting feels like roaming through a world of fantasy. One of the first—and still most impressive—of the many testaments to its magic was written by the British art critic Walter Pater in 1869, who regarded the *Mona Lisa* as the archetype of femininity, a force that preceded creation and would live well beyond it. Mona Lisa's eyelids may look "a little weary," but it is no wonder:

She is older than the rocks among which she sits;
Like the vampire,
She has been dead many times,
And learned the secrets of the grave;
And has been a diver in the deep seas,
And keeps their fallen day about her
And trafficked for strange webs with Eastern merchants;
And, as Leda, was the mother of Helen of Troy,
And, as St. Anne,
Was the mother of Mary;
And all this has been to her but as the sound of lyres and flutes,
And lives
Only in the delicacy
With which it has moulded the changing lineaments,
And tinged the eyelids and the hands[1]

Less lofty commentators have focused on finding out whose face was on the picture. There is still disagreement on this issue today. Most experts now concur with Leonardo's first biographer, Giorgio Vasari, that a Florentine woman named Lisa Gherardini posed for it. Gherardini's husband, a silk merchant named Francesco del Giocondo, probably commissioned the work to celebrate the imminent birth of their son Andrea. If that is the case, the *Mona Lisa* is the portrait of a pregnant woman.

But Leonardo never parted with this painting. And no one knows how the painting was transformed during the years Leonardo spent reworking it. Some researchers think that Leonardo kept the painting for himself because after all the changes he made, Lisa Gherardini was barely recognizable on it. The Italian literary scholar Carlo Vecce claims that the Mona Lisa we see today was a courtesan, namely Isabella Gualanda, whose clientele was drawn from the upper echelons of society while Leonardo was living in Rome. When a rich patron commissioned a portrait of this woman, the story goes, Leonardo simply recycled the unfinished painting of Lisa Gherardini. While it is certainly possible, the idea that this much-admired painting actually portrays a high-class prostitute has not been substantiated.[2] To his credit, Vecce sticks quite close to the historical sources; he is the author of the most detailed Leonardo biography to date.[3]

Lillian Schwartz, a New York artist, came up with an even bolder theory, which became the subject of a cover story in *Scientific American* in 1995.[4] Using image editing software, she concluded that Leonardo and Mona Lisa were one and the same person. As the Tuscans were fond of saying in Leonardo's era: "Every painter paints himself." And this, in Schwartz's view, is precisely what Leonardo did. When he worked on the unfinished painting for years without a sitter, he used his own face as a model.

Turin self-portrait

Schwartz conducted a computer analysis of the most famous of all of Leonardo's self-portraits, the original of which is a red chalk drawing now housed in Turin. The artist is an old man. Flowing hair and beard frame his face, which appears deeply skeptical and even a bit mocking. The corners of his mouth are turned down, and he has prominent cheekbones. His face is lined with wrinkles across his forehead, at the corners of his eyes, and the area extending from his nostrils to the outer edges of his lips. The upper lip is thin, little more than a line, as though there were no incisors beneath it. The deep-set eyes are piercing, but the barely visible pupils are not trained on the viewer; they are fixed on a point somewhere in the distance.

The expressions on these two pictures could hardly be more different. Moreover, Mona Lisa is looking to the left, and the old man to the right. But when Schwartz flipped the self-portrait and superimposed the two images, they fit exactly. The distance between the eyes, the size of the mouth, even the cheekbones of the old man and the young woman are identical. The deviations amount to less than 2 percent. And the two pictures feature the exact same prominent brow, which protrudes in a manner that is typically male. Schwartz claims that Leonardo even encrypted a clue that he was portraying himself: Along the upper edge of Mona Lisa's black bodice, the artist drew countless knotted cloverleaf patterns in a wickerwork design. The Italian word for wickerwork—*vinco*—is nearly identical to the name of Leonardo's birthplace.

Leonardo was a master of concealment; that much is certain. He loved entertaining people with fanciful tales and puzzles, and there are dozens of clever wordplays and picture puzzles tucked away in his manuscripts. Now and then he also encoded notes about his inventions and plans for the future to shield them from prying eyes. But first and foremost he sought to conceal *himself* from his fellow man. On the rare occasions that he made reference to his feelings and desires on the six thousand extant pages of his diaries, he obscured his identity by substituting animals for people, for instance, and assuming the role of a mythical figure.

Even so, art historians consider Lillian Schwartz's theory implausible. They dismiss the idea that the portrait of the *Mona Lisa* is that of Leonardo himself, and point out the lack of historical evidence for this theory. The wordplay with the knots proves nothing, they contend, and the fact that the faces fit together so well simply reflects a similarity of artistic technique.

Perhaps Schwartz was just concocting an amusing game involving a painter and his most famous model—two larger-than-life figures who make it difficult for us to distinguish reality from invention. But neither Schwartz nor her critics can explain why it is that in surveys today more than 85 percent of people, when asked to name a famous work of art, respond with the *Mona Lisa*.[5] (In second place is Van Gogh's *Sunflowers* series, named by a mere 4 percent of respondents.) In religious portraits, a story of a miracle invariably precedes veneration of a subject's artistic representation. But no one has claimed that Mona Lisa, the subject of the portrait to end all portraits, performed miracles. So it must be Leonardo's special way of painting that is responsible for the extraordinary fascination that this work of art holds for us.

THE ARTIST AS NEUROSCIENTIST

One of the first to marvel at the *Mona Lisa* was Raphael. This painter, whom we today associate primarily with lovely pictures of the Virgin Mary, must have had access to Leonardo's workshop in Florence. In any case, the Louvre has a document the size of a sheet of paper on which Raphael drew the unfinished *Mona Lisa* with quick strokes of the pen. The woman portrayed here displays the features as we know them today, but she is unsmiling. Her face seems narrower, more feminine, and younger, and there is no background landscape. This was evidently how Leonardo's painting looked in about 1504.

Raphael's impressions from Leonardo's studio were fresh in his mind when he painted the *Lady with a Unicorn* and the *Portrait of Maddalena Doni*. Both subjects are seated on a balcony in front of an open landscape. Their left shoulders are rotated toward their viewers, and

Raphael, Lady with a Unicorn

their overall pose is strikingly similar to the *Mona Lisa,* right down to the positions of their hands. (This unique pose was Leonardo's invention and is found nowhere else in the art of the period.[6]) Raphael's technique is flawless; although he was barely over twenty at the time, he was already regarded as a great master. In contrast to Mona Lisa, the fair-haired lady with the unicorn is a beauty by today's standards. If she were to step out of the picture frame and walk down the street, she would be sure to collect admiring glances.

Nonetheless, the woman with the mythical beast on her lap has never achieved worldwide fame. If you stand in front of Raphael's picture, you soon notice that this painting is far less compelling than its model. The difference goes beyond the magic of the names *Mona Lisa* and Leonardo. The lady with the unicorn is certainly beautiful and the skill of her creator estimable, but the painting fails to move us.

The effect of the *Mona Lisa* can be summed up in two words: She lives. The British art historian Martin Kemp, a Leonardo expert, has provided this apt description of how her face engages her spectators: "She reacts to us, and we cannot but react to her. Leonardo is playing upon one of our most basic human instincts—our irresistible tendency to read the facial signs of character and expression in everyone we meet. We are all intuitive physiognomists at heart. No matter how many times our expectation of character on the basis of facial signs may be proved false, we cannot stop ourselves doing it."[7]

Leonardo himself considered it his chief goal to arouse feelings in spectators. Artists, he said, are "the grandsons unto God," because they could "dismay folk by hellish fictions" if they so desired.[8] But how can a dead piece of canvas stir emotions? Leonardo contended that spectators unconsciously project themselves onto the figures on the picture, not as a mere mental exercise—or even consciously—but in a direct fashion that allows them to experience the emotions of the people on the canvas within their own bodies. Smiling and yawning are known to be contagious because we unintentionally imitate the movements of others; we can also suffer inner torment just by seeing someone wracked with pain.

Leon Battista Alberti, a guiding intellectual force in Renaissance art, had written an influential book on painting back in 1435 that urged artists to make the most of this effect. Leonardo concurred: "The painter's most important consideration is for the movement of each figure to express its state of mind—desire, disdain, anger, sympathy, and so forth. . . . Otherwise art is not good."[9] And if the work is successful, it triggers physical manifestations in the spectator: "If the picture depicts horror, fear, flight, sorrow, weeping and lament, or enjoyment, pleasure, laughter, or similar conditions, the minds of those who regard it should make their limbs move in such a way as to make the spectator feel that he is in the same situations as the figures on the picture."[10]

In the past few years, brain research has proved that this seemingly implausible idea really does hold true. Neurophysiologists have even isolated specific brain cells that enable us to empathize with other people while we observe them. Because these neurons mirror the motions of others within our own bodies, they are called mirror neurons. These neurons make our facial muscles break into a smile when we see a happy person. The brain then interprets these muscle movements as an expression of our own pleasure—and actually makes us experience good feelings.[11]

Leonardo structured his pictures accordingly nearly half a millennium ago without the benefit of these modern neuropsychological insights. "Most painters are also neurologists," explains London scientist Semir Zeki, an expert in the neurobiology of vision. "They are those who have experimented upon and, without ever realizing it, understood something about the organization of the visual brain."[12]

NOSES FROM THE CONSTRUCTION KIT

How are facial expressions and human emotions connected? Leonardo spent a great deal of time pondering this question. Only a painter who knows the subtlest variations in facial expressions can portray them convincingly enough to effect an emotional impact on the viewer.

Leonardo's notebooks feature the full spectrum of faces, in virtually every shape and expression. Vasari reports that Leonardo often followed a person around for an entire day on the street if he had a striking appearance. Thus the study of the notebooks becomes a journey through the gamut of the human countenance. There are young women and old men, with faces ranging from the aristocratic to the uncouth. We see joy, devotion, pride, and bitterness. Some heads are fully realized, with light and shadow; others are hastily sketched with just a few strokes of the pen. Still others have extremely distorted features, like caricatures, as though Leonardo was aiming to grasp certain facial expressions by exaggerating them.

Elsewhere we find a whole catalogue of human noses. Leonardo created a system to classify the many shapes of noses, from the aquiline to the bulbous: First they were sorted by basic types, such as straight or rounded, second by how they are curved, both above and below the center, and whether these curves were convex or concave—or neither. Using variables of these kinds, he explained, the painter could not only form a mental image of an unknown face, but also create new faces from a set of component parts.[13]

Above all, Leonardo wanted to know how facial expressions are formed. He dissected the heads of cadavers to expose the facial muscles and found that the lips were actually muscles that compress the mouth, while lateral muscles draw back to widen it when we laugh. He identified the cranial bones where these muscles begin and how the skin of the face alters its shape as they move. He even went so far as to ascertain the interplay of these muscles with the brain, discovering nerves that guide muscle movements and thus bring about the expression of feelings.[14]

No other artist of his era came close to penetrating this deeply into the mysteries of human nature. The knowledge Leonardo gained enabled him to juggle the features of Mona Lisa and the feelings of her viewers so masterfully. For example, the features of the young woman are not symmetrical: the left corner of her mouth is higher than the

Grotesque heads

right, and the shadow above her left eye is more pronounced. Each side conveys a different mood. If you cover the left half of Mona Lisa's face, she seems serious, but the other side displays a distinct smile.

Facial expressions often contain subtle asymmetries of this kind because the brain is divided into two hemispheres that target the two sides of the body in mirror image. The left side of the brain controls the muscles of the right side of the face, while the right side of the brain is in charge of facial expressions on the left. And because the right hemisphere is more directly responsible than its counterpart for processing emotions, feelings are usually expressed more prominently on the left side of the face. We normally fail to register this difference

because we look at faces as a whole. Experiments conducted during
the past few years have clearly established these connections.[15]

But Leonardo was keenly aware of these subtle effects, and he employed them to make Mona Lisa's face appear inscrutable by exaggerating the natural differences between the two sides of the face, thus
making the viewer wonder what the young woman might be thinking
or feeling. As Paul Ekman and J. C. Hager have demonstrated, facial
asymmetry becomes more pronounced when a person masks annoyance
with a smile or otherwise feigns feelings. What does Mona Lisa wish
to hide from us?[16]

Leonardo did all he could to heighten the mystery. Even if each side
of the face is considered independently, the lack of sharp outlines makes
it difficult to figure out what it expresses, and the transitions between
the various parts of the face and between light and shadow are blurred.
Where we expect the skin of Mona Lisa to be, we are actually seeing
only unbounded patches of color; from the red on her cheeks to the
olive-green on her chin, the shades blend without our being aware of
it. This effect, known as *sfumato*, makes us think that the face is moving
in relation to us; actually, though, it is our own gaze that does not
linger in any one place, because Leonardo does not offer it anywhere
to alight.[17]

Leonardo evidently knew which subtle deviations would convey a
very different impression. A slight modification of the area around
the mouth is enough to make a happy face look sad—and vice versa.
The Russian-American visual neuroscientist Leonid Kontsevich produced metamorphoses of this kind by placing a blurring filter of "random visual noise" over Mona Lisa's mouth on a computer monitor to
make her lips and the adjacent areas of the cheek and chin look as
though they are on a snowy television screen. Sure enough, some of
the resultant images suggest such torment that we might think Lisa

"What makes Mona Lisa smile?"

Gherardini had just spent weeks coping with devastating news.[18] That is how strongly we react to the slightest of variations when reading faces. Of course, Leonardo had already worked this blurring effect into the original painting; Kontsevich had merely to enhance it. The expression on Mona Lisa's face remains an unfathomable enigma. And because the look on another person's face automatically triggers emotions in the viewer, every encounter with this picture becomes an emotional roller coaster.

Pyramidal Law

Leonardo was able to manipulate our perceptions so brilliantly because of his unique ability to track his own. He noticed that a burning piece of wood flying through the air leaves a trail of light in the eye. His notes describe the movements of a dragonfly: "The dragonfly flies with four wings, and when the anterior are raised, the posterior are dropped."[19] Pictures taken on today's high-speed cameras prove that he was essentially correct, apart from the fact that during a dragonfly's descent, the front pair of wings is ahead of the back pair by an eightieth of a second, while the upward movement is synchronized. But who could blame Leonardo for this minor inaccuracy? It is amazing that he was able to detect the phases of wing movement with the naked eye at all. Normally we do not perceive even movements that are eight times slower—it takes humans an average of about a tenth of a second to register images.

Was Leonardo really blessed with an "inhumanly sharp eye," as British art historian Kenneth Clark claimed? Perhaps he was simply able to draw the correct inferences from minuscule distinctions. Leonardo may have noticed a tiny imbalance in the flight of the dragonfly—which in itself would be quite astonishing—and figured out its implications. His notebooks are full of reflections inspired by details other people would likely deem insignificant and ignore. Leonardo, however, refused to take anything for granted. His mind worked like that of a child seeing everything for the first time and always wondering why things are the way they are and whether it might be possible for them to be some altogether different way.

For Leonardo, seeing something with his own eyes was the starting point of all knowledge, but he did not put blind faith in his vision. Precisely because he examined everything so scrupulously, he knew how tricky human perception could be. In countless passages in his note-books he remarked that some objects simply cannot be the way they appear. The subtlest irregularities caught his eye: that we regard build-ings as bigger in the fog, that we have crisp vision in only one small area of our field of vision,[20] and that the colors at the edge of a surface are brighter and more sharply defined than in the center.[21]

An artist who understands how to portray these effects artistically can create amazingly realistic paintings. However, in order to apply the rules of optics, you first have to grasp them.[22] In Leonardo's view, "the painter who draws by practice and judgment of the eye without the use of reason is like a mirror that copies everything placed in front of it without knowledge of the same."[23]

Leonardo began experimenting with optical instruments in the very early years of his career, perhaps even during his apprenticeship to the painter Verrocchio. He designed concave mirrors and machines to pol-ish them, as well as a floodlight with a lens that clustered candlelight.[24] He spent years refining the rules of perspective, which were quite im-precise at the time; his subsequent study of spatial representation led him to the laws of optics. Using a perspectograph, Leonardo was able to establish that objects appear only half as large when they are twice as far from the viewer—which leading authorities of antiquity and even many of Leonardo's contemporaries disputed.[25]

Leonardo used the term "pyramidal law" to designate the manner in which objects appear to grow or shrink in relation to our distance from them. Light rays drawn from the eye of the viewer to the corners of an object form a pyramid. Although Leon Battista Alberti had es-tablished this fact back in 1435, he failed to recognize its broader im-plications. Leonardo realized that an immutable geometric law was at work here, namely that the apparent size of an object increases or de-creases according to its distance from the viewer. Later he applied this

Perspectograph

principle to many other problems. Numerical relations that could be sketched with a few quick strokes of the pen must have been quite an eye-opener for Leonardo, whose limited education had never allowed him to master even the basics of arithmetic, for they provided him a point of access to science that built on his extraordinary visual talent.

We find the *Mona Lisa* so riveting because it incorporated many of the optical rules Leonardo had discovered and enabled him to bring enormous depth to the picture, which can make the young woman seem like an almost incorporeal being. Viewers who focus on the background find that Lisa Gherardini is like a spectral vision floating somewhere in the ether between themselves and the infinitely distant landscape.

In the notebook now known as the Codex Leicester, Leonardo recorded not only his observations about how proportions change in relation to distance, but also how light is transformed as it passes through the atmosphere as "minute and insensible atoms" scatter it.[26] He was mistaken only in his belief that the atoms of the air itself scatter sunbeams and not only, as he thought, those of steam. To reach this conclusion, he spent years studying light diffraction during periods of haze and with various types of clouds, and even the origins of weather itself. We see the result of this research in the blue and hazy mountains behind Mona Lisa, which fade into a boundless depth.[27] Leonardo explained this effect in terms similar to the proportions described in his pyramidal law: "If one is to be five times as distant, make it five times bluer."[28] And the peaks are lighter than the valleys, because Leonardo knew that the atmosphere grows "thinner and more transparent" at higher altitudes.[29]

Still more remarkable is how the light pours over Mona Lisa's body and plays with her fingers, each of which is finely shaded like a miniature sculpture. The hands project far forward to counterbalance the landscape in the distance, which augments the painting's sense of depth. The folds of the sleeves sparkle like sunbeams on the waves of the sea. Most importantly, the illumination makes Mona Lisa appear both animated and mysterious; the distribution of light and shadow foils any attempt to construe her frame of mind. Obviously Leonardo calculated the brightness of each and every square inch of his painting to achieve a particular effect. Nevertheless, no detail seems contrived or calculated; the light that falls on the young woman appears quite natural.

IN THE LIBRARY OF HER MAJESTY

The *Mona Lisa* displays the culmination of Leonardo's optical ideas and experiments, but his sketches allow us to follow the master step by step on his path of discovery. Seventeenth-century merchants sold many of these items in Melzi's valuable collection to the British royal family; today they are in Windsor Castle. A staff member there led me into a quiet room high above the Thames, the ceiling of which was elaborately ornamented with rosettes. A frame had been set up to hold the drawings while I examined them, and I was supplied a magnifying glass and white cotton gloves (visitors are not allowed to touch the originals with bare fingers). Without further ado, the woman opened a glass case and took the first pages and a mount out of a cardboard box.

Landscapes, studies of anatomy, architecture and rocks, portraits, maps, and visions of the end of the world—the librarian had prepared a cross section of Leonardo's oeuvre, and whenever I wanted to view the next page, I gave her a sign and she placed it on the frame. Some drawings were in pen and ink, others in red chalk, coal, chalk, or a combination of media, and on nearly all of them I saw details that are not captured on even the best reproductions. These works were at my exclusive disposal for an entire day, and sometimes I got the feeling I could commune with their creator, which was a pleasant contrast to my experience with the Louvre crowds.

One of the pages, half the size of a standard sheet of paper, shows the profile of an elderly man.[30] His wrinkled face, hooked nose, jutting chin, and protruding lower lip do not lend him a handsome appearance. The old man is facing a set of light rays, which Leonardo drew as a series of straight lines. All the rays merge at one point, which is evidently the sun. The uppermost ray meets the top of the man's scalp, and the lowest touches his chin. The remaining rays illuminate his forehead, nose, and mouth, and Leonardo marked all the spots where a ray makes contact with his face with a letter in mirror writing. There was no way I could read the extensive commentary on the page, which was also in mirror image; still, I had a good idea of what Leonardo was hoping to accomplish in this drawing, namely to figure out how the brightness of each spot on the face depends on the angle at which the sunlight meets the skin. The top of the head and the chin, which the light merely grazes, have to appear darker than the base of the nose and the forehead, where the rays come straight down.

Sure enough, the comments in mirror writing describe these very connections, as I learned while reading a transcript that I came across

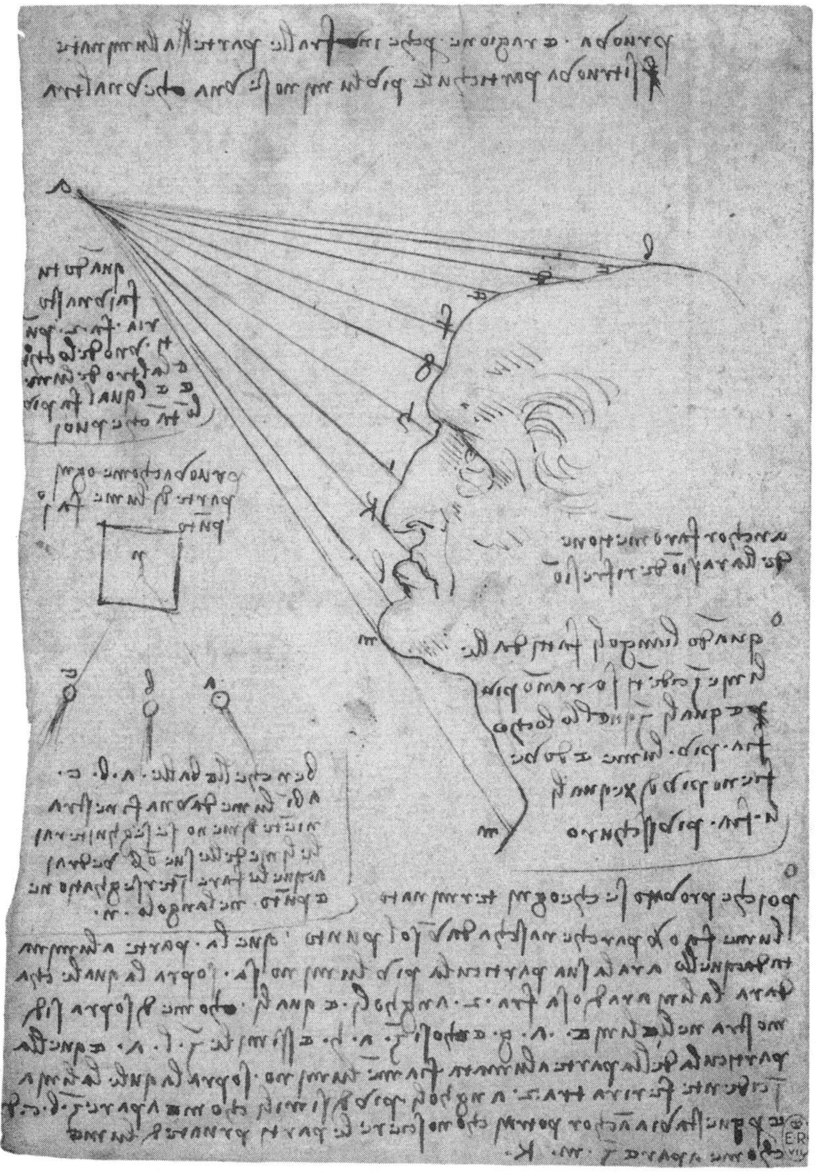

Head of a man showing how rays of light fall upon the face

later in the Berlin State Library, and the facsimiles of other notebooks housed there reveal that Leonardo spent years trying to gain a precise understanding of light and shadow and calculating degrees of brightness. One sketch in the Codex Arundel even analyzes the sun's reflection of light on waves in the water—a problem that remains one of the most challenging in computer graphics today. The *Mona Lisa* has more in common with current attempts to construct images synthetically than with the traditional painting that was standard in Leonardo's era.

We nearly always recognize computer-generated images for what they are when we encounter them in films, video games, and even in museums; by contrast, the light on Mona Lisa seems quite natural. But a closer look reveals that something is not quite right: The woman is sitting on a loggia, as the bases of the columns still visible at the corners of the picture indicate. Therefore the illumination would have to come primarily from the open side of the balcony toward the landscape, so we ought to be seeing Mona Lisa against the light. But in Leonardo's painting, she is illuminated from the front upper left corner, a direction from which a vaulted soffit ought to have cast its shadow. Leonardo, however, used the laws of optics to such perfect effect that the illusion is not conspicuous. And we are not bothered in the least by the fact that light would never really make the subtlest curves of Mona Lisa's body stand out so prominently. We simply accept that the young woman looks more real than reality itself. Leonardo did not paint this picture in accordance with reality; he created a new one—a virtual reality.

"How the Scintillation of Each Star Originates in the Eye"

Leonardo himself provided the key to the mystery of his painting with tiny picture, smaller than a passport photo, on the margin of the

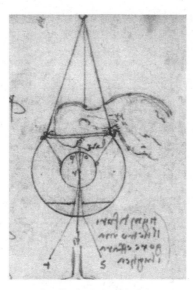

*Glass bowl as a model of the
human eye*

third page of the collection known as Notebook D, which is housed
in the Institut de France in Paris. In this picture, a man with a bare
torso is bending forward and immersing his face in a round glass bowl.
The bowl, containing a small amount of water at its base, is suspended
from two ropes. Its light rays travel across the glass of the bowl, are
refracted in the water, and then reach the man's eyes.[31]

Leonardo used this somewhat odd sketch to figure out how vision
works by scrutinizing the manner in which images enter the eye. The
candle is an example of an object that emits light. The round bowl
represents the eyeball. The light comes through the outermost layer
of the eyeball, the cornea, which in Leonardo's sketch corresponds to
the side of the glass bowl. Then the rays make a sharp bend, and just
as the lens of the eye refracts light in reality, the water on the curved
base of the bowl refracts the light. When the rays leave the lens again
in bundled form, they travel to the back of the eyeball and produce an

image on the retina. When the man holds his head into the bowl, he can observe precisely what happens in the retina of a real eye.

Now Leonardo could use this setup to conduct all kinds of experiments. What would happen, for instance, if the candle were moved farther from the bowl? How would the path of the rays change if more water were added? We do not know whether Leonardo actually carried out these experiments or whether he was using the sketch as a model to puzzle out these issues.

His earlier experiments were aimed at determining how the incidence of light alters the appearances of things—flat lighting reduces brightness, the light on remote summits is blue, and so forth. Now his investigations took an important step forward by exploring the process of seeing itself. Leonardo was on his way to understanding how our own perception determines our experience. The images we see are not simply there; they arise within the individual, in the interplay between ourselves and the world. Only someone who knows how the eye functions can understand what is seen: "The order of proving that the earth is a star. First explain the mechanism of the eye, then show how the scintillation of each star originates in the eye."[32]

Leonardo wrote these lines in 1508, the year he devised the experimental setup with the glass bowl. The *Mona Lisa* was still a work in progress, and Leonardo was now sixty-three years old. His discoveries about sight came to represent both the pinnacle and the legacy of his life as a painter and researcher. Had he not realized that a work of art is ultimately created not on the canvas, but in the eye of the viewer, he would have been incapable of producing the magical effect on viewers of the *Mona Lisa*. But to get to that point, Leonardo had spent decades studying the laws of optics. Step by step, he had to free himself from the biases of his era, conduct experiments, and make missteps, until he finally arrived at a rough idea of how images come into the head.[33]

He conducted major experiments with the camera obscura, a device that was well known to the painters of his era. Leonardo describes how he cast light on the opposite wall in dark rooms through a little hole and there saw the outside world standing on its head. These experiments brought him to the realization that the eye functions like a camera obscura. The pupil corresponds to the hole through which the light falls; the image originates on the retina. Later on, he drew a camera obscura and an eye directly on top of each other.[34] The sketch illustrates one of Leonardo's strengths—drawing parallels between the known and the unknown—to which he owed many of his most original achievements.

And the lens? Leonardo knew that glass lenses were capable of focusing light rays and concluded that the lens of the eye has no other purpose. And since he was also aware that a curved water surface refracts light, he drew water on the base of the glass bowl. Even though he did not know the laws of refraction, he was still the first to understand this principle of vision.

Almost, that is. Throughout his life, he could never get over his astonishment that man sees everything right side up even though the images in the eye ought to be upside down the way they are in the camera obscura.[35] He never realized that the inverted image later reverts in the brain.

The originality with which Leonardo applied the laws of optics and perceptive psychology explains why his *Mona Lisa* appeals to people far more than its copy, Raphael's *Lady with a Unicorn*, as a simple comparison of how the two artists painted the faces reveals. Raphael portrayed what he saw. He may have idealized the features of his model somewhat, but he did not go beyond what is immediately visible. His artistic awareness of the young woman essentially ended at the level of her skin. What might be going on behind it, let alone in the mind of a viewer, was of little interest to Raphael. Thus his painting is what it appears to be—lifeless.

Leonardo, the visionary, dug deeper. He exposed the layers beneath the facial features to understand where facial expressions originate. He wondered how an image takes shape on the retina and what feelings it arouses in the person gazing at it. And he knew how to put the knowledge he gained to artistic use. Raphael was an exceptionally gifted painter, but Leonardo probed beneath the surface.

And his intellectual curiosity did not stop at the questions that pertained directly to painting. That, too, is reflected in the *Mona Lisa*—not so much in the figure of Lisa Gherardini, but rather in the landscape behind her back, which in its way holds at least as many secrets as the disconcerting smile on the woman in the foreground.

It would appear that Walter Pater's effusive claim that the painting portrays epochs long before living memory was not so far off the mark. Still, Leonardo's prehistorical vision is reflected not in the face of the young woman, as Pater thought, but rather in "the rocks among which she sits." While painting the *Mona Lisa*, Leonardo was deeply engaged in geological studies of how mountains, rivers, and living beings originated. He regarded the constantly changing earth as a kind of organism. The extensive river landscape behind Mona Lisa appears to incorporate his theories, and perhaps we respond so powerfully to this picture because it seems to herald a very distant past. This setting would surely have looked less imposing if Leonardo had not sought to fathom the formation and fading of the earth.

The noblest aspiration of Renaissance art was to reproduce nature to perfection—to paint things precisely as they are. Leonardo broke with this endeavor. His quest to understand nature and people aimed at *recasting* reality. Accordingly, he did not adhere to a traditional sense of realism in his art, or, for that matter, in his designs of turbines, robots, and flying machines. His desire to investigate nature had originated in a pursuit of artistic perfection, but as the years went by, his intellectual quest increasingly broke away from its practical application to art and took on a life of its own. Once Leonardo started asking questions, he could not stop.

Waterfall

WATER

FOR MANY YEARS I KEPT a postcard-size pen-and-ink drawing over
my desk. From a distance all I could make out was a whirling something
that held a strange fascination for nearly everyone who came to visit
me. Only up close could they see that this odd image was actually a
torrent of water breaking through a rectangular opening in a wall and
pouring down into a pool. The stream of water is no more than a set
of curved lines that resemble a well-coiffed ponytail. Spume forms
where these lines strike the surface of the sketched water in the pool.
Little waves shoot up, break, and tumble. Around the periphery, the
water streams in large spirals. The whole pool is in a state of upheaval.

The bubbles on the water, which have combined to form rings, look
like blossoms with a funnel-shaped vortex opening out in the center—
like a chasm heading into the depths. And the surface of the water
curves to form a valley where the torrent enters the pool.

Viewers can even look right through the maelstrom, X-ray-vision-
style, and see that the current on the surface amounts to a minute por-
tion of the movement in the pool. The air bubbles and funnel are only

the external indications of a much greater turbulence below. The farther down you look, the mightier the flow becomes and the more the water spirals. A modern viewer may be reminded of the spectacular images of solar protuberances or collisions of two galaxies that astronomers are sometimes able to capture on film.

This is how Leonardo da Vinci portrayed the impact of water on water in about 1506. I had discovered the picture in a folder with cheap prints that circulated in my high school art class. The reproduction was so poor that it did not even hint at the brownish color of Leonardo's ink. The lines appeared blurred, and the explanations in mirror writing that Leonardo had inserted under his drawing were missing.

Even so, the picture held my attention. I tried to imagine where I might re-create this drama for myself. Wouldn't the same thing happen in the bathtub as the water pours in, or even in a teacup when you add milk? So many mysteries are revealed in the most mundane activities if you look carefully enough. Leonardo's drawing seemed to me the very symbol of how tiny a sliver of reality we tend to register. Standing at the edge of a basin, we may notice the waves at the surface, but we don't ponder what lies beneath.

When I was finally able to examine the original in the Royal Library at Windsor Castle, I realized that my reproduction conveyed only a rough idea of the intensity with which Leonardo saw and depicted the world. The longer I studied Leonardo's pen strokes, the more they drew me in. The lines stood out so sharply that they radiated a peculiar dynamism, as though the artist had just finished drawing them. I saw some of the very fine lines merge into what seemed like a three-dimensional image—almost like a hologram. Some currents receded into the background, while others pressed forward, forming curlicues that spiraled out toward the viewer. It seemed more and more incredible that I was looking at a flat object, a somewhat graying piece of paper mounted behind a thin pane of acrylic glass.

The drawing is a snapshot of shapes that disappear in the very next moment, never to recur in the same way. Leonardo succeeded in capturing the liveliness of inanimate nature. And yet the current is not a reflection of reality, but a fiction. Just as the *Mona Lisa* played with the laws of perception to animate the woman's face, here, too, the artist aimed higher than merely depicting the visible world; he sought to explain it.[1]

Leonardo highlighted what he considered the essential elements, emphasizing some elements and omitting others. Air bubbles on the water, for instance, never appear as perfectly round and crowded together as in this picture. Leonardo apparently believed that the raging of the water, no matter how chaotic it might appear, adheres to a mysterious order. Under the sketch of the torrent, he noted, in mirror writing, "Water entering a pool moves in three ways, and the air pushing into the water creates a fourth movement."

But how does order arise in the whirling water? Today this question would go straight to scientists, and the discipline of hydrodynamics would be there to provide an answer. In Leonardo's era, this field did not exist. No one thought of focusing on the way water flows, let alone of drawing pictures of turbulences or describing these kinds of phenomena in words. And that was only one of Leonardo's many pioneering ventures. In fields as far-flung as optics, geology, and anatomy, he was the first to describe problems that generations of researchers after him would tackle. Even more than his virtuosity with the paintbrush, it is this versatility that we admire today in Leonardo, the universal genius, the man who apparently knew, and could do, anything and everything.

His mythic status notwithstanding, experts continue to debate whether Leonardo merits the status of a scientist, let alone of the first scientist. For some, he is a true pioneer of the modern study of the world, while others consider him an outstanding artist who only dabbled in science. However, the drawing of the torrent of water reveals that art and science are far more interrelated than many believe. Both explore an unknown reality, and both attempt to make it comprehensible to man. If there is one central theme linking Leonardo's wide-ranging interests, it is water. *The Annunciation, The Virgin of the Rocks,* the *Madonna of the Yarnwinder,* the *Mona Lisa*—again and again Leonardo painted his figures in front of rivers and lakes. As an engineer he planned to redesign the major watercourses in Italy. As a naturalist he studied fossils and discovered that his homeland must once have been the bottom of a gigantic sea. In the final years of his life, he used deeply moving words and images to portray the Flood as the end of the world. The range of Leonardo's disposition and his unique way of thinking are revealed not in the *Mona Lisa* or in the *Last Supper*, but in his studies, sketches, and descriptions of water.

REMAINS OF A LOCK

During a visit to Milan, I traveled out to the elegant Brera district. My hosts had told me that a lock built by Leonardo near the San Marco Church was on display there. I spent quite a while wandering through streets lined with boutiques and bars. It was late in the afternoon, and the cars were so tightly wedged together, motors running, that I often had to squeeze sideways between the bumpers.

I tried to console myself with the thought that even Leonardo had complained about the cramped conditions in Milan (a "huge gathering of people who herd together like goats on top of one another and fill every part with their stench"). The Church of Santa Maria delle Grazie, which Leonardo was commissioned to embellish with his *Last Supper*, and the lock I was looking for were still way before the walls of the city at the beginning of the modern age. Even so, Milan was then one

Ideal city

of the most densely populated metropolises of Europe, with nearly 200,000 people crowded into a tiny area.[2] To alleviate these conditions, and presumably also to cope with the plague epidemic he experienced here in 1485, Leonardo proposed an "ideal city" with dual-level streets. The houses would have two entrances, one atop the other. The lower level would be reserved for deliveries and servants. Leonardo pictured covered carriage routes and canals on this lower tier, with a drainage system for sewage. In his vision, the bourgeoisie would go about its business in loggias and gardens on the pedestrian boulevards above this level, undisturbed by noise and stench.

I finally entered a passageway that looked quite promising, and emerged at a long plaza. It was quieter here; the sound of cars at a multi-lane intersection could be heard only at a distance. A street led down the narrow end of the square, then ended abruptly. I walked for a few feet and peered into a ditch full of brambles and willows. Here were the remains of a canal, with two rotted wooden lock gates on a brick foundation separated by exactly the length of a barge. Atop the gates, two cats were basking in the sun. Down below I saw large open wooden hatches with bolts. The bolts, hatches, and gates formed a complicated linkage system up to the banks of the canals. Evidently this device was once used to open and close the hatches. I tried it out, but the hinges were rusted solid.

According to a plaque, the canal was still navigable in 1960, then the water was rerouted to subterranean pipes. It has not been used for transportation since then—and does not begin to resemble Leonardo's vision of covered carriage routes in his ideal city. In 1497, Ludovico Sforza, the Duke of Milan, had commissioned the construction of the lock where I was standing to connect a higher Alpine canal with the waterways in the city.

A painting in the Gallery of Modern Art in Milan by a now-forgotten nineteenth-century artist named Cherubino Cornienti portrays the fictitious scene of a proud Leonardo explaining the canal to the ruler, who is standing at the edge of the lock. But not all experts are convinced that this idyll is historically accurate, and some even doubt that Leonardo designed it.

Be that as it may, there is evidence that this structure was Leonardo's only invention to have survived into our era. His notebooks contain several pages of sketches of the exact wooden hatches, bolts, and posts that the lock gate still has today. You can even make out the brick foundation and a recess in the wall of the canal into which the gate folds when open.[3] The hatches and their sophisticated mechanism were not used in any other structure during this early era of technology. Fifteenth-century locks nearly always had primitive lifting doors that needed to be pulled upward like the blade of a guillotine—there was no evidence of swinging gates, let alone recessed hatches.

The skeptics argue that the famous architectural theorist Leon Battista Alberti had described locks with swinging gates twenty years earlier,[4] and that not a single document proves that Leonardo actually directed the construction of the locks of San Marco. Perhaps, they say, he was simply copying what others had devised.[5]

Lock near the San Marco Church in Milan

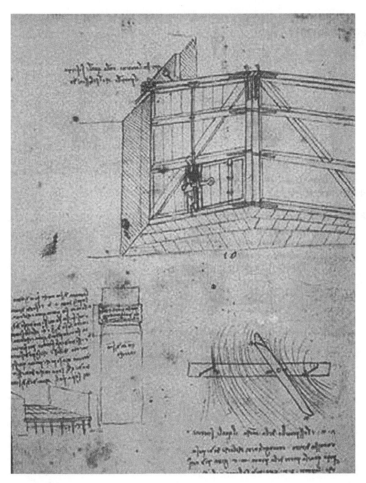

Lock gate

Most likely the dispute will never be resolved, primarily because Renaissance engineers tended to transmit their technical knowledge orally. No one knows how many ideas for the lock at San Marco were adopted from others and how many improvements Leonardo himself added. Still, Alberti provided only explanations of how to mount gates that are easy to use under hydraulic pressure, but he mentioned neither double lock gates of the kind that are standard today nor recessed hatches to equalize the pressure. And he did not describe a complete closing mechanism. All three principles, however—double doors, hatches, and closing mechanism—were used in San Marco, and it is hard to imagine that Leonardo would have drawn this lock in such detail if it had not been his own design.[6]

Whether or not he personally designed the lock at San Marco, he fully grasped the principle behind it, as the notebooks also reveal. Under a particularly exquisite drawing of the closing mechanism, Leonardo sketched the flow lines along which the water passes through the hatches into the lock chamber.[7]

Leonardo was also well aware of the challenges inherent in this construction. To avoid undercurrents, he recommended mounting the hatch not in the exact center of the lock gates, but a couple of inches away, so that the difference in pressure could interact with the closing mechanism to make the door gently swing open automatically and let in water as soon as the gate opened.[8] If, on the other hand, the water were to stream into the lock chamber too quickly, a dangerous swell of water could build up, which "would spill into the ship, fill it instantly, and sink it."[9] He also advised recessing the open gates in the wall, as was done in San Marco, to prevent eddies from forming at their edges and eroding the bank reinforcements over time.

Leonardo's extraordinary *Mona Lisa* put his years of research on the laws governing perception to optimal use. The drawings of the lock at San Marco reveal his similarly intense devotion to studying the mechanics of currents. In both cases Leonardo sought solutions to practical problems—how to create a startlingly lifelike portrait in the one instance, and how best to hoist ships in the other. Thus his studies of vortices and locks had more in common with the *Mona Lisa* than with the learned treatises of his university counterparts, who studied these issues on a purely theoretical level.

SEEKING EMPLOYMENT FROM THE TYRANT

Unlike the scholars of his era, Leonardo earned a living by promising his employers spectacular works of art and technology. His studies of hydraulic engineering were especially valuable for Milan, because the city owed its prosperity to water. The canal at San Marco, which is choked with weeds today, was then only one of many waterways in this metropolis, which bore a strong resemblance to Amsterdam or Venice. On canals that stretched across the Po Valley, ships made their way to the lakes at the foothills of the Alps or into the Mediterranean. On their return from the north, the barges transported marble for the construction of the immense cathedral.

Business in Milan textiles and weapons boomed. The success of the metalworks and textile industries was made possible by the rivers in Lombardy, because water power was the only reliable energy source. Animals and wind were too undependable, and steam engines and motors lay so far beyond the capabilities of technology that even a Leonardo could not picture them. Gristmills, saws, hydraulic presses, bellows, forge hammers—wherever there was a machine, a course of a river was sure to be nearby.[10] According to the French historian Jean Gimpel, water power was just as important to that era as oil was to the twentieth century. And the farmers in the vicinity of Milan benefited from Alpine water making the land fertile and enabling them to grow mulberry trees, which provided food for silkworms, and thus making possible a highly profitable industry.[11]

Leonardo was well aware of this when he applied for a position at the court in Milan in about 1482. We do not know exactly what made him decide, at the age of thirty, to give up his career as a freelance artist in Florence, which had begun so promisingly, and to try his luck in Milan. Perhaps he feared that his unhurried style of working would make it difficult for him to maintain his position in the highly competitive art market. In the transition period between the late medieval and the modern ages, artists were still regarded as craftsmen; just as a metalworker received money for making a railing, a painter was paid for furnishing a portrait or an altarpiece according to specified guidelines and deadlines. Leonardo often took years to complete his paintings, which made it difficult for him to live from the sale of his works.

In contrast to the situation in Florence, Milan offered Leonardo a realistic chance of finding support from a patron, namely Ludovico Sforza, one of the most elusive and unscrupulous rulers of the Renaissance. An unknown painter portrayed his face with fleshy but severe features that radiate resoluteness and self-confidence.[12] His fur hood features a golden *M*, the initial of Ludovico's epithet, *il Moro*, which can mean both "mulberry tree" and "Moor"—a reference to his dark complexion. Ludovico was the son of a mercenary leader who had staged a coup and made himself ruler. Now, Ludovico ruled Milan successfully with an iron fist. The economy flourished, and the city became a leading Italian power. A steady job at the court of il Moro would enable Leonardo to pursue his interests without having to worry about selling his artwork.

A detailed and remarkably self-assured application to il Moro spelled out in ten points what he was willing to provide in exchange for a

Ludovico Sforza, known as
il Moro—The Moor

position at the court. The first nine provided specifics of the horrific weapons and other military equipment he would construct. He wrote that he would be good at building armored cars, catapults, and bombs that would instill great fear in the enemies of his new employer and would inflict even greater damage. In the tenth point, finally, Leonardo claimed that "in time of peace" he would prove a first-rate architect and "conduct water from one place to another." Almost as an afterthought, he then offered to build a colossal bronze horse, an equestrian statue, "which shall endue with immortal glory and eternal honor the auspicious memory of the Prince your father and of the illustrious house of Sforza."[13]

Ludovico, the ragamuffin among Italian rulers, was in sore need of glorification. Although he had no right to call himself "duke," he used the title anyway. He was from a family of parvenus and had usurped his nephew's throne. Ludovico's incompetent brother, Galeazzo, was assassinated in 1476, and there is considerable evidence that il Moro had helped engineer the conspiracy from his exile in France. He proceeded

to wrest control of the government from his sister-in-law, guardian of
Galeazzo's underage son Gian Galeazzo, while she acted as regent,
and he held them both in confinement for nearly two decades. In 1494,
Gian Galeazzo, like his father, fell victim to an attempt on his life. This
time there was no doubt that Ludovico was the person responsible.

To win over the powerful families of Milan for himself, il Moro organized splendid galas; to confer legitimacy on his rule, he sought to
make Lombardy a center of intellectual life. He appointed prominent
scholars, such as Dimitrios Castrenos of Greece, to his court, and the
first Greek book—a grammar book—was printed in Milan. A court
poet named Bellincioni hailed Milan as the rebirth of ancient Greece:
"Come, I say, to today's Athens in Milan, for here is the Ludovican
Parnassus."[14]

Humanists such as Francesco Filelfo also contributed to il Moro's
intellectual propaganda. The poet wrote a *Sforziade* in the style of
Homer—an epic poem in hexameters telling the story of Ludovico's
ancestors. And the duke commissioned the preeminent architects Do-
nato Bramante and Francesco di Giorgio to design cathedrals in Milan
and Pavia.

Leonardo served as a kind of technical adviser to Sforza. A document
written in the 1490s refers to him as *Ingeniarius Ducalis* ("ducal engineer"). His duties ranged from supervising shipping routes and military
equipment to tending to the water pipes in the duchess's bathroom.
(Several of Leonardo's sketches illustrate these plumbing tasks.) He
set to work on the promised 23-foot-tall equestrian statue and organized pageants for il Moro. He was given a workshop at the palace in
Milan, the Corte Vecchia, but he was not a part of the royal household.
Hierarchically speaking, an engineer was above a painter, but still a
craftsman. He most likely ate his meals at the table for the household
staff, with the masons and gardeners, but at least he did not suffer the

same indignity as his Florentine colleague Domenico Ghirlandaio ten years earlier, whose meals consisted of his patrons' leftovers. Times were changing.

Love Nest in the Mill

The duke's pet project was a model farm named La Sforzesca (derived from his family name, Sforza) in the plain eighteen miles outside of Milan, where Ludovico installed a broad network of main and subsidiary canals to enhance rice cultivation. An inscription in Vigevano, the nearby town where Ludovico was born, hails his achievement here: "The desert waste became a green and fertile meadow; the wilderness blossomed like a rose." The ruler had built a small country palace for himself and his wife, and he enjoyed falconry. A visitor from France even wrote that life on the country estate felt like paradise.

Even so, the trip to La Sforzesca is monotonous. From the lock at San Marco you cross through Milan on streets that were once canals until you get to the spot where the water, which was routed through pipes under a fish market, reemerges from below. You then follow a waterway called the Naviglio Grande, which takes you west for an hour by car. I passed by fields and buildings that might be factories, warehouses, or shopping centers.

The model farm is now in ruins. An enormous courtyard filled with debris surrounds four towers with ramshackle stables between them. Small stone houses adjoin one of the stables, and a construction fence runs along them. During my visit, smoke was rising from one of the chimneys. I crossed a road with clattering trucks and came to a Renaissance church. It was locked. Next to it I saw another courtyard, which was part of the palace. An alarm went off as I approached the passageway, so I slipped into a bar in one of the stables, where several

La Sforzesca

men were drinking espresso laced with grappa and talking in a dialect I couldn't follow. Some of them also held liqueur glasses, and all had bad teeth. I wondered whether these people were surprised to see me, and what sort of impression the flamboyant stranger Leonardo must have made on the local farmworkers back in his day.

The barkeeper told me that people say Leonardo had spent quite a long time here and lived in the ducal palace, but he did not know many specific details.

Leonardo made several references to the model farm in his notebooks. In describing a canal construction project, he wrote: "On the second day of February, 1494, at the Sforzesca, I have drawn twenty-five steps, each of two thirds of a braccio high and eight braccia wide."[15] We are not told whether Leonardo was designing a new set of steps or merely drawing an existing one.

A later note explains how steps were used to obtain fertile land beneath the Sforzesca: "One hundred and thirty steps . . . down which the water falls . . . dried up a swamp."[16] The trick was to slow down a torrential stream by directing it over the steps. Once the water moved slowly, it no longer carried away the soil. Instead, the mud settled, and new fields formed over time. The duke's engineers, perhaps even Leonardo himself, had put nature to good use.

Leonardo also examined the gristmills in the vicinity, calculating their daily output and estimating the costs of new mills that could use water power more efficiently. He even reported the discovery of a prehistoric ship ten arm's lengths under the earth.[17]

From La Sforzesca I headed over to the Mill of Mora Bassa, which Duke Ludovico once gave to his wife, Beatrice, as a wedding present (although the barkeeper informed me that Ludovico used the mill, which was still surrounded by woods at the time, for secret trysts with his mistress, Cecilia Gallerani). The duke also commissioned Leonardo to paint Cecilia's portrait. The painting in question is the famous *Lady with an Ermine*, which now hangs in Krakow. Cecilia, who was just seventeen years old at the time, may have been the most beautiful woman Leonardo ever painted. The artist included the upper part of her body in frontal pose. She is clad in a simple but elegant velvet dress; in the center of the painting, Cecilia's slender fingers are petting a furry white animal. But the young woman is not looking at the viewer; her head is turned toward her shoulder, and her rather girlish, yet flawless, features appear in three-quarter profile.

A golden net covers her forehead. Her light brown hair comes down over her cheeks and enhances her finely etched appearance. A smile plays around Cecilia's thin mouth, and her alert gaze suggests a high level of intelligence. She spoke fluent Latin, composed sonnets, and earned praise as a singer. It is said that Cecilia liked Leonardo.

Cecilia Gallerani

In any case, he was later a regular guest in her apartment at the ducal palace in Milan, and she had a major role in helping the Tuscan painter become one of Europe's preeminent naturalists and writers. Leonardo made the acquaintance of the country's top scholars in her salon.

Leonardo had great difficulty accepting his status as craftsman. He considered painters far superior to men who dirtied their hands to earn their pay. His notebooks rattle off arguments about the superiority of painting over the other arts: Music does not last, while paintings do; poems cannot be touched, but paintings can. The painter, we are told, is more elegant than his major rival, the sculptor: "The painter sits in front of his work at perfect ease. He is well dressed and moves a very light brush dipped in delicate color. He adorns himself with the clothes he fancies; his home is clean and filled with delightful pictures and he often is accompanied by music or by the reading of various beautiful works to which he can listen with great pleasure."[18]

LEONARDO BECOMES A WRITER

While a regular visitor to Cecilia's salon, Leonardo developed in yet another area that would henceforth set him apart from his fellow artists: He began to write. His notebooks now included stories in addition to sketches, projects, and observations. The duke's engineer invented fables and riddles suitable for entertainment at the court. He also tried his hand at so-called prophecies, gloomy images that ostensibly predicted the future but actually described the current state of affairs. Since he was not especially skilled at language—Leonardo had had a limited formal education and spoke the dialect of his Tuscan homeland—he decided to enlarge his vocabulary systematically. Now more than thirty-five years old, he began studying up on standard Italian. In Codex Trivulzianus, a collection of his notes from the years he spent in Milan, the reader suddenly comes across endless word lists. And because a more varied vocabulary would be helpful for his scientific work, Leonardo compiled lists of technical terms, including a set of sixty-seven words describing the movement of water. Another manuscript, which Leonardo composed during the same period, made reference to waters intersecting, surging, upwelling, and swelling, with careful distinctions drawn between water that was eddying and pushing away, and between the meeting and merging of two flow paths.[19] He later studied Latin, although he did not get beyond the basics. He also acquired a small reference library. By the end of the 1490s, he owned more than forty books, as we know from a list in his notebooks.

Knowing full well that university scholars would not regard him as an equal anyway, he decided to mount a counterattack:

I am fully aware that the fact of my not being a man of letters may cause certain presumptuous persons to think that they may with reason blame me, alleging that I am a man without learning. Foolish folk! Do they not know that I might retort by saying, as did Marius to the Roman Patricians: "They who adorn themselves in the labors of others will not permit me my own." They will say that because I have no book learning, I cannot properly express what I desire to treat of—but they do not know that my subjects require for their exposition experience rather than the words of others.[20]

Leonardo aimed to develop a whole new approach that relied not on traditional knowledge, but on his own perceptions. And he knew that he had at least one important authority to back him up. Hadn't the philosopher Aristotle defined sensory perception as the basis of all true knowledge? When Constantinople fell in 1453, the Greek original texts by this ancient thinker came to the West, and reliable translations were now available. Leonardo owned several books by and about Aristotle.

As an author, he sought to put into practice what the philosopher had proposed more than eighteen hundred years earlier. For his first work, Leonardo was planning a book about water. Even his early notes invoked the poetic hold of this element on man.[21] They are punctuated with sublime and pithy formulations, such as this: "Sea, universal lowness and sole resting-place of the roaming waters of the rivers."[22]

Leonardo hoped that his writings would inspire other researchers and artists "to study the many beautiful motions that arise when one element permeates another."[23] While most of his other notes were brief and to the point, Leonardo waxed eloquent when writing about water: "It goes round and round in continuous rotation, hither and thither from above and from below, it never rests in quiet, either in its course or in its own nature. . . . So it changes continually, now as regards place, now as regards color, now it absorbs new smells or tastes . . . now it brings death, now health."[24] It would be impossible to overstate the significance of this element, he contended, because "water is the driving force behind all of nature."[25]

WATER MUSIC

On my way to the Mill of Mora Bassa, I tried to appreciate Leonardo's special connection to water so that I would find it easier to see the world through his eyes. It is nearly impossible to picture this area as it once was, so densely wooded that Duke Ludovico was able to use the mill as a hidden love nest. Today the area is wide open. The only relatively tall plants are the mulberry trees that Ludovico planted along the canals to make Lombardy a center of silk manufacturing.

It was a clear day in February when I strode through the Lomellina, as this plain is called, and saw the snowcapped peaks of Monte Rosa illuminated on the northern horizon. Leonardo, a pioneer in mountaineering as well, probably climbed up to a height of nearly 10,000 feet.[26] In any case, his notebooks mention in passing that he climbed up the "Monboso" to explore the origin of all the waterways of Europe. The base of this mountain, he wrote, is the point of origin of the four rivers that flow over the entire continent in the direction of the four compass points. By the "four rivers," Leonardo was referring to the Rhône, the Danube, the Rhine, and the Po. We do not know the origins of this odd theory, although Leonardo may have taken it from the historian Flavio Biondo's atlas of Italy, which is the first recorded use of the name "Monboso" for the Monte Rosa.[27]

He wrote that when the air rises on the mountain slopes, humidity builds up. Of course the Monte Rosa is so high that precipitation rarely falls as snow, but rather as hail that piles up to form an immense mass of ice. Leonardo evidently reached the glacial region. The sun, he wrote, shone far more brightly than in the plain. And the air up here had a strange deep blue color, which Leonardo correctly attributed to its low humidity.

The sight of the Monte Rosa reconciled me somewhat to the plain, if only from afar. People like me, who have grown up in the mountains, can easily feel lost in a landscape devoid of hills. Everything seems to look identical. The eye seeks and fails to find a focal point (there is not even a forest) and winds up looking off into the distance. What could an artist from the pleasantly undulating landscape of Tuscany find appealing in this monotony? Leonardo spent twenty-three years in the plain in Lombardy, more time than he had in Florence. And these years utterly transformed his art and his research.

After about an hour, I began to get a sense of the richness of the Lomellina. Its rice fields were interesting after all—just very different from the ones I'm used to. You can take in a landscape not only with your eyes, but also with your ears. In the canals and drainage channels along the fields, the water gurgled, roared, whispered, and trickled in constantly changing patterns. A variety of obstacles in the channels produced still other sounds. Here a waterfall cascaded over a little weir, there a rivulet crossed under the path in a pipe and rippled out into a rice field. In another spot, groundwater bubbled up out of the ground, then collected in a basin. And at nearly every junction there were weirs of various designs—orchestras among the hydraulic engineering works into which a river splashed down, then settled in, only to resurface in the underflow with a gush, a gurgle, or a roar. Leonardo regarded the sounds of water as music, and even pondered how they could be created systematically. His later project for a hydraulic organ has been preserved.[28]

Peering into the water was even more riveting than listening to it. The water cascaded down in white stripes, waves swirling into braids behind bridge piers and intersecting like the sides of a triangle when approaching a constriction. Currents of water rose up above the flow, pushed underneath it, and formed hilly landscapes of foam in the whirlpool basin of a dam. All the shapes from Leonardo's manuscripts, and more, were in evidence. You could see them from many angles and watch one shape glide into another. Leonardo faced the challenge of capturing the waves, eddies, and currents on a two-dimensional sheet of paper.

The idea of studying nature for its own sake was alien to Leonardo's contemporaries. It would not have occurred to people in the Middle Ages to call a landscape or even a plant "beautiful." A cornstalk was useful, a poppy a mere weed, and a lily nothing more than a symbol of the purity of the Virgin Mary.[29] When Petrarch, the Tuscan poet, described the rapture he experienced during his famous ascent of Mont Ventoux in southern France in 1336, he did not devote a single word to the view he enjoyed at the summit; instead, the reader learns how nature whetted his appetite to open a book he had brought along about St. Augustine, whereupon the mountain hiker began to contemplate all the foolish mistakes in his life and the insignificance of mankind as a whole. Even when Leonardo's fellow artists began to move away from the tradition of painting their figures of saints in front of a gold background and instead situated them in front of mountains, rivers, and gardens, the landscape was nothing more than a template.[30] Every object had a meaning, like a prop on a stage. A mountain stood for the crucifixion, a river for the baptism of Christ, a garden for the fertility of the Blessed Virgin.

Leonardo broke away from this kind of symbolism when he was still a young man. His first known and dated drawing (August 5, 1473)

Arno Valley drawing

features a river landscape as its central image. Just twenty-one years old at the time, he created the first landscape drawing in the history of European art. Beyond that, however, he also portrayed water in a manner unusual in painting: as a force that shaped the earth.[31] In the foreground of the picture a stream gushes down out of a cave. The cascade has made deep carvings into the rock, and in the valley below the water has eroded a gorge.

The *Baptism of Christ* (Plate III), which Leonardo painted a few years later together with his mentor Verrocchio, also features a waterfall, which flows into the Jordan between John the Baptist and Jesus. Leonardo was still feeling his way toward this new type of motif, and the torrent is portrayed somewhat awkwardly.[32] Foam spraying into the air anticipates his later pen-and-ink drawings. Through the surface of the water, John and Jesus can be seen seeking firm footing on the stones of the riverbed. Eddies have formed around the ankles of the two men. Viewers feel as though they are themselves standing in water, because the Jordan occupies nearly the entire front edge of the picture, then flows out to the horizon.

Evidently Leonardo was already enthralled by nature's inexhaustible abundance of shapes and creatures, which emerge, evolve, and fade away in some mysterious way. The things that were unfolding before his eyes—light shimmering in the leaves of a tree, intersecting ripples from skipping stones, marvelous life inside the human eye—so riveted him that he had no time for

Waterfall (Detail from The Baptism of Christ)

otherworldly matters. Aren't discoveries of this sort far more exciting and poetic than the lives of the saints?

This was the unexplored treasure he set out to mine in his art—a whole world that no one had ever captured on paper or canvas. But would he have been able to grasp the dynamics of water as successfully back home in Tuscany? The steep streambeds full of curves and stones cascading down from the mountains into the Arno Valley make it difficult to study the currents, and the chaotic swirling of water does not allow for a good overview. Lombardy, where nature is tamed, offered Leonardo the opportunity to grasp its laws. The absolutely straight lines and vertical banks of the watercourses here enabled him to study flow patterns, current formations, and the emergence of waves. An environment that offered few distractions allowed him to focus his attention on the essentials.

Single File Through an Alley

Leonardo's insatiable thirst for knowledge gained new momentum during his stay at the La Sforzesca model farm. It was here that he realized that conventional technological methods would fall short in designing mills and canals for the duke.[33] In drawing up his plans for the lock, he was guided by the principle that working *with* the forces of nature—not *against* them—would be the only way to design optimal hydraulic plants. First, however, he had to figure out the laws that governed these forces.

At the outset, Leonardo followed the typical path of those who come up against the limits of their knowledge, namely looking things up in books or seeking expert advice. But Leonardo quickly realized how fragmented and incomplete the standard wisdom was. The science of liquids, for instance, had barely moved ahead since Archimedes supposedly ran naked through the streets of Syracuse in Sicily yelling "Eureka!" after discovering in his bathtub why some bodies sink and others swim.

So Leonardo embarked on his own quest for the laws of nature, using very simple means. A dewdrop helped him fathom the mystery of surface tension: "If first you take a cube of lead of the size of a grain of millet, and by means of a very fine thread attached to it you submerge it in this drop, you will perceive that the drop will not lose any of its first roundness, although it has been increased by an amount equal to the size of the cube which has been shut within it."[34] And he explored the laws of pressure with a wine cask: "If a cask is filled four braccia high with wine and throws the wine a distance of four braccia away, when the wine has become so lowered that it has dropped to a height of two braccia in the cask, will it also throw the wine through the same pipe a distance of two braccia, that is whether the fall, and the range

Loss of pressure in a water cask

that the pipe can throw, diminish in equal proportion or no."[35] If we substitute the modern term "energy" for "range," Leonardo was right on target: The force of the water decreases along with the water level (though this does not hold true for the range of the jet). And by capturing on paper the current and waves in the canals, he gained insight into hydrodynamics.

Leonardo understood that all physics can be explained by laws of motion; that is, by mechanics, and he sought the simplest examples to highlight general problems. The jet pouring from the wine cask stands for water that powers a mill; the straightened canal for a winding river. The only way to understand nature is by asking the right questions. It is crucial to select the right detail from the overall picture of the universe.

Leonardo was thus one of the first to use a simplified experiment to grasp the rules of a complex reality, which remains the most important method today.[36] A good scientist approaches nature the way a caricaturist approaches the features of a politician: Both simplify and overdraw their objects until the essence clearly emerges. The drawing over my desk is also a caricature of a waterfall, albeit of a highly artistic nature.

Some of Leonardo's discoveries are still considered valid, and two of them even inspired American historian of science Clifford Truesdell to regard Leonardo as a forefather of fluid mechanics.[37] Leonardo may have come across the first of these while observing water in a narrowing canal and noticing that the river flowed more rapidly there. After the constriction ended, the speed slowed down again. The speed therefore depended on the breadth and depth of the riverbed—and more generally on the surface the current crosses.

Leonardo explained why this was so with an innovative thought experiment: The reader is asked to picture a group of men sidling through an alley as though they were dancing the Polonaise.[38] The rule is that the men can never lose physical contact. Now the alley expands out into a street that is four times as wide. At all times the street has to accommodate all the men who enter it from the alley; the flow cannot break off. That is Leonardo's key insight. Even today, all of hydrodynamics is based on this principle, the "principle of continuity." Without the principle of continuity, weather forecasts and airplanes would be unthinkable.

His second principle similarly reveals Leonardo's powers of observation and his refusal to take anything for granted. He wondered why the water in the center of a vortex rotated much more quickly than at the outer edges. It seemed strange to him, because a wheel worked the opposite way. A nail on a tire moved much faster than one on the hub. Evidently the movement of fluids proceeded according to different laws. Leonardo was able to guess the correct correlation: The speed of the water depends on the path on which it moves around the center of the vortex.[39] The shorter the path, the faster the speed—a correlation anyone can verify by watching a bathtub drain.

Liquids swirl in a drain, and water particles squeeze through a canal just like men through an alley. Leonardo thought in pictures. He owed his highly significant discoveries to this pictorial approach, though it also led him astray at times, because looks can be deceiving. A sheet from the year 1500, for instance, has drawings of the arm of a scale, the trajectory of a stone cast upward, a jet of water that tapers toward the bottom, and a device to measure the water pressure. At the top is this remark, in mirror writing: "All forces are pyramidal."[40] Throughout nature, he sought the ratios he had come across while studying perspective and called his findings "pyramidal law." Just as objects twice as far away seem to dwindle to half their size, he noted, other sizes change proportionately to each other. Balance scales confirm this idea: If you double the weight of an object, the counterweight on the other arm of the scale has to be moved twice as far away from the suspension, in accordance with lever law. Also, the pressure of a jet of water doubles with the water level in the container. Matters are not quite so simple when considering the speed of a stone cast upward and the diameter of a jet of water flowing downward. These decrease with the square root and with the fourth root of the height, respectively. And the range of a jet of water pouring from a cask changes with the square root of the water level in the container. But Leonardo did not know how to perform these arithmetic operations.

Because many of his theories are incorrect, some art historians tend to discount his significance as a researcher. However, this dismissive attitude does not do him justice—and betrays a lack of information as well. In natural science, errors are not only admissible, but invaluable. Only when a theory proves contradictory does it give rise to new experiments and thus to progress. In all eras, the greatest minds have also claimed quite a bit of nonsense along the way. That Isaac Newton believed in the alchemy of gold production does nothing to diminish his achievement of having founded modern physics.

While Leonardo's experiments paved the way for modern research, he was not a scientist in today's sense of the term—not because he was often wrong, but because his working method was too different from the standard method in modern laboratories. Instead of relying on visual perception, today's scientists strive wherever possible to count and to measure. Leonardo appreciated the value of mathematics, but his notebooks contain unsuccessful attempts at even simple division. His pencil remained the major instrument of his thought processes.

Natural scientists today seek to establish connections. They are not satisfied with a theory until its hypotheses can be confirmed—or refuted—in experiments. Leonardo, by contrast, described, and based his conclusions on, what he saw, but he did not try to fashion a coherent theory from his findings. He did not even carry out systematic series of experiments. Instead, his interest leaped from one topic to the next.

But Leonardo's noncoordinated and comprehensive approach is precisely what enabled him to lay the foundations for a new, broader scope for science, and it provided a way out of the dead end in which science was caught as a result of its overdependence on book learning. Ultimately, this approach grew out of Leonardo's background in crafts-manship, where results took precedence over reading. Even later, when he acquired a literary education, he shied away from launching into extended theoretical discussions; none of the ideas in the notebooks fills more than a single page.

Ever the consummate craftsman, he preferred to explore every new insight with an eye to how it could be implemented. And if he found he was getting carried away with his ideas, he would caution himself to stick to practical applications: "When you write about the movements of water, think about specifying its practical uses for each project."[41]

At the Mill of Mora Bassa, where Cecilia Gallerani (the lady with the ermine) seems to have enjoyed the company of the duke, visitors today can see how Leonardo envisioned the fruits of his research. Enterprising residents have turned the ruins into a museum, and the giant water wheel still turns out front. A cabinetmaker from Leonardo's hometown of Florence provided two dozen wooden models of machines Leonardo once designed in the service of Duke Ludovico, including pumping stations powered by water, clock mechanisms, construction cranes, flying machines, a spring-driven automobile, and huge catapults—the enormous engines of war that Leonardo had promised his ruler.

Most visitors react with a combination of fascination and disbelief to the fact that the same man who painted *The Last Supper* and the portrait of the beautiful Cecilia designed all this equipment as well. Leonardo would never have described himself as a universal genius, because he regarded art, technology, and science, which we now consider such dissimilar endeavors, as a single pursuit of the human mind.

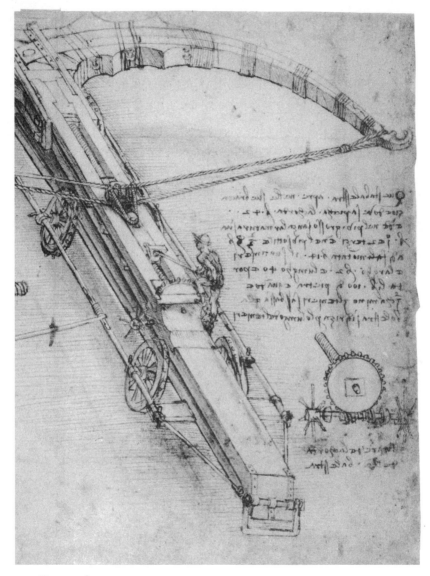

Giant crossbow

WAR

ONE OF VASARI'S LOVELIEST ANECDOTES about Leonardo concerns the artist's love of animals: "Often when he was walking past the places where birds were sold, he would pay the price asked, take them from their cages, and let them fly off into the air, giving them back their lost freedom."[1] Did Leonardo, who had an exceptional desire for freedom and himself tried to fly, feel a special rapport with birds?

A letter from the west coast of India addressed to the Florentine regent Giuliano de' Medici in 1515 is revealing. A seafarer named Andrea Corsali reported that he had discovered gentle people clad in long robes who lived on milk and rice, refused any food that contained blood, and would not harm any living creature—"just like our Leonardo da Vinci."[2] Corsali was describing the Jains, known for their extreme nonviolence; in the twentieth century they would have a profound influence on Mahatma Gandhi.

Of course Corsali would not have been reminded of the artist far away if Leonardo's attitude had not seemed so remarkable. That a person would display empathy at all was quite unusual in this era, which had been devastated by violence. But the idea of actually forswearing the consumption of meat out of simple consideration for other creatures was unheard of in the West.

Vasari, who later wrote a biography of Leonardo, may have known these and other reports about customs in the Orient. In the Buddhist countries of Southeast Asia birds are offered for sale in front of some temples even today so that people who want to ensure good karma can buy their freedom and send them soaring into the air. Vasari's account of Leonardo's bird liberation may have been no more than an appealing embellishment to his text.

Still, there is no doubt that Leonardo had a deep-seated aversion to all violence, as several passages in his notebooks confirm. His attitude certainly had more in common with the ethos of Eastern nonviolence than with the harsh customs then prevalent in the Christian West. Precisely because he respected the value of every creature, he was firmly convinced of the sanctity of human life. In reference to his anatomical studies, he wrote: "And thou, man, who by these my labours dost look upon the marvelous works of nature, if thou judgest it to be an atrocious act to destroy the same, reflect that it is an infinitely atrocious act to take away the life of man."[3]

Leonardo's words make it difficult to grasp the gruesome fantasies his mind was capable of in designing his engines of war. On hundreds of pages, Leonardo sketched giant crossbows, automatic rifles, and equipment to bombard strongholds with maximal destructiveness. The sole function of these devices was to kill and destroy. He did not just record the technology, but provided graphic descriptions of the devastating impact of his inventions. In one sketch, archers are running away from an exploding grenade, which Leonardo referred to as "the deadliest of all machines."[4] In another, a war chariot with rotating scythes as large as men is mowing down soldiers and leaving behind

Scythed chariot

a trail of severed legs and dismembered bodies.[5] The battle plans
Leonardo drew up are equally chilling. On Sheet 69 of Manuscript B,
housed in Paris, we read about his preparations for chemical warfare:

> Chalk, fine sulphide of arsenic, and powdered verdigris may be thrown
> among the enemy ships by means of small mangonels. And all those who,
> as they breathe, inhale the said powder with their breath will become as-
> phyxiated. But take care to have the wind so that it does not blow the
> powder back upon you, or to have your nose and mouth covered over with
> a fine cloth dipped in water so that the powder may not enter.[6]

His involvement in the wars of his era extended well beyond the
design of weapons and began even before he signed on with the in-
famous, bloodthirsty Cesare Borgia in 1502. How could a man whose
sense of empathy is said to have inspired him to free birds from their
cages come up with ideas of this sort?

On one occasion, Leonardo justified his military activities with a
statement that a modern-day reader could easily picture coming straight
from the Pentagon: "When besieged by ambitious tyrants, I find a
means of offense and defense in order to preserve the chief gift of
nature, which is liberty."[7]

Doubts are certainly warranted here; after all, his first employer,
Ludovico Sforza, was not exactly a champion of freedom. The historian
Paolo Giovio, a contemporary of il Moro, called him "a man born for
the ruin of Italy." That might sound harsh, but without a doubt, "the
Moor" was a major reason that Italy lost its freedom for centuries and
became a battlefield for foreign powers.

Ludovico, an inveterate risk-taker, sized up his position on his very
first day in power and realized that he was surrounded by enemies. In
his own empire his right to rule was in dispute, since he owed his power

to the violent murder of his brother, for which no one had been charged, and the arrest of the sister-in-law. Moreover, Venice and the Vatican tried to exploit Ludovico's insecure position, and they armed for war. In March 1482, the Venetians attacked Ferrara, which was an ally of il Moro. At this time, Leonardo arrived in Milan and in his famous ten-point letter of application promised il Moro a whole new arsenal of weapons. Two years later, Ludovico was able to defeat the Venetians.

But il Moro, who was focusing all his efforts on legitimating his rule once and for all, needed a seemingly endless supply of weapons. Over the next few years, his dodges would determine not only the further course of Leonardo's unsettled life but also result in the so-called Italian Wars, which lasted sixty-five years and brought about the political collapse of the country.

The disaster ran its course when Ludovico sought a strong ally against Naples. The king of Naples, Ferdinand I, had meanwhile given his daughter's hand in marriage to the legitimate heir to the throne in Milan, Gian Galeazzo, and was quite indignant when he realized that Ludovico had no intention of ceding power to his son-in-law. Ludovico encouraged Charles VIII of France to invade Italy to overthrow Ferdinand. What followed was a bloody farce: Charles was asked to invade Lombardy with forty thousand soldiers, whereupon Gian Galeazzo was murdered. Two days later, Charles declared il Moro the legitimate duke of Milan. But the latter showed no gratitude. When the Neapolitans rebelled against the French occupation in the following year, the opportunist switched sides and entered into an alliance with Venice and the pope. The French were expelled and suffered great losses.

Just a few decades earlier, wars had been highly ritualized battles with relatively few casualties, but now they were developing into horrific bloodbaths. The handgun had been widely adopted; a few years later, Leonardo would contribute a wheel lock, which was one of the handgun's first effective firing mechanisms.⁸ And there were growing numbers of portable cannons on battlefields. Since the earlier stone balls had been replaced by metal projectiles, the firearms shot more effectively than ever before, as Charles VIII's soldiers proved when they demolished the ramparts of the mighty castle of Monte San Giovanni Campano with small cannons within hours, before attacking Naples. Until then the battle was won by the side that had more and better soldiers. From this point on, technology was key.

Leonardo had promised marvelous weapons to il Moro and was granted a tremendous degree of freedom in return. As the engineer of the duke, he received a fixed salary and no longer had to rely on selling his art on the market. This was the only way he could pursue his research interests and continue to perfect his paintings without any pressure to meet deadlines. We owe the magnificence of the Milan *Last Supper*, the studies of water, and his explorations of the human body to Leonardo's clever move of offering himself up to one of the most unscrupulous warlords of his era. During his first seventeen years in Milan, serving Ludovico, he sketched the great majority of his weapons, among them his most dreadful ones.

All the same, Leonardo's interest in weapons went far beyond the steady job they brought him. His drawings reveal an unmistakable fascination with technology. In the end, his inventions were the product of his inexhaustible fantasy, which gave rise to paintings, stories, projects to transform entire regions, tools—and weapons. One of these weapons, which he designed in Milan, looks like a water mill, but is actually a gigantic automatic revolver. Leonardo arranged four crossbows in a compass formation, with one pointing upward, one downward, one to the left, and one to the right. The wheel was powered by four men running along its exterior to turn it at breakneck speed. An ingenious mechanism with winches and ropes caused the bows to tighten automatically with each turn. The marksman crouched in the middle of the mechanism and activated the release. In one version, the wheel was equipped with sixteen rather than four crossbows. Leonardo devoted himself to refining the driving mechanism as well.[9]

Even so, in comparison with the truly revolutionary firearms of the era, this contraption looks charmingly old-fashioned. At least for the years until 1500, Kenneth Clark was probably right in claiming that Leonardo's knowledge of military matters was not ahead of his time.[10] Even Leonardo's most spectacular weapon, the giant crossbow he invented in 1485, was not really pioneering. With a 98-foot bow span, this monster was intended to stand up to cannons, to fire more accurately, and to save the soldiers from often fatal accidents with exploding gunpowder. There is no evidence, however, that anyone attempted to construct this giant crossbow during Leonardo's lifetime. More than five hundred years later, when a British television production undertook this project, the results were pitiful. Specialized technicians were brought in to build a functionally efficient weapon using twentieth-century tools, guided by Paolo Galluzzi, one of the leading experts on Renaissance engineering. Since they were required to restrict their materials to those that were available in the Renaissance, they opted to build a bow with blades made of walnut and ash that would be five times larger than any before. A worm drive designed by Leonardo himself had to muster a force equivalent to the weight of ten tons to tighten this enormous spring, thus making it possible to catapult a stone ball over 650 feet. But when British artillerymen tried out the construction on one of their military training areas, the balls barely left the weapon. After a mere 16 feet in the air, they plopped to the ground. Video recordings showed that they could not detach properly from the bowstring. When the technicians added a stopping device to the string (not drawn by Leonardo), the range increased to 65 feet—

still hardly sufficient to produce anything but guffaws on a Renaissance battlefield. And the fact that the replicators had made the bow thinner than in Leonardo's design came back to haunt them—the wood broke.

When you look at many of Leonardo's drawings from his years in Milan, it is hard to shake the feeling that Leonardo had no intention of supplying serviceable weapons. It seems to have been far more important to him to impress his patron—especially when he emphasized the enormous dimensions and the impact of his weapons. As the most talented draftsman of his generation, he knew how to create a dazzling effect. Leonardo enjoyed an outstanding reputation as a technician of war because he was a great artist. He portrayed the details of his designs so meticulously, using the effects of perspective, light, and shadow so skillfully, that it was easy to mistake reality for wish. The drawing of the giant crossbow features not only the knot of the string and the details of the trigger mechanism, but also the soldier handling the weapon. Like the face on the *Mona Lisa*, Leonardo's war machines seem alive.

THE PHYSICS OF DESTRUCTION

While Leonardo proved a master of illusion in designing weapons, he also made concrete contributions to military development. Military commanders needed to figure out how to put the latest firearms— mobile cannons—into action. How should they shoot? With bows and crossbows, the shooter simply aimed straight ahead; the range of the new firearms, by contrast, meant that the trajectory curve had to be determined to make the cannonball hit its target. But no one had a clear idea about the laws governing the paths of cannonballs. Progress on this matter could determine the outcomes of wars.

Traditional physics offered little help, because this discipline still adhered to the ancient view that a body moves only while a force acts on it. But if that were so, a cannonball would come to a standstill just after leaving the barrel of the cannon. The seemingly plausible concept of "impetus" was introduced: The cannon gives the ball its impetus, and only when the impetus is completely used up as it flies through the air does it fall to the ground. The cannoneers of the time were well aware that the impetus theory could not be correct; anyone who relied on it was off the mark. The error is that gravity sets in immediately to begin pulling down on the cannonball.

Leonardo's interest in this question went far beyond its military implications. He was determined to figure out the laws of motion. He kept going around in circles because he could not relinquish the idea of impetus and because the crucial concept of the earth's gravity was still unknown at the time. His notebooks document how bedeviled he was by the laws of motion. His explanations of mechanics were riddled with inconsistencies; at times he argued both for and against impetus within the space of a single paragraph.[11]

But then he had a brilliant idea of how to determine the trajectory of projectiles not by conceptualizing, but by observing: "Test in order to make a rule of these motions. You must make it with a leather bag full of water with many small pipes of the same inside diameter, disposed on one line."[12] One sketch shows the small pipes in the bag pointing upward at various angles, like cannons that aim higher at some points and more level at others. The arcs formed by the spurting water correspond to the trajectories of the cannonballs. Leonardo's trajectories were accurate in both this sketch and others.[13] By means of a clever experiment—not involving mathematics—he had discovered the ballistic trajectory that Isaac Newton finally worked out mathematically some two hundred years later.

This little sketch offers a glimpse inside Leonardo's mind. He was able to link together fields of knowledge that appeared utterly unrelated.

From the laws of hydraulics, which he had investigated so exhaustively, he gained insights into ballistics. His thoughts ran counter to the conventional means of solving problems. Instead of attacking the matter head on, formulating the question neatly, and penetrating more and more deeply below the surface, Leonardo approached the problem obliquely—like a cat burglar who has climbed up one building and from there breaks into another across the balconies. Leonardo was unsurpassed in what is sometimes called "lateral thinking," which enabled him to explain the sound waves in the air by way of waves in the water, the statics of a skeleton by those of a construction crane, and the lens of the eye by means of a submerged glass ball.

Leonardo's experiments with models also represented a new approach. Since he neither understood how to use a cannon nor was able to observe the trajectory of an actual cannonball up close, he used a bag filled with water as a substitute. Of course an approach of that sort is unlikely to yield a coherent theoretical construct, because similarities between different problems are always limited to individual points, and Leonardo was far too restless to pursue every last detail of a question. Still, his models yielded astonishing insights. The French art historian Daniel Arasse has aptly called him a "thinker without a system of thought."

In an impressive ink drawing, Leonardo illustrated the damage that could be inflicted by applying his insights into ballistics.[14] A large sheet in the possession of the Queen of England shows four mortars in front of a fortification wall firing off a virtual storm of projectiles. Not a single square foot of the besieged position is spared from the hundreds of projectiles whizzing through the air. For each individual one, Leonardo marked the precise parabolic trajectory, and the lines of fire fan out into curves like fountains. Ever the aesthete, Leonardo found elegance even in total destruction.

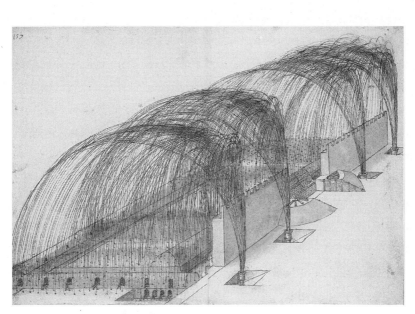

Saturation bombing of a castle

It is difficult to establish to what extent Leonardo's knowledge of artillery was implemented on an actual battlefield. When Ludovico had Novara bombarded in February 1500, the mortars were so cleverly positioned that the northern Italian city quickly fell. In the opinion of the British expert Kenneth Keele, il Moro was using Leonardo's plans for a systematic saturation bombing.[15]

Leonardo's close ties to the tyrants of his day offer a case study of the early symbiosis of science and the military. Now as then, war not only provides steady jobs and money to pursue scholarly interests, but also prompts interesting theoretical questions. Even a man as principled as Leonardo was unable to resist temptations of this sort. He was not the first pioneer of modern science and technology to employ his knowledge for destructive aims. Half a century earlier, Filippo Brunelleschi, the inspired builder of the dome of the Florence Cathedral, had diverted the Serchio River with dams to inundate the enemy city of Lucca. (This operation came to a disastrous end; instead of putting Lucca under water, the Serchio River flooded the Florentine camp.) Leonardo's struggle to strike a balance between conscience, personal gain, and intellectual fascination seems remarkably modern, and brings to mind the physicists in Los Alamos who devoted themselves heart and soul to nuclear research until the atomic bomb was dropped on Hiroshima.

Of course we cannot measure Leonardo's values by today's standards. We have come to consider peace among the world's major powers a normal state of affairs now that more than six decades have passed since the end of World War II, but we need to bear in mind that there has never been such a sustained phase of freedom from strife since the fall of the Roman Empire. In Italy, the Renaissance was one of the bloodiest epochs. The influence of the Holy Roman Empire had broken down, mercenary leaders had wrested power from royal dynasties, and a desire for conquest seemed natural. War was the norm, and a prolonged period of peace inconceivable.

Leonardo's refusal to regard death and destruction as inescapable realities is a testament to his intellectual independence from his era. As far back as 1490 he was calling war a "most bestial madness."[16] And one of his last notebooks even contains a statement about research ethics. While describing a "method of remaining under water for as long a time as I can remain without food," he chose to withhold the details of his invention (a submarine?), fearing "the evil nature of men who would practice assassinations at the bottom of the seas by breaking the ships in their lowest parts and sinking them together with the crew who are in them."[17] The only specifics he revealed involved a harmless diver's suit in which the mouth of a tube above the surface of the water, buoyed by wineskins or pieces of cork, allows the diver to breathe while remaining out of sight.

Leonardo must have had his reasons for withholding particulars about the dangerous underwater vehicle. Perhaps his ideas were still quite vague, or he was afraid that imitators might thwart his chances for a promising business. But the key passage here is Leonardo's statement about the responsibility of a scientist. He was the first to assert that researchers have to assume responsibility for the harm others cause in using their discoveries. Insights like these, and his high regard for each and every life, were quite extraordinary at the time. It is amazing that he embraced these ethical principles—but not surprising that he repeatedly failed to live up to them, at least by today's standards.

AMORRA, ILOPANNA

War would continue to chart the course of Leonardo's career. When King Louis XII ascended to the throne in Paris and formed an alliance with the pope against il Moro, a new invasion by the French was just a matter of time. On April 1, 1499, Leonardo paid up the employees in his workshop in Milan, and on September 6, French and papal troops occupied the city. The cover of Leonardo's Notebook L, which is housed in Paris today, features this bitter comment: "The duke has lost his state, his property, and his freedom, and none of his projects was finished." This last clause seems to refer in part to the projects the duke had commissioned Leonardo to build, in particular the giant equestrian statue. More painful still was the loss of his position at the court, which had offered him high status and a steady salary. Ludovico himself had departed for Austria.

At this time, Leonardo wrote a strange note to himself: "Find Ingil and tell him you will wait Amorra, and will go with him Ilopanna."[18] He evidently wrote this message in code to ensure that it could not be made out if it fell into the wrong hands. Leonardo does not appear to have considered his adversaries very clever; decoding this text is simply a matter of reading it backwards:

Ingil= Ligny
Amorra= a Roma (to Rome)
Ilopanna= *a Napoli* (to Naples)

So Leonardo wanted to join Ligny, the mercenary leader, on his way from Rome to Naples. Louis of Luxembourg, Count of Ligny, was an influential cousin of the king of France. Leonardo figured he had found himself a new patron. Perhaps as a small favor to Ligny, Leonardo sketched a map of Lombardy.[19] But his hopes were dashed when Ligny left for France empty-handed in the wake of political disputes. More-over, rumors started circulating that il Moro, equipped with new troops by Maximilian I, head of the Holy Roman Empire, was returning to Milan and intended to punish collaborators harshly.

Leonardo decided to flee. On the page with the Ligny note, he jotted down a few items he would need to prepare: "Have two trunks covered ready for the muleteer. . . . Buy some tablecloths and towels, hats, shoes, four pairs of hose, a great coat of chamois hide, and leather to make new one. The turning-lathe of Alessandro. Sell what you cannot carry."[20]

On December 14, he deposited six hundred florins in a bank in Milan with instructions to transfer it to his account in Florence, and left the city in the nick of time. A few weeks later, Milan was back in Ludovico's hands. Those who had cooperated with the French feared for their lives.

Leonardo made it safely to Venice. He was quite welcome there, because this maritime power on the Adriatic Sea feared an attack by the Turks. The senate dispatched him to the border area of Friuli to take measures to prevent an onslaught of Ottoman troops from the northeast. Leonardo returned with a report that suggested inundating the valley of the Isonzo River to block an invasion. He was an expert on the subject of water, and most likely he knew the details of Brunelleschi's attempt to force Lucca to its knees by means of an artificial flood. It is not clear what specific measures Leonardo recommended to the Venetians, because only fragments remain of a draft of a letter to the "illustrious Lords," as he customarily called his patrons.[21] The basic idea was to build a giant dam in the riverbed with gates that could be used to raise and lower the water level quickly. Later references to construction at the Isonzo indicate that his plan was carried out at least in part.[22]

Even so, Leonardo's stay in Venice was no more than an episode. He could not gain a foothold in this city, where policies were determined by a few influential merchant families and benefices were already assigned, so Leonardo decided to return to Florence, where he knew the customs. By Easter, he was back in his hometown. Now that he was nearly fifty years old, he would have to build a new life for himself. But competition among artists was stiff, and Leonardo, who had attained so much independence in Milan, had little desire to paint pictures according to the wishes of patrons, as his colleagues did. Instead, his next employer was Cesare Borgia—a man feared throughout Italy.

PACT WITH THE DEVIL

Cesare was the commander of the Vatican troops and an illegitimate son of the reigning pope, Alexander VI, alias Rodrigo Borgia, who had bought his way into office by bribing the electors, as was customary at the time. He aimed to start a dynasty.

It was common knowledge that Alexander and Cesare had no moral scruples. Beginning on July 19, 1497, when Cesare's older brother Juan

Bartolomeo Veneto, a portrait said to be of
Lucrezia Borgia

was found stabbed to death and floating in the Tiber, the Borgias, who
were originally from Spain, did everything in their power to stand up
against the long-established Roman clans. Anyone who got in their
way was simply done away with. "Every night four or five murdered
men are discovered—bishops, prelates, and others—so that all Rome
is trembling for fear of being destroyed by the Duke [Cesare]," the
Venetian ambassador reported just as Leonardo was planning naval
wars in Venice.[23]

The third member of this grim family enterprise was Cesare's sister
Lucrezia. Her role was to marry the right men. Her contemporaries
called her a bewitching beauty. (The Städel Museum in Frankfurt
houses the enchanting *Ideal Portrait of a Woman*, by Bartolomeo Veneto,

which may be a portrait of Lucrezia Borgia.) As soon as the marriages had served their political purpose, the pope would annul them. At the age of 13, he married off his daughter for the second time, to a cousin of Ludovico Sforza, in order to secure an alliance between the Vatican and Milan. Four years later, when the power of il Moro began to dwindle, the pope proclaimed that the marriage had never been consummated, and that the husband, Giovanni Sforza, was impotent. That claim could not be leveled against the next husband, who was from the royal dynasty of Naples, because Lucrezia had borne him a son, so Cesare had his brother-in-law strangled before his eyes.

It fell to Cesare to use the money and the soldiers of the church to conquer a territory to rule in central Italy. His adversaries feared the undeniably talented Cesare, although he was a mere twenty-five years old. Envoys reported that he was consumed with ambition, but he was also quite eloquent and engaging. Soldiers praised his horsemanship, his strength, and his courage. A contemporary painting in the Uffizi Gallery in Florence shows him in profile with well-proportioned features; his mouth, framed by a well-groomed full beard, is half open, as though he is engaged in conversation. The most compelling feature is Cesare's piercing gaze.

The portrait must be highly idealized, because Cesare was suffering from syphilis, which had disfigured his face and given him a repulsive look. A series of three drawings by Leonardo that appear to be of Cesare Borgia seem more realistic. They, too, highlight the full beard and the expression in the eyes, but they convey a totally different impression. His beard is so wild and his glance so shifty-eyed that his portrait instills not fascination, but fear.

After a blitzkrieg that lasted less than eighteen months, this man controlled nearly all of central Italy. On June 4, 1502, Arezzo, spurred on by Borgia, rose up against its neighbor Florence, which until then

Cesare Borgia

had been superior in strength. In Leonardo's hometown, there was widespread panic of becoming Cesare's next victim.

Leonardo signed on with Borgia at this very time. Perhaps he used the turmoil surrounding the rebellion to switch unnoticed to the side of the enemy. We do not know what enticed him to do so. A single note making reference to Cesare's promises is all we have to go on: "Borges [Borgia] will get the Archimedes of the bishop of Padua for you."[24] The reference is to a manuscript with texts by the famous Greek mathematician and physicist, which the pope's son had probably stolen from the library in Urbino not long before.

The prospect of receiving a rare manuscript can hardly have sufficed to entice him to work for a tyrant who was notorious as the most brutal mercenary leader of the time and was even threatening Leonardo's hometown. According to political scientist Roger Masters, Leonardo seems to have switched sides with the full knowledge of the Florentine government, and possibly even on its behalf.[25] A note by Leonardo suggests that the enemy camp had approached him for information. We know that he swiftly produced a map of Arezzo and the surrounding areas that specified the distances between the locales and fortifications. But it is unclear whether he did so on behalf of Borgia or for the Florentines.[26] Florence had now paid an exorbitant thirty thousand gold ducats in protection money to buy off Borgia. Leonardo's employment in enemy headquarters would thus have served as a supporting measure to learn of Borgia's intentions ahead of time, and Leonardo was traveling through Italy on a double assignment—working for Borgia *and* spying for Florence.

It is difficult to picture Leonardo, who was introverted and always out for his own interests, as a secret agent. It is more likely that personal motives drove him to accept his new post as Borgia's "architect and general engineer," in the words of a pompous letter of appointment dated August 18, 1502. His financial situation in Florence was dire, and his bank statements make it abundantly clear that he was living from the money he had saved in Milan. Now the opportunity arose to gain the patronage of the son of the pope, a man with an apparently brilliant future ahead of him.

Was Leonardo also attracted to Cesare's commanding personality? The two men had almost certainly known each other from when Borgia had occupied Milan as the leader of the papal troops in collaboration with the French.[27] Cesare was an affable young conqueror, open to excesses of all kinds, besotted with power and eager for quick victories; Leonardo, an aging artist and researcher who was withdrawn, unruffled, and intent on fathoming the mysteries of the world, who abhorred violence and spent years on each of his great works. It would be hard to imagine a greater contrast between two characters, aside from the fact that each was considered the undisputed genius of his era in his respective arena. Neither bothered about taboos, and both had lightning-quick minds. Leonardo clearly preferred the intelligence of a Borgia (as he had the shrewdness of il Moro) to the mediocrity of the patrician families and clergymen who had been his business partners in Florence. And a capable tyrant, who did not have to answer to anyone, could more easily be persuaded to sponsor bold projects than bourgeois committees looking to shield their own interests.

The new position was certainly alluring. Leonardo was in charge of the entire network of fortifications in Borgia's sphere of control. Not even il Moro had given him this much responsibility. He galloped through central Italy and checked the positions. Within just a few weeks, he had inspected Piombino, Urbino, Pesaro, Rimini, Cesena, and Porto Cesenatico.

The town of Imola, located in a plain southeast of Bologna, is the best place to view the results of Leonardo's activities. Today Imola has become synonymous with the Formula One San Mariono Grand Prix, but it is so unchanged from the way it was in Leonardo's day that if you take a walk in the center of town and picture it without all those bicycles, you feel as though you have been transported back in time. In the arcades, which cast shade along the paved main streets, you hear the echoing voices of people going about their business or stopping to chat. No one is in a hurry. Cars are not allowed in the downtown area, there are no modern buildings, and even the town gates and sections of the ramparts are still standing. For centuries, this place was of paramount strategic significance, because this was the key control point for the routes leading into Romagna, which was fiercely contested, and the Adriatic ports.

The Rocca Sforzesca, Borgia's winter quarters

Heading west from the center of town, I arrive at a large open square that must have been used as a field of fire. At the end of it, ramparts rise out of a ditch, with smooth and uniform reddish walls that extend for more than three hundred feet until they come to an end in a circular tower at each of the four corners of the fortress known as the Rocca, the fortifiable stronghold in a town, its "rock" of refuge. The whole structure is so out of place here that it might as well be a spaceship from another galaxy. In the past, the ramparts must have looked even more disconcerting, because as Leonardo's drawings show, even the openings over the parapet walks, a good 65 feet above the ground, were covered by wooden lids.

Cesare Borgia set up his headquarters behind these walls in the winter of 1502 after seizing the Rocca.[28] He owed his success in large part to a betrayal, because the fortress was considered impregnable. It is still easy to see why today. The only way inside leads over a stone bridge first on a man-made island, where the intruder, in full view and shooting range of the defenders, steps onto a second bridge, at the end of which the entrance gate finally looms up. Inside, a corridor leads along 40-foot-thick ramparts. When I reemerge into the light, I find myself in a courtyard surrounded by parapet walks and casemates. Leonardo must have spent the cold months of 1502 in these vaults among Borgia's entourage. The general, who, according to chroniclers, threw wild parties at night, planned to restructure the Rocca as a permanent military base and possibly make Imola the capital of his future empire.[29] As Borgia's general engineer, Leonardo must have been chiefly responsible for this project. Several detailed drawings of the Rocca confirm that this was the case. Evidently Borgia hoped to remodel the fortress to make it truly impregnable and to transform it into a magnificent noble residence.[30]

Leonardo's precise survey of the area has ensured that his name will forever be associated with Imola. Weeks of hard work resulted in nothing less than the first city map the world has ever seen. It is a masterpiece of graphic design (Plate II). Portrayed as a circular vignette with very fine strokes indicating the compass points, Imola resembles the pupil of the eye. The roofs of the houses, each individually painted in water colors, have a reddish hue; the main streets, in white, contrast with the yellowish-green municipal gardens and the wheat-colored fields outside the fortification walls. A moat, which varies in color from bright blue to silver, divides the city from the country, and the Santerno River flows past the minutely detailed gravel banks in such dynamic flow lines that you can almost hear the crunch of the pebbles when the waves hit. "It is far from being a lifeless object, a blandly flat record of measured features. It perceptibly stirs with life," writes the Oxford art historian Martin Kemp. "Under the touch of Leonardo's pen and the scrutiny of his eyes, nothing remained inert, not even a flat map."[31]

Leonardo's map of Imola opened up a new perspective on the world. Until then, pictures were largely restricted to images that the eye could see. Leonardo's depiction of Imola, by contrast, while oriented to reality, abandoned the realm of natural sensory perception. His abstract rendition was so revolutionary that it would take more than 450 years until people would next view their world from a similarly alien perspective—when they saw our blue planet rise from the moon.

Today we are so accustomed to using maps to find our way around—and now we even have satellite images of the surface of the earth—that the magnitude of Leonardo's achievement can be appreciated only by those who compare it to one of the standard city maps of that era. The old illustrations nearly always pictured the areas they were mapping at a diagonally downward angle, as though the draftsman were looking at the streets and houses from a high mountain. Even though walls and roofs—and often trees—could be made out in those pictures, they had a strangely distorted perspective. Finding your way around with a map like that would be just about impossible, because the setting looks different at varying angles. Moreover, distances can never be accurate in a picture of this kind.

Leonardo chose to forgo any obvious similarity with what he saw, and he depicted Imola as though he were aloft above the town. Because Leonardo was not able to assume this position in reality, he applied mathematical methods (still used today) to derive a true-to-scale layout of the houses and streets on the basis of surveying data. To get these data, Leonardo and his assistant must have paced off every street and every house. A drawing in the notebooks displays two different wheelbarrow-like carts with gear mechanisms on the axles to count the wheel revolutions and thus record the distances.[32] Sketches attest to this surveying work.

Reproductions of the maps give us no more than a hint of the extreme precision Leonardo must have employed. The original, which is housed in Windsor, conveys a more accurate impression; to recognize the true value of this masterpiece, you need to examine it with

Cyclometer

a magnifying glass. Every courtyard, and even the entrances to the houses, can be made out.

Leonardo's map of the town is accurate to within a few feet, and because Imola's town center has changed so little since Borgia's age, I was able to use a copy of it to find my way around without any difficulty, though the river banks, so stunningly portrayed on this map, are gone today, having been replaced by the race track. It was also odd to see that the main street in town, the Via Emilia, which is elegantly curved on the map and takes up the bends of the river so harmoniously, actually runs straight as an arrow. Did the artist distort the direction of this street for aesthetic effect?

Leonardo's talents as a cartographer were unquestionably invaluable for Borgia. Art historian Martin Kemp has established a link between the map of Imola and sketches of lines of fire that Leonardo drew during the same period of time: "Presented with a map of the Imola kind, Cesare could have literally grasped matters in his own hands, formulating plans of action, ordering the dispositions of forces and weapons even more accurately than was possible on the spot. For good measure, Leonardo has added the compass bearings and distances of neighboring towns."[33] He must have produced similar maps of at least two additional cities, Cesena and Urbino; the preparatory sketches in his notebooks have been preserved.[34] And the maps of entire regions and of the area surrounding Arezzo, which Leonardo also drew, made it possible to organize military campaigns with record precision. Leonardo may not have provided his employer any sophisticated killing machines, but he did give him a far more effective weapon: information.

STRANGLED AT DAWN

Leonardo must have met Niccolò Machiavelli in the fortress in Imola as well. Evidently the two men became friends; at any rate, they worked together on at least three later projects.[35] Leonardo and Machiavelli, who had to spend time with Borgia as a Florentine envoy, were certainly kindred spirits. Both were loners, and both struggled mightily to grasp the nature of reality. Leonardo and Machiavelli were prepared to defy

traditional wisdom and taboos. When in doubt, they relied on observation. Neither engaged in metaphysical speculations about the ultimately inexplicable facets of life. Leonardo focused on nature and art,
and Machiavelli on people and their life in the community, namely the
state. Leonardo forever transformed art, and Machiavelli man's notions
of power and politics.

The very mention of Machiavelli's name was chilling during his lifetime and still is today, since it is associated with utter ruthlessness,
particularly because of his most famous book, *The Prince*. In reality,
however, Machiavelli was merely being blunt in describing what he
observed while serving as secretary of the Florentine government and
as a diplomat. Suspiciously often, accusations against Machiavelli were
leveled from the Church and from the aristocracy. While others
sounded off about the meaning and lofty aims of their rule, he straightforwardly laid out techniques for retaining power.

Machiavelli so admired Cesare Borgia's skill that he made him the
hero of *The Prince*. He considered the events of December 1502 (which
Leonardo in all probability witnessed) a stroke of genius.[36] To gain
complete control over occupied Romagna, Borgia granted complete
authority to his deputy, a cruel man named Ramiro de Lorqua. As
soon as calm and order were restored, Borgia no longer considered
such a harsh regime necessary. On the morning of December 26, he
had Ramiro arrested, brought to the main square in Cesena, and cut
in two. He then ordered the corpse and the bloody executioner's sword
to be placed on display. "The brutality of this spectacle left the people
both stunned and appeased."[37]

Borgia needed to win over the civilians because he was in deep trouble. Some of his mercenary soldier leaders had formed a covert alliance
against him, and the rebels were about to topple him. (Possibly Borgia
had doubts about Ramiro's loyalty by this point as well.) Cesare sum-

moned the renegades to Senigallia for a reconciliation meeting and demanded that all troops be withdrawn in advance from this newly conquered small town. On the morning of New Year's Day, he appeared before his mercenary soldier leaders, accompanied by a single mounted escort, and greeted them cordially. But during the banquet, his small group barricaded the town gates and surrounded the palace in which the party was feasting. On New Year's night, two of the leading renegades were strangled with a garotte, and the others were arrested (and later killed). Meanwhile Borgia's soldiers were looting the town, as Machiavelli reported to Florence. The ever-audacious Cesare was at the height of his power.

The sources show that it is likely (though not certain) that Leonardo was still with Borgia at this time. We do know that he resigned no later than the first weeks of the new year, but the reason is unclear. Had Borgia's machinations become unbearable to him during these final days of December? Was he afraid of falling victim to this unscrupulous man himself? He had had a good relationship with Vitellozzo Vitelli, one of the two mercenary soldier leaders executed on New Year's night. (When Leonardo signed on with Cesare, Vitellozzo Vitelli was leading the rebellion of Arezzo.) Or Leonardo may have sensed that the era of the Borgias would soon come to an end. When Cesare's father, Pope Alexander VI, died in August 1503, his successor, Julius II, relieved the son of his post as commander of the Church state. Borgia fled to Spain and was killed in a melee. He was only thirty years old.

By March 4, 1503, Leonardo was back in Florence. A bank statement documents his withdrawal of fifty gold ducats from his account on that day—evidently he had not received his pay from Cesare. Ultimately, the military campaigns yielded no income for him. Everything he designed for the son and military commander of the pope progressed no further than the planning stage.

Even so, his military adventure was a formative experience in his life. In 1504, the Florentine government sent Leonardo to Piombino, which had reverted to its previous ruler, so that he could design a better way to fortify the seaport. The sketch he drew about a year later reveals his intense dedication to the problems of static warfare. The trip was almost certainly initiated by Machiavelli. Going far beyond his actual assignment, Leonardo drew a ring-shaped citadel quite unlike its Renaissance counterparts; it has more in common with twentieth-century defensive structures used in the two world wars.

A model is on view at the National Museum of Science and Technology in Milan. It was part of the very first major Leonardo exhibit in 1939. The Mussolini regime laid claim to the master from Vinci with a grand spectacle, using his genius to confirm the superiority of the Italian mind to the world once and for all.

The fascist organizers of this exhibit had thousands of drawings to choose from, but it was no accident that they picked this design for a fortification, because the model they produced conveys one key point to anyone who looks at it: This fortress has to be impregnable. Even Leonardo's most gruesome engines of war are not as spine-chilling as his vision of defense in a modern war. It looks especially menacing if you kneel down a little and look at the vast installations from the perspective of an attacker. The entrenchment is like a streamlined bulge, protruding from the ground so minimally that even a hurricane would not damage it. Furthermore, all the walls are curved, and there are no edges. Where could enemy forces attack? Viewers see nothing but a monotonous series of tiny square openings, each of which appears to contain artillery aimed straight at them.

Once you return to a standing position and view the model from above, you see that the fortification forms three concentric rings, each in the shape of an inflated bicycle inner tube. While conducting his ballistic studies, Leonardo had noticed that a cannonball causes far less damage on a crenallated surface than on a flat one.[38] A straight wall, in contrast to a curved one, is easy to bombard frontally. Geometry was Leonardo's response to the destructive force of cannons. But even if attackers had been able to blow up the outer wall of the fortification, they would not have accomplished very much—the defenders would simply retreat into the inner rings, and the battle would go on.

THE BEAST WITHIN MAN

The grim determination and the violence and cruelty that Leonardo must have experienced in the war were reflected in his painting. In the same year that he returned from the expeditions with Borgia, Machiavelli, on behalf of the municipal administration, commissioned a monumental fresco of the Battle of Anghiari, which had ended in victory for Florence, to decorate the council hall—a colossal hall in the Palazzo Vecchio, the building on the city's main square, which is topped by a high tower, and now displays a copy of Michelangelo's *David* at its entrance. Never had Leonardo been offered such a glorious assignment.

The Florentines were hoping for a fresco that glorified their ability to defend themselves. Instead, Leonardo created the first painting in the history of art that deliberately and drastically highlighted the horrors of war. His fresco, along with Goya's *Execution of the Rebels*, his etchings about the Napoleonic War, and Picasso's *Guernica*, represents one of the most stirring images of all time.

There is particular irony in the fact that this painting, which portrayed destruction so graphically, was itself destroyed. The decomposition of the work began while Leonardo was still working on it. To avoid the fate of the *Last Supper* fresco in Milan, which had already started peeling, Leonardo had mixed new types of primers and colors to add to linseed oil, but they proved utterly useless for mural painting. The colors did not dry in the council hall, and when Leonardo tried to heat the room using iron tubs filled with glowing coals, the colors simply ran and merged. Leonardo lost his patience with the project. He broke his contract with the city fathers and abandoned his artwork, which, though unfinished, was already crumbling. In the end, the city council settled on Giorgio Vasari, Leonardo's first biographer, to paint over the remainder.

These unfortunate circumstances notwithstanding, we still have a good idea of how the fresco might have looked. For one thing, we have Leonardo's own sketches of details of his painting. For another, the Louvre has on display a copy of *The Battle of Anghiari* by Peter Paul Rubens, which is based on an older engraving. Although Rubens's drawing is not in full color and reproduces only a detail of the destroyed painting, it conveys a good sense of the fresco as a whole (Plate V). Instead of portraying a traditional battle scene, Leonardo directed our attention right to the focal point of the battle, to the cavalrymen fighting for what appears to be the standard of Milan, and brought the viewer up so close that the soldiers no longer appear as men in uniform representing a state power, but as creatures in the throes of death.

Here is the description by Vasari, who painted over Leonardo's masterpiece in 1563:

> Rage, fury, and vindictiveness are displayed both by the men and by the horses, two of which with their forelegs interlocked are battling with their teeth no less fiercely than their riders are struggling for the standard. . . . An old soldier . . . grips the staff with one hand and with the other raises a scimitar and aims a furious blow to cut off both the hands of those who are gnashing their teeth and ferociously defending their standard. Besides this, on the ground between the legs of the horses there are two figures,

foreshortened, shown fighting together; the one on the ground has over him a soldier who has raised his arm as high as possible to plunge his dagger with greater force into the throat of his enemy, who struggles frantically with his arms and legs to escape death.[39]

Even Rubens's cartoon conveys how this battle erases all differences between friend and foe, and even between man and animal. The horses have human-like faces, while the features of the combatants are so contorted that they do not appear human. They are filled with the raw emotions of fear and belligerence. The horseman on the far left is even fused with his steed to suggest a centaur-like creature. He is leaning so far forward that the upper part of his body covers up the horse's head. On his back there is a shock of hair—precisely where a horse's mane would be—and the head and arms of the man emanate from a mass of flesh that could be man or monster.

War brings out the beast in man. In one of Leonardo's short stories, which he collectively called *Prophecies*, Leonardo predicted that man would see creatures on the earth who were forever locked in battle and who "set no bounds to their malice."[40] They would tear the trees in the forests from the ground and spread death, affliction, suffering, and terror among all living beings. "There shall be nothing remaining on the earth or under the earth or in the waters that shall not be pursued and molested or destroyed, and that which is in one country taken away to another."[41]

The title of this piece is "Of the Cruelty of Man." It is tempting today to construe these lines as a foreshadowing of the all-out wars in the twentieth century—or even as a vision of a nuclear end to the world. But Leonardo did not intend his *Prophecies* as a glimpse into a distant future. He was straightforwardly depicting his own era as a period in which people lost no time implementing scientific innovations

Soldiers' heads, a preliminary drawing for the Battle of Anghiari *fresco*

to wage war. Leonardo was playing a unique double role at this turning point in history: As one of the first modern researchers, he resolutely served the military—and as an artist he unsparingly described the business of destruction.

IV

THE DREAM
OF FLYING

To get to the top of Monte Ceceri, you walk steadily uphill from Fiesole through a dense and unvarying forest of pines, cypresses, and holm oaks until you suddenly find yourself standing in front of a quarry wall gaping open between the trees. This is where the master builders of the Renaissance in Florence acquired sandstone for their palaces. You climb the final few feet along bare rockfaces to get to the summit, which is crowned by an iron stele in commemoration of Leonardo, who is said to have tried out his flying machines on this spot.

I made my way here on a hot evening in June. Although the sun was already going down, it was still stiflingly hot in the valley. There was not a hint of a breeze, and the air was so milky that it absorbed the fading light like murky water. Even so, I was able to look out over the landscape dozens of miles beyond the quarry. Monte Ceceri rises over Florence like a pulpit. It is the highest peak of a range of hills on the northern boundary of the Arno Valley. Where would a paraglider take you from here? Circling over the Arno Valley and the roofs of Florence, a flier could gain height, glide into the hills of Chianti, which

Experimental study for the flying machine

View of Florence from Monte Ceceri

appeared in a bluish blur in the distance, and perhaps soar over to the Monte Albano Ridge, where the small town of Vinci is situated. Eventually the milky sky would simply envelop the flier.

But a flier who went into a tailspin right at the start would likely plunge over the edge of the quarry and crash onto sharp rock ledges at the base of the hillside. The architect and mathematician Giovanni Battista Danti had the good fortune of landing on the roof of the Church of Santa Maria Nuova when he donned feathered wooden wings in 1498 and plummeted from a tower in Perugia. Several sources indicate that he suffered no more than a broken leg.[1]

The Arno River and the lights of Florence glistened a quarter of a mile below me. Between them the cathedral dome loomed up like one lone, enormous molehill, three times as high as any of the houses in the city. Leonardo's contemporaries must have found this view breathtaking. For over a millennium, the concrete dome of the Pantheon in Rome had remained unsurpassed; then, in about 1430, Filippo Brunelleschi succeeded in building a dome that stood some 350 feet

Daedalus on the Florence Cathedral

in the air, more than double the height of the Pantheon. (In Verrocchio's workshop, the young Leonardo would later work as an apprentice on the gilt ball to be placed atop the lantern of the dome.)

Brunelleschi's achievement was mankind's greatest triumph over gravity to date, and his creation made him one of the most famous men of his era. When he died in 1446, he was buried under his dome, and the chancellor of the republic of Florence contributed an epitaph that compared the deceased to Daedalus—the great architect of antiquity who is said to have learned how to fly, although it cost him the life of his son. The high-spirited Icarus came too close to the sun with the wings his father had fashioned for him, and plunged to his death.

The notion that people could fly was no more than a dream for the builders of the cathedral in Florence. Daedalus's deeds were considered a symbol of what the bold human mind can achieve. The Greek hero was commemorated on the church tower on a relief of a bearded man gazing upward and clutching giant birds' wings, his feet lifted off the ground.

Leonardo regarded the legend of the ancient birdman not as a dream, but as a promise. To realize it, all that was needed was a machine that would enable man to imitate the incomparable elegance of the flight of birds. Form and function, art and technology would merge in an invention of this kind. Could there be any greater challenge for the researcher and artist Leonardo? It was a matter of approaching flight with scientific curiosity, observing the way birds of prey glide so carefully that the underlying mechanism becomes apparent, counting how many times falcons beat their wings as they begin their nosedive, figuring out how swifts attain their amazing speed, drawing clouds to discover indications for upwinds and downdrafts, and, finally, being guided by the wings of the eagles and buzzards in constructing wings. The results portended euphoria and immense freedom as well as extraordinary sources of inspiration for art. The eyes of the painter, no longer fixed on the earth, would see the world from a near-divine perspective.

This pioneering adventure would take place on Monte Ceceri: "The first flight of the great bird from the summit of Monte Cecero will fill the universe with wonder; all writing will be full of his fame, bringing eternal glory to the place of its origin."[2] To understand this dramatic pronouncement on the cover of Leonardo's codex on the flight of birds, you have to read on. On page 18 of this volume, where Leonardo jotted down his notes about flying, we find the explanation: "From the mountain that bears the name of the great bird, the famous bird will take its flight and fill the world with its great fame."[3] Only one mountain in this entire area bears the name of a "great bird," namely *Cecero*, an old Florentine word for "swan."

Leonardo wrote these lines in about 1505, the year he returned from the war and tackled the disastrous *Battle of Anghiari* fresco. His effusive tone may stem from his great longing to leave behind the atrocities he experienced in his military campaigns with Borgia and the humiliating failure of what was probably the most prestigious commission of his career. It is as though he was dreaming of soaring up into another world.

Was he merely contemplating this spot for his initial flight—or did the "bird" actually take wing? Leonardo certainly spent time at Monte Ceceri and the surrounding areas on several occasions and made a detailed study of the wind conditions there. His notebooks provide information on this subject: On March 14, 1505, for instance, he observed the flight of a large bird of prey near Fiesole, but his notebooks make no mention of attempts at flight. Even today, though, people around here say that once a giant bird rose into the air on Monte Ceceri and vanished in the distance, never to be seen again.[4] Did the legend originate in the fate of a man who flew over the quarry into the depths, suspended from enormous wings? Girolamo Cardano, the preeminent physician and natural philosopher of the Renaissance, featured a description of Leonardo's attempts at flying; Cardano's text even implies that Leonardo crashed.[5] Cardano had apparently learned of these events from his father, Fazio, who was friends with Leonardo.

At any rate, the time was ripe for experiments of this kind. Drawings made by engineers in Siena in the mid-fifteenth century show men sailing through the sky with primitive wings, suspended from pointed parachutes.[6] By 1500, tales of aerial acrobats began to proliferate. There was talk of leaps with man-made wings in Nuremberg and Scotland, and mocking tales poked fun at both the audacity of the intrepid fliers and the public's hankering for sensations. In the now-classic stories about Till Eulenspiegel recorded during this era, the legendary trickster decides to entertain the people of Magdeburg by preparing to fly: "There at once arose such a clamor in the city that young and old gathered at the market place, hoping to see him do it. Well, Eulenspiegel took up his position on the roof of the town hall, flapping his arms, and acting as if he really meant to take off."[7]

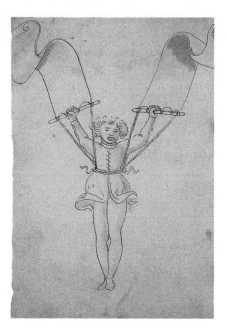

Drawing of a "birdman" by an unknown
draftsman from Siena

Just a few decades earlier, it would have been unthinkable for people to place such fervent hopes in soaring up into the skies. In antiquity, conquering gravity was left to the gods, in the Christian West to the angels, a few saints, and of course Jesus and Mary. All others had to be content with the view, represented by Saint Augustine in his *City of God*, that a particular element was intended for each creature to inhabit—the earth for humans, the sky for birds. The utmost ecstasy possible for man's soul would be to float through the spheres of paradise after death, as described in Dante's *Divine Comedy*. But anyone trying to emulate Christ's Ascension was clearly in league with demons and thus guilty of heresy, deserving of the kind of punishment purportedly meted out to the early Christian sorcerer Simon Magus when he levitated up into the sky. Peter prayed to God to make Simon fall, and

Simon came crashing down to earth and broke his legs. He was stoned to death by bystanders.[8]

But once the intellectual revolution gained steam in the first half of the fifteenth century, this kind of reasoning was no longer a deterrent. The fall of Constantinople had resulted in the relocation not only of entire libraries of ancient manuscripts to Italy, but also of scholars who understood them; suddenly there were alternatives to Church doctrine. Technology was developing rapidly, surpassed only by the pace at which artists invented ever-new forms of expression. Wealth abounded, cities had become independent of the central power, and there seemed no good reason to endure limitations. Trade with the non-Christian new rulers of the eastern Mediterranean was blossoming, and the news from Spain was that Christopher Columbus had discovered the sea route to India. Nearly anything seemed possible—even flying.

The Church had preached humility for over a millennium, but now the Florentine philosopher Marsilio Ficino was contending that man's dignity arose from his ability to transform himself and his world according to the dictates of his will and that the highest good was creative power. Ficino, with whom the young Leonardo spent a good deal of time, even maintained that the human soul should strive to return to its natural state of perfection.[9]

Leonardo's contemporaries recognized that he had come further down this road than anyone else. Who better to be the first human being to challenge the supremacy of gods in the sky? Conquering the force of gravity with knowledge and resourcefulness meant coming that much closer to perfection. The dream of the Renaissance was crystallized in man's yearning to fly.

Leonardo made it his mission to realize this dream, and in 1505 he recorded the following vision, just as he was planning to launch his "great bird" at Monte Ceceri: "To write thus clearly of the kite would seem to be my destiny, because in the earliest recollections of my infancy, it seemed to me when I was in my cradle that a kite came and opened my mouth with its tail, and struck me within upon the lips with its tail many times."[10] That Sigmund Freud chose to interpret these words as a statement of Leonardo's intensely erotic attachment to his mother and of his nascent homosexuality (mistranslating the Italian *nibbio* (kite) as "vulture" in the process) reveals more about Freud than it does about Leonardo. It is highly unlikely that this story reflected an actual childhood memory; as far as we know, Leonardo told it for the first and only time when he was a fifty-three-year-old man. The point was probably to emphasize that he was one of the chosen few, striving for eternal fame as the builder of the "great bird," as we learn on the cover of his notebook about the flight of birds.

Leonardo's ambition was also an outgrowth of an epoch in which people strove for esteem as never before. As the British historian Peter Burke has pointed out, the literature of the Renaissance brimmed with words like "competition" (*concertazione*), "emulation" (*emulazione*), and "glory" (*gloria*).[11] Just two generations earlier, the ill-fated Icarus had been considered guilty of hubris, but the tide turned by the sixteenth century, as evidenced in this sympathetic statement by the Neopolitan poet Luigi Tansillo: "This one aspired to the stars, and if he did not reach them, his life faded, but not his daring."[12] And Leonardo made a note of Dante's cautionary words in the *Inferno*: "He who goes through life without achieving fame leaves no more vestige of himself on earth than smoke in the air or foam on the waves."[13]

The folk legend about Monte Ceceri fits so perfectly with Leonardo's vision of flying that we might well share the art historian Ludwig Heydenreich's hunch that Leonardo, the consummate storyteller, concocted the glorious legend of the swan himself. Another possibility is that he knew the story from his childhood and chose this spot for his experiments to make it seem like the fulfillment of an old myth. In either case, the coupling of this story with Leonardo's attempts at flight would have enhanced his own fame.

While I was coming down from Monte Ceceri, I asked a woodsman who was gasping for breath as he made his way upward about this story, and he told me that Michelangelo—Leonardo's archrival—is said to have broken his legs here while flying.

Alone Against Gravity

Would anyone spend half a lifetime drawing flying machines without the slightest intention of putting them to the test? For over three decades, Leonardo threw himself headlong into filling his notebooks with hundreds of sketches of man-made wings, propulsion mechanisms, and birds' wings. He jotted down notes about the flight of birds, pondered airstreams and the forces on a flying body, and wondered how a human could survive a crash.

All the same, many biographers and art historians have declared Leonardo's flying machines "technical utopias," by which they mean that he merely dreamed of flying but did not actually believe that his ideas could be realized, and that he did not attempt to execute his designs. Arguments of this sort emphasize that no extant document substantiates any attempt at flight, but they tend to disregard the numerous references in his notebooks to preparations for this kind of experiment. It is hard to imagine that a mind as curious as his would leave things at a merely theoretical level. We have to assume that Leonardo tried out some of his designs.

The doubts are certainly understandable, though. Leonardo's drawings of flying machines seem so far removed from anything people had previously produced that it is easy to come away thinking that Leonardo was merely daydreaming. But once we realize how intensively he grappled with the problem of flying, we get a sense of just how seriously Leonardo really took it—and how bold his fixation was. In the decades he spent working on flying machines, aerodynamics, and the physical structure of birds, he was all on his own. The science of his era was not in a position to contribute virtually anything of value on these subjects.

How far can a gifted individual go alone? Leonardo's attempts to conquer the sky were a test of the boundaries of the human mind.

"Board up the large room above . . ."

Leonardo had his first documented encounter with the dream of flying as a young man in Florence. In 1471, his mentor Verrocchio was involved in the preparations for a spectacle honoring the visiting duke of Milan. In three churches in the city, angels with flapping wings, pulled by invisible cables, floated over the heads of the faithful, and a Christ soared up to the heavens.[14] Soon afterward, Leonardo began to draw machines for the stage; the graphic arts collection in the Uffizi Gallery still has his first sketches on red paper. The aerial screw he designed appears to have been intended for the theater as well; its unique construction gave some later historians of technology the idea of hailing Leonardo as the inventor of the helicopter, although there is no evidence that he believed his contraption would ever rise into the air on its own.

These early sketches of flying machines seem especially alluring because they blend realistic ideas with absurd fantasies. The young Leonardo drew the most implausible designs—feathered wings that spread out as they opened up, and a kind of treadmill in which a standing man would use cranks and pedals to operate paddles over his head, working so vigorously that he would effectively row his way into the air.

Aerial screw

Yet Leonardo soon went beyond mere special effects. In about 1487, he designed a skeletal structure for wings on which the pilot's out-stretched fingers were separated by webbing,[15] and complex steering mechanisms enabled the pilot to engage each finger joint of the wings individually.

Clearly he was planning to construct wings even at this time. He noted down every last detail of the materials he would need. The skele-tons would be made of "fir, and reinforced with limewood"[16] and covered with the "skin of the sea hen" (a flying fish), or, if that were not available, with normal skin.[17] Leonardo also built an entire arsenal of measuring instruments for his experiments. The notebooks feature anemometers to gauge the wind force, inclinometers to measure slopes, and a giant device resembling bellows used to test whether individual wings pro-duced enough lift to raise a 200-pound man into the air (see illustration at the beginning of this chapter).

But the more research he did, the more questionable these designs began to seem. Leonardo started to wonder whether the human mind was capable of creating a workable flying machine without relying on a model. He reasoned that it would be safer to let nature be his guide:

"Although human subtlety makes a variety of inventions . . . it will never devise an invention more beautiful, more simple, or more direct than does nature, because in her inventions nothing is lacking, and nothing is superfluous."[18]

Leonardo studied birds and bats (he even made himself a note to "dissect the bat"[19]) and examined the movements of butterflies and flies. Birds, he wrote, *are* flying machines.[20] In doing so, incidentally, he anticipated the fundamental insight of Otto Lilienthal—the first successful aviator—who collected extensive data on sparrows and storks and wrote an entire book on their art of flight before attempting his own first takeoff from the Mühlenberg mountain near the village of Derwitz, outside of Potsdam.

Leonardo's designs reflect the way their inventor increasingly modeled his creations on the workings of nature. With his unique powers of observation, he had figured out that birds make headway by flexing their wings.[21] As photographs with high-speed cameras reveal, the tips of the wings work like little propellers: When they are lowered, their leading edges are pulled downward, and when they are raised, the edges rise, which is how the wings, like the rotor blades of a helicopter, produce lift and forward thrust at the same time. Although Leonardo did not know the principle of the propeller, he sensed that his flying machines would have to imitate the flexing of birds' wings, so he planned for a large number of joints in the wings.

But how does a bird soar up into the air? The answer—by beating its wings—seems so obvious at first that any further thought on the subject appears pointless. Leonardo was never able to move beyond this plausible but incorrect explanation. The air, he reasoned, is compressed under the bird, and as its body escapes the resistance, it is pushed aloft.[22] He therefore equipped nearly all his constructions with wings that could be raised and lowered using muscle power.

Study of the flight of birds

When Leonardo began his systematic study of the anatomy of humans and birds in about 1490, he realized that, by body weight, humans are much weaker than birds. More than half of a bird's body mass is concentrated in its pectoral muscles, as compared to a tiny fraction in humans. Leonardo set out to compensate for this disadvantage by making the most of the pilot's arm and leg strength with slings, stirrups, and foot spars. On several sketches we see prone figures positioned in a frame, their legs drawn up and their limbs anchored to the machine. Even the head is used for steering within an enclosure. The would-be pilot is thus strapped to an instrument of torture and equipped with wings that are clearly far too small. The drawings he made during his early years in Milan look heroic, yet somewhat desperate.

The shortcomings of the construction and of human anatomy did nothing to stop Leonardo from coming up with concrete ideas for a test flight. Above the somewhat unclear drawing of a flying device with giant wings, placed on a ladder, we read his thoughts about secret locations for his experiments in the Corte Vecchia in Milan: "Board up the large room above, and . . . you will have space upon the roof above. . . . And if you stand upon the roof at the side of the tower the men at work upon the cupola will not see you."[23] At one point he was considering launching the artificial bird's first long flights over a body of water and equipping the pilot with an inflated wineskin to use as a life preserver.[24] Later he designed leather bags "tied after the fashion of the beads of a rosary" and fastened to the pilot to cushion his landing. "If you should fall with the double chain of leather bags which you have tied underneath you so manage that these are what first strike the ground."[25]

What finally made him question whether it was possible to fly using muscle power: failed attempts at flight, theoretical insights, or both? Whatever the case, Leonardo started to realize, during his final years in Milan, that beating wings were insufficient for flight. Humans were simply too weak to rise into the sky on their own power. Once, in about 1495, he broke away from the model of the birds with two designs, at least one of which would have had a good chance of success.[26] The first is a sphere with circular sails, the pilot floating through the air in its middle as though suspended within a bubble. The second drawing features a rigid wing that bears a striking resemblance to a modern stunt kite. Unfortunately Leonardo did not pursue this promising idea.

Instead, he returned to studying nature. He noticed that the larger the bird, the less frequently it flapped its wings. Now he saw a solution that made it possible to remain aloft for hours, and even to rise, with far less use of force: An eagle draws on the force of the wind, and uses its wing movements almost exclusively for the purpose of steering. Leonardo must have observed birds executing their maneuvers on countless solitary hikes, his notebook attached to his belt. Sketches show vultures in various wind conditions circling in the sky and eagles beginning their nosedive by adjusting their wings. Still other birds glide down in wave movements or use thermal activity to spiral upward.

In the flying machines Leonardo was now constructing, there was less emphasis on thrust, but movable, adjustable wings continued to be of paramount importance. Still, the ropes and guide pulleys would now serve primarily to steer the "bird" by flexing its wings. The flying machine would soar through the air, elegant as a swallow, with an occasional beating of wings by the pilot to help it along. Leonardo had understood that in gliding the critical element is achieving the optimal shape of the wing. Only then can the wings transform the force of the headwinds into lift. The book about the flight of birds and other sheets reveal the most astonishing plans: Leonardo designed wings with an aerodynamic profile and thought about the airstream at the outermost edges of the wings, where modern engineers attach upwardly curving pieces on top of their jets, called "winglets," to conserve fuel. Later he even made a sketch of how the air swirls under the curved interior surface of a bird's wing.[27]

The drawings give us a good indication of how the "great bird" lifting off from Monte Ceceri might have looked.[28] With its curved, partially movable wings and a smaller steering wing at the tail it would have resembled a giant kite or eagle from afar. Under the wings, at the precise center of gravity of the construction, the pilot would be attached to a gondola in a standing position and would steer the device by flexing his upper body. One of Leonardo's most profound insights was that birds steer the direction of their flight by shifting their body weight and flexing their wings. An entire section of the codex about the flight of birds treats these delicate problems of equilibrium.

"LEONARDO COMPLICATED MATTERS"

To see the kind of glider Leonardo might have built, I traveled to Bedfordshire, England. It took me a good hour of driving through villages

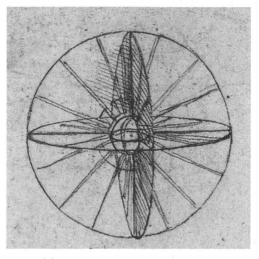

Glider

to get to the abandoned Rotary Farm. There, seven men who enjoy tinkering with aviation devices are spending their days assembling historical flying machines using original parts. Steve Roberts, a precision mechanic, who until several years ago serviced the printing presses for the *Times of London*, accompanied me into a big barn with so many biplanes that I felt as though I were standing in a World War I hangar. Roberts explained to me that these vintage planes were always ready for takeoff, and even the machine guns could still shoot. I saw one of his colleagues fiddling with a strange vehicle that had a spluttering motor on its loading area. It was a machine to start up old propellers, the man said. Did I know what it took to get your hands on an original set of coil springs in good condition for a 1915 carburetor control cable? He finally struck gold at a scrap dealer in Australia.

Producers from the London television station that had arranged for the construction of the giant crossbow had come here back in the summer of 2002 to see the design engineers, bringing with them Martin Kemp, the Leonardo expert from Oxford. The scholar produced several

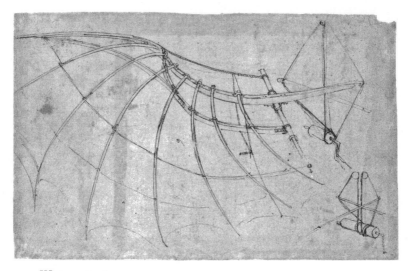

Wing construction

drawings from the notebooks and asked Roberts if he thought that something constructed on the basis of these designs could fly.

"I felt like saying 'never,' because the drawings seemed far too absurd," Roberts told me, "but I decided to hold back a bit, and we embarked on the project of building a flying machine according to Leonardo's designs." The hobbyists had three months to complete the machine. The greatest challenge was trying to forget everything they knew about airplanes and to consider only how Leonardo would have proceeded. "Since we were restricted to the materials he had available to him as well, we opted to construct a frame out of poplar, hemp ropes, and a linen wing cover. We made glue from a component of rabbit skins. Leonardo almost never provides measurements on his drawings, so we made the flying machine the size a man would just about be able to carry."

The wing designs that Roberts and his colleagues studied generated too little propulsion, and the project began to seem hopeless. "But then, Kemp showed us a sketch with a covering around the leading edge of the wing that allowed a good airstream to form. Leonardo quite clearly intended this. We just had to simplify his plan: Instead of two movable wings on the right and left we built one single rigid piece. Leonardo complicated matters." The mechanic thus changed the historical design in a small but significant way by departing once and for all from the concept that birds fly by flapping their wings, which Leonardo had found so difficult to relinquish.

Under the ceiling of Roberts's barn was a brownish wing more than 30 feet wide, with a pyramid-like frame dangling from the middle, where the pilot would be suspended. The whole thing resembled one of today's hang gliders, but the sweeping S-shaped wing made it far more elegant.

When Roberts tested the construction on the roof of a special-purpose automobile that was traveling against the wind, nothing happened at first, but when the headwind reached nearly gale force, the wing moved upward, instilling new hope in the television crew, which had begun to have its doubts about Leonardo and the broadcast after the fiasco with the crossbow. Now they needed to find a pilot who was lightweight, but strong enough to take a run-up with this heavy structure. But who would be willing to face a storm with Leonardo's wings?

The Intrepid Judy Leden

Judy Leden had not only won the world championship in hang gliding three times, but she had also paraglided from the highest active volcanoes in the world. She had sailed over the valleys of the Himalayas with flocks of vultures, and in Patagonia she took to the air with giant condors. The forty-seven-year-old described the experience of flying as though she were realizing Leonardo's dream of making man fly like a bird. "For me, it is like entering into another state of mind. I am aware of the sun, the wind, and the pressures on the wing. I stop *thinking* about how the interaction of the elements affects my flight—I *feel* it physically. Over the years I've actually developed a kind of bird brain. When I leave the ground, I'm not just floating through the air; I'm feeling and thinking the way a bird does."

She tells me that she did not hesitate for a second when she got the offer to make the maiden voyage with the glider: "I considered it a great privilege to learn for myself whether Leonardo would have been able to fly." Even though the TV documentary clearly shows that Leden gasped when Roberts's first model fell to the ground like a ripe apple during a test flight, she held to her promise.

One stormy October morning, the team at the hills of the southern English coast was ready for takeoff. "I had a silly discussion with my husband, who wanted me not to go into the sky in this storm," Leden recalled. "We have two small children. But the glider was only able to fly with strong headwinds." Assistants used long ropes to hold onto both ends of the wings, because Roberts was afraid that the glider might otherwise rise at breakneck speed, topple over, and crash. "I ran up, took off right away, and climbed above the treetops, until the ropes slowed me down and I sailed down the hill. It was scary when the wing began to swing around in the air—but I landed safely on my feet at the edge of the hillside. It was fantastic."

All the same, the experienced pilot struggled mightily to handle this contraption: "Of all the devices I have ever flown, this was the hardest to control. Since the wing was stiff, you couldn't steer. I felt as though I were in a car traveling at a hundred miles an hour with the steering wheel unbolted. I literally had to learn how to fly all over again." While Leden was learning to maneuver it, there were dramatic landings. The glider was thrown off course and its nose or wing wound up buried

Judy Leden's maiden voyage with the Leonardo glider

in the ground. "But after my best start, I flew thirty feet high and more than six hundred fifty feet in length, which beat the records of pioneers Lilienthal and Wright. Leonardo was an incredible genius."

Does this mean that Leonardo would have been able to build a functional airplane nearly five hundred years before Lilienthal? Leden hesitated before replying, "Well, if he succeeded in building a plane, he surely paid for this success with the life of his test pilot." Now it was my turn to gasp. The fact that the British experiments turned out so successfully and exceeded expectations was thus due solely to the skill of both Leden and design engineer Roberts. An inexperienced pilot would have plunged to his death even without a crisis. The shock of feeling the earth disappear under his feet would have been enough to make him lose control.

Still, it seems highly doubtful that one of Leonardo's gliders of this kind ever soared into the air. For one thing, Leonardo—in contrast to the British hobbyists—had not taken the crucial step of fusing the two movable wings into a single one. But even if he had combined the rigid hang glider he had designed in 1495 with aerodynamically ingenious wings, a test flight would most likely have been doomed to failure. Leonardo had not grasped the fact that the pull upward can develop only if the pilot gets a running start. Instead, he pictured his flying machines taking off the way small birds do. A sparrow can generate enough flux by beating its wings to lift its slight weight up, but a bird as large as a swan has to run to create sufficient air movement on its wings to lift off. And a human being needs a good deal more lift.

Thus, a daredevil taking off from the slope of Monte Ceceri would certainly have plunged into the quarry. There is no doubt that Leonardo was aware of dangers of this kind. Is that why he kept his attempts secret? Or did he ultimately shrink back from this hazardous enterprise?

After 1506, Leonardo made just one more sketch of a device for human flight (which he definitely did not build). Apart from this single sketch, however, he did not pursue the matter again, but he redoubled his efforts to study the mechanics of the flight of birds and wind flow. He had evidently come to terms with the fact that he understood far too little about the basics to fly himself. We would love to know what caused his change of heart, but there are no notes on this subject. What had Leonardo attempted before 1506—and how many times? Was there even a tragedy on Monte Ceceri that made him give up?

FLYING DOES NOT MEAN FLAPPING WINGS

Leonardo had everything he needed to build a functional glider, as the trials in England prove. He went to incredible lengths to achieve this goal. For the crucial question—the wing profile—he had even found solutions that come astonishingly close to those used today, yet in all likelihood, he never flew.

Why was he bound to fail? Leonardo himself provided the answer: "Those who are enamored of practice without science are like a pilot who goes into a ship without rudder or compass and never has any certainty where he is going."[29] Leonardo wrote this comment a few years after his confident proclamations about a big swan soaring into the sky over Florence.

He had ventured into areas of physics in which his visual way of thinking no longer sufficed. Leonardo was able to provide brilliant descriptions of what he saw, but he could not join all his observations together into a comprehensive theory that would provide practical solutions.

He continued to pursue the seemingly obvious solution—that humans could fly like birds—even though his own research had long since indicated otherwise. Although he came to recognize the significance of gliding, he never stopped reflecting on the wing movements of birds. Again and again he designed contraptions with movable wings that were too unstable to work. He never seriously considered the possibility that the solution might lie in a rigid wing, since every bird was able to raise and lower its wings.

Unlike most of his contemporaries, Leonardo knew that he needed to question what he saw, but, being the extremely visual person that he was, he neither could nor would forgo this type of perception altogether. But science is the business of disengaging yourself from the obvious: The world is not flat, and birds do not remain in the air because they flap their wings, but only because their wings are shaped like an aerofoil, to take full advantage of updrafts. A bird is both pushed and lifted upwards.

Because the wings face against the direction of flight, the air passing above the wings moves more quickly on its upper surface than the air on its underside.[30] This creates a subpressure above the wing, forcing the body to rise. Faster-moving air has a lower pressure and results in lift. That is the secret of flight.

Although Leonardo understood so much else about airstreams and water flow, he never made this connection, but he took an important step in the right direction when his research about water made him realize that a current gets faster when constricted. He even had all the tools to measure the undertow of the more rapid current, yet it took two hundred years after his death for the Swiss physicist Daniel Bernoulli to come up with this idea. Leonardo's mind was unprepared to look for the proper physical quantities. His ideas about the pressure of fluids and gases were far too vague; he was in sore need of a theory—not that he could fathom what such a theory might have conveyed. Compared with later researchers, Leonardo was lacking less in technology and knowledge than in a method of organizing his knowledge.

It is thus all the more astonishing that he got as far as he did—single-handedly and without knowing the rules of the game his successors used to tease out the secrets of the world. After its beginnings in the sixteenth century, science quickly developed into a giant parlor game. From the outset, hundreds of scholars in Europe took part in it, and today there are millions of men and women throughout the world whose discoveries follow a set procedure: reconcile a new idea with others' observations and corroborate it with experiments and measurements. If the idea turns out to be sound, it is published and others can test it and develop it further. The system is so successful precisely because it works even when the players are no better than average. No individual researcher need be a genius—it requires only the addition of a few more pieces to the big puzzle while relying on previously published findings.

As a result, an ample foundation of well-organized knowledge was in place by the seventeenth century. Even the father of modern physics, Isaac Newton, who was ordinarily not given to modesty (and was anything but an average scholar) explained his success by claiming he was able to see farther than others because he was standing on the shoulders of giants.

Leonardo was larger than life, but his feet were planted firmly on the ground. While later researchers were able to enjoy a productive exchange of ideas, his communications were restricted largely to jottings in his notebooks. And instead of conducting systematic experiments to test his ideas, he kept up a kind of interior monologue. It is fascinating, and often touching, to trace the way he kept questioning his ideas and discovering contradictions—and often arriving at better insights. But just as often, as with his imperfect understanding of the flight of birds, he lacked the interaction with others that might have helped him get past an intellectual impasse.

His attempts at flight did not go beyond the technical capabilities of his era, but his approach was quite novel. Still, nothing would be more unfair than to call him a "utopian," as people often do. Only researchers who know how to dream advance the progress of mankind.

Leonardo's quest for the truth was arduous and solitary. By the time of his final visit to Monte Ceceri, he must have known that it would be left to later eras to fulfill his greatest dream. He himself would never enjoy the fame of being the first human to fly. The only reward for his efforts was his increasingly profound understanding of the mysteries of nature. But this prospect was enough to keep him exploring the flight of birds for another dozen years. He was extraordinarily tenacious. His notes contain only a single remark that appeared to cast doubt on the advisability of forging ahead with his work: *O Leonardo, perché tanto penate?*[31] Oh, Leonardo—why do you torture yourself so?

Toward the end of his life, he found an easier means of approaching the object of his greatest yearning. His first biographer, Giorgio Vasari, noted in amazement that Leonardo began to construct artificial birds, little toys that flew over the heads of his visitors, as if to poke fun at

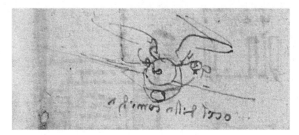

Small mechanical bird

his own dream of flying: "He experimented with a paste made out of a certain kind of wax and made some light and billowy figures in the form of animals which he inflated with his mouth as he walked along and which flew above the ground until all the air escaped."[32]

In 1506, the year of the apparent failure on Monte Ceceri, Leonardo left Florence, the place where he had experienced so many disappointments, and, after considerable wavering, took up residence in Milan again. Two years later, he made a sketch of a small mechanical bird consisting of a cylindrical trunk and two essentially useless wings. It looks like one of those Chinese plastic toys you see everywhere these days. The bird is mounted on a slanted cord, and as it slides down, its wings are set in motion. But the flight is mere illusion. After thirty years of tireless work, Leonardo's dream of flying had reverted to what it was in the first days of his research—a flight of the imagination.

ROBOTS

MARK ROSHEIM LIVES IN A bright green, wood-framed house near the Minneapolis airport. A tin-can robot greeting visitors at the front stoop is the only distinguishing feature of Rosheim's home in a sea of single-family dwellings with gable roofs and carports. Rosheim is a lean man in his late forties who bears the traces of his Scandinavian heritage. The tidy living room is furnished with upholstered armchairs and a smoked glass coffee table. A reproduction of Leonardo's Turin self-portrait hangs next to the fireplace. Rosheim lives alone.

On the coffee table I saw a column-like object about as long as my forearm, with dozens of intertwined pieces of steel. I assumed this object was a work of art, but my host informed me that it was a humanoid robotic joint. This construction gives an artificial claw the mobility of a human hand. Rosheim has a patent for it and for countless other components to make human-like machines. Mechanics construct the mechanical shoulders, wrists, and arms, as well as complete robots, in the rear wing of the house—but Rosheim felt that the workshops were too messy to be shown to visitors. He told me that he has been

Spring

Mark Rosheim with his reconstruction of
a spring-driven car

able to sell some of his inventions to NASA and that he has received some funding from the Pentagon.

Rosheim taught himself the art of engineering after a few short months in a mechanical engineering program at the University of Minnesota. He applied for his first patent at the age of eighteen. When he was trying to figure out the right proportions for a robotic shoulder joint, he found a phenomenally precise model in Leonardo's *Vitruvian Man*, the famous drawing of a man inscribed in a circle and a square, and Rosheim became a confirmed Leonardo fan and bibliophile. He opened a cabinet in his living room that held facsimiles of all six thousand extant drawings by Leonardo, stored in leather-bound cases. Rosheim proudly announced that he had several copies of a group of rare reprints and that his collection was unsurpassed in the entire Midwest.

Then he rolled in a black wooden frame on three wheels from the next room. The machine was flat, about the size of a stove top, with a jumble of wooden gears, springs, cams, and levers, and bore a resemblance to a giant clock mechanism. Rosheim turned a wheel to wind up a spring, placed the little car back on the floor, and let go. The vehicle began to move straight ahead, then turned and executed a bold but precise slalom between the couch, the floor lamp, and the fireplace.

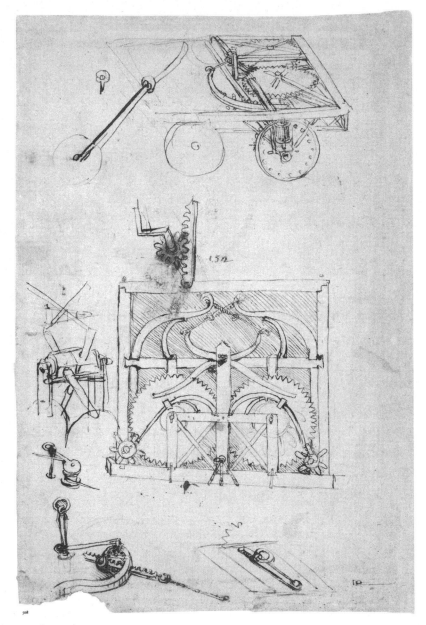

Spring-driven car

Rosheim stopped it, tinkered with the mechanism, and exchanged a couple of cams. After he wound it up again, the car charted a different course over the rug. "You are seeing what is likely the oldest programmable automaton in the world," Rosheim explained, adding that he built it according to plans by the young Leonardo.

As if this were not startling enough, Rosheim went on to say that Leonardo had made still more inroads into twenty-first-century-style technology. Leonardo had designed a mechanical man driven by cables and even digital components of the kind found in computers today. All it takes to recognize this is a careful reading of Leonardo's notebooks. "Leonardo," Rosheim explained, "was a pioneer of robots and computers."

Had this man from Minneapolis gotten too caught up in his studies? He would not be the first to be carried away with notions of genius and to make untenable claims when contemplating the notebooks. There are few technological achievements that have not been attributed to Leonardo at one time or another. He is said to have come up with the ideas for bicycles, helicopters, submarines, and paddle steamers— even automatic rotisseries.

Nowadays, people who regard Leonardo as a futurist of the early modern period are viewed with suspicion. Just as we can no longer look at the *Mona Lisa* without preconceptions, we find it difficult to take Leonardo's inventions at face value once inundated with marvelous stories about them. Enthusiasm for Leonardo, who seems so far ahead of his time, has a long history. The initial wave of euphoria crested in about 1880, when the first scholars studied Leonardo's technical drawings and were startled to discover cutting-edge innovations of their own era in Leonardo's jottings. A couple of decades later, though, it became apparent that many of Leonardo's designs could not function in practice.

A search for evidence that anyone had built machines according to the practicable sketches ensued, and when nothing turned up, Leonardo was dismissed as a dreamer. His star as an inventor sank still further in the second half of the twentieth century, when historians of technology came across more and more construction plans from the early modern period and compared them to Leonardo's ideas. They discovered that much of what the master had sketched was also found in the work of his contemporaries. Now experts cast doubt not only on his scientific achievements, but on his aptitude as an engineer.

Was Leonardo da Vinci a revolutionary, a dreamer, or someone who just copied the ideas of clever contemporaries? Even today, each of these views has its proponents, and many scholars find elements of all three in his designs. Leonardo Olschki describes his namesake as follows: "His scientific and technological work is little more than a mass of eloquent literary fragments and realistic drawings, of ingenious projects that would hardly have withstood a practical test."[1]

But Rosheim is confident he has proved that Leonardo was far more than a mere Jules Verne of the Renaissance.

HANDBAGS AND WATER HEATERS

One of Leonardo's most spectacular extant plans, a machine to shear cloth, was conceived in about 1490.[2] The idea was to have an automaton perform the laborious task of trimming the nap off woolen cloth by carrying out three simultaneous tasks on four pieces of fabric stretched across a frame in parallel rows: The scissors would open and close, then move across the cloth after every cut, whereupon the device would bring in more fabric from the reel. A mechanical control system for such a complex sequence would pose quite a challenge even to a mechanical engineer today. Leonardo's plans for this device were metic-

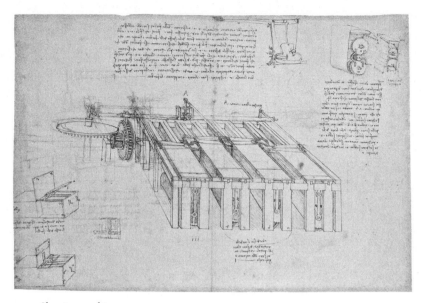

Shearing machine

ulously executed. Even Bertrand Gille, a French historian who was otherwise quick to disparage Leonardo's technical achievements, was full of admiration for these sketches: "There is no doubt, as a single glance will be enough to show, that these sketches are, from the technical point of view of course, the best drawings of Leonardo da Vinci which have come down to us."[3]

Leonardo developed dozens of appliances of this kind, from a file-cutter (one of his first machines) to a device for grinding concave mirrors (one of his last). He found the notion that machines could perform highly complex tasks nearly as exhilarating as the idea of flying. In this respect, Leonardo was pursuing the same goals as engineers in the industrial age. Even his aim of cutting costs sounds modern. When designing a machine to produce needles, he made careful calculations to find out how much money the implementation of his invention would yield annually if it were used for twenty working days a month: 60,000 ducats.[4]

He was one of the first engineers to advance the process of automation. The astonishing brilliance of his technical achievements is often played down by art historians, who reduce this aspect of his creativity to a mere outgrowth of his artistic prowess, and skeptics like to point out that there is no documentation to confirm that any of Leonardo's designs were implemented. The latter claim is true only up to a point: In a codex that was discovered in the Biblioteca Nazionale Marciana in Venice in 1953, a clockmaker named della Golpaja described a water wheel that Leonardo made for the wealthy Bernardo Rucellai. The description matches one of Leonardo's sketches.[5]

In addition, there are statements by contemporaries, such as the painter Lomazzo, who noted after the death of Leonardo that "all Europe [was] full" of his inventions.[6] Toward the end of the sixteenth century, Don Ambrogio Mazenta reported that workmen in Lombardy were using Leonardo's machines to polish crystal, iron, and stone and that "there is one [machine] much used in the cellars of Milan, for grinding large amounts of meat to make *cervellato* [sausage made with pork meat and brain] with the help of a wheel turned by a boy."[7] Both statements are of questionable value, however: Lomazzo's wording is vague, and Mazenta, who himself owned Leonardo's notebooks, is not considered a reliable source.

However, the manuscripts leave no doubt that Leonardo was a highly practical draftsman who was much in demand. Water heaters, locks, ladies' handbags, hydraulic lifts, looms, and hundreds of other items that appear in his notebooks are anything but technical utopias; they were clearly made to be used in the workplace and elsewhere. Historian of science Bern Dibner wrote, "Leonardo's notebooks often read like a modern mail-order catalogue that offers an ingenious tool or gadget for every conceivable purpose."[8]

And there is no reason to believe that the devices depicted on Leonardo's sketches were never built. While flying machines might be the stuff of dreams, the only reason to draw practical items such as hydraulic lifts and water pipes would be if commissioned to construct them. It is not surprising that Leonardo was much sought after: His reputation as an outstanding engineer was sure to have preceded him.

The question of which parts he invented and which he took over from others will likely never be answered. This uncertainty was already evident in the discussion about the San Marco lock in Milan. There was no orderly system of publication in the Renaissance to use in reconstructing the development of technology. Although the Republic of Venice had enacted the world's first patent law in 1474, it was universally ignored. Plagiarism was the order of the day. In any case, the success of an engineer depended far less on his wealth of ideas than on his ability to produce a needed piece of equipment. The employers wanted solutions, not strokes of genius. They did not care whether an engineer had thought up a particular mechanism by himself or adopted someone else's idea. We wonder about Leonardo's significance as an inventor today because of our interest in learning about him as an individual. Back then, the question was of little consequence.

When historians of technology, such as Paolo Galluzzi in Florence, began a systematic comparison of Leonardo's manuscripts with the notes of other Renaissance engineers, the result was as expected. The master had openly helped himself to the work of his peers. Many of his designs bore a strong resemblance to older notations by Francesco di Giorgio Martini and Taccola. Both men worked in Siena, where engineering had thrived even in the century before Leonardo's birth. Manuscripts from this city featured diving bells, parachutes, and paddle steamers.[9] These ideas were subsequently often falsely ascribed to Leonardo because his manuscripts were known, while the designs of others had been consigned to oblivion. In praising Leonardo, people were effectively praising the inventiveness of an entire century.

Findings of this sort tend to dishearten those with a romantic bent who embrace the notion that a genius of the stature of Leonardo was of his era in body, but centuries ahead of his time in mind. But of course Leonardo was a child of the fifteenth century. His writings and drawings are not merely the legacy of an extraordinary individual, but a unique testament to the capabilities of the era in which he lived. This realization should not detract from our admiration for Leonardo, but rather help us recognize the supposed dreamer for what he was: a realist who took a practical approach to testing the limits of what could be achieved. And Leonardo's very reliance on established knowledge enhanced his chances for success—whereas his attempts at flight were doomed to failure because they lacked a scientific foundation.

Even more than in his innovative designs, Leonardo was pioneering in his grasp of technology. His precursors, who were still under the sway of the Middle Ages, regarded engineering as a craft. They put their faith in tradition, and new inventions came about by trial and error. An engineer did not set down his knowledge for posterity—he just passed it on by guiding his pupils. Whole cathedrals were built by relying on past experience in placing more and more weight on a supporting structure until at some point it collapsed. The brilliant architect Brunelleschi departed from this practice, using a new type of shuttering process—which he had tested out systematically on a model—to construct the immense dome for the Cathedral of Florence. It was a sensation.

Leonardo similarly rejected the haphazard approach of his colleagues. He did not want simply to turn out machines without investigating why one construction worked and another did not. Just as Leonardo studied nature and the laws of vision to enhance his artistic skills, he devoted himself to physics to find optimal technical solutions. In doing so, Leonardo was the first to lay a scientific foundation for engineering.

Leonardo showed the absurdity of the many attempts then under way to build a perpetual motion machine. In systematic thought experiments he devised various pieces of equipment that supposedly functioned without an energy supply and realized that they all had to come to a standstill at some point. The dream of a machine that performed a job without expending energy, he found, would never be fulfilled—just as it would be hopeless to try to turn dross into gold. "O speculators about perpetual motion, how many vain chimeras have you created in the like quest? Go and take your place with the seekers after gold."[10]

A sensational discovery in 1965 shows how sketchy our understanding of Leonardo's thinking remains to this day. Scientists in the National Library of Madrid happened upon two long-lost manuscript collections. The two notebooks, bound in red kid leather, had been in this spot all along, but had been assigned an incorrect catalogue number, and no one noticed that they contained original texts by Leonardo. This discovery revived the hope that additional works by Leonardo were tucked away in archives and would resurface one day, and it also shed new light on other extant writings.

The first of the two manuscripts, now referred to as Codex Madrid I, is a virtual anatomical atlas of technology. The author chronicled the machines of his era, reduced to their component parts. He filled page after page with views of couplings, flywheels, connecting rods, valves, and cams. The codex contains the first known drawings of ball bearings and worm drives. (The Italian historian of science Ladislao Reti was exaggerating only slightly when he claimed that of all the

138

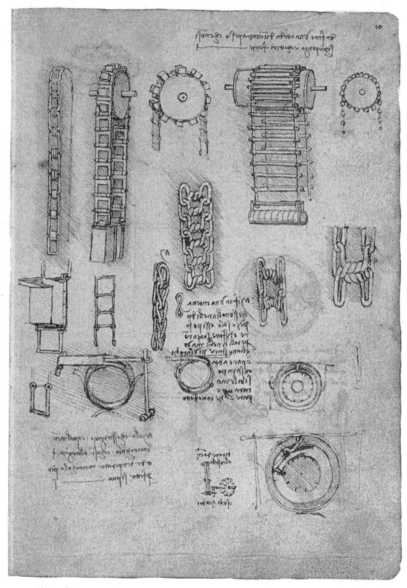

Chain drives

elements of machines now in use, the only one missing was the rivet.)
Evidently Leonardo was planning to publish these as a book. In contrast to the hastily drawn sketches in most of his other manuscripts,
these drawings seem so meticulous that they could easily pass as a
printer's copy.

The manuscript from Madrid confirms the modern nature of
Leonardo's ideas about engineering. His way of thinking about machines differed quite significantly from that of his contemporaries, the
way a biologist's perspective on an ear of corn differs from that of a
farmer. The farmer sees the plant as a whole entity, knows from experience how to handle it, and tends to stick to tried-and-true methods
of cultivation. The biologist, by contrast, breaks down the plant into
its component parts, analyzes the inflorescences, places them under
the microscope, isolates individual cells, and perhaps gets as far as the
genetic makeup in the cell nucleus, thus determining species and sub-
species, clarifying the relationship to other plants, and using this information to develop better methods of cultivation and new varieties.

In the same way, a screw was not just a screw. Leonardo regarded
its thread as an inclined plane wrapped around a cylinder and the screw
as a kind of wedge, and proceeded to determine how for both parts
the angle of inclination had to be set to lift weight most effectively.
Compared with the sketches of the aerial screw, diving bell, or giant
crossbow, these studies may not seem very spectacular, but they—not
his fanciful designs—are what made Leonardo the first engineer of
the modern era.

Leonardo was also a pioneer in the field of technical drawing. He
had realized that the current language no longer sufficed to describe
these increasingly sophisticated machines and to draw up construction
manuals for them. Using elevation, exploded views, and isometry, he
formulated an entire vocabulary of technical drawing, which is still in

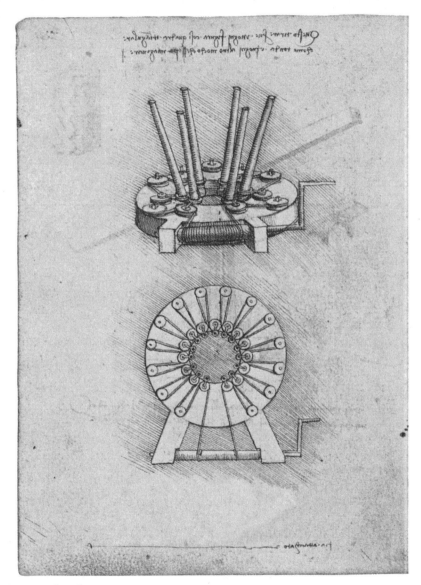

Lifting device

use today and remains the most important tool for engineers even in our era of computerized design.

His sketches attest to his extraordinary ability to think three-dimensionally. Leonardo seems to have had no difficulty turning three-dimensional shapes every which way in his mind. Early studies of the automatic car, the successor of which now winds about on Rosheim's carpet, show how brilliantly Leonardo met this challenge.[11] Gears, worm threads, levers, and bearings on these sheets can be viewed from the front, then from the side at an upward angle, then from behind. Some of the sketches seem like quick jottings, as though Leonardo had drawn them while lost in thought—the way we doodle while talking on the telephone.

Leonardo probably drew on older models for this vehicle as well. Francesco di Giorgio Martini from Siena, one of the most prominent engineers of the Renaissance, had drawn several cars for passengers to operate with a crank. But his designs are of clumsy vehicles—rolling cabins in which he planned to install man-size cogs and gears. In the interior, di Giorgio Martini wasted quite a bit of space between the various mechanisms. Leonardo, by contrast, was able not only to replace the cranking passengers by a spring drive and to provide for an automatic steering device—he also fit the entire device, which was now far more complex, into a flat frame. Leonardo had aspired to and achieved a goal pursued vigorously by today's engineers: reducing the size of technology.

Of all his many talents, his ability to work with the concept of space may have had the most significant effect on his creations. The powerful impact of his paintings derives from the way he makes viewers experience space in ever-changing fashion. To a person standing in the refectory of the Convent of Santa Maria delle Grazie in Milan, *The Last Supper* seems like a natural extension of the walls out to the horizon;

Mona Lisa, by contrast, seems to be hovering in front of the water in the background.

Since Leonardo drew no distinctions among art, science, and technology, his technical designs are more than mere construction guides—they overwhelm and enthrall the viewer. The French art historian Daniel Arasse wrote that at some point, Leonardo fell victim to his own rhetoric, and regarded his visions as reality—which would also explain why he spent decades designing one flying machine after another.[12]

The Performance of the Mechanical Lion

Let us not forget that Leonardo earned his living by conjuring up dreams and illusions. After all, his primary task at the court was to entertain his patrons. Thus it was quite logical that his extended efforts at flying eventually resulted in a little mechanical bird, which was evidently designed to delight the guests of the French governor of Milan. During the period that Ludovico Sforza was still ruler of Milan, Leonardo had already proved a success as an entertainer. When il Moro arranged a brilliant political match between Isabella of Aragon and his nephew Gian Galeazzo in 1490, Leonardo was asked to devise a spectacle with the theme of "paradise on earth." He had seven actors costumed as planet deities float from the sky to greet the bride. The spectacle was such a success that the guests referred to the wedding reception as the Paradise Festival. From then on, Leonardo enjoyed the monarch's highest regard.

His mechanical lion was a sensation as well, as we learn from several documents. Michelangelo Buonarroti the Younger, a nephew of the famous artist, describes the appearance of this automaton at a banquet honoring the king of France's entry into Lyons in 1515. The lion is

Face of an animal; possibly a sketch of the mechanical lion

said to have walked a few steps, then risen on its hind legs and opened its breast, revealing a bouquet of lilies, the coat of arms of the French royal family.[13]

A performance of this kind in an era when the laws of mechanics and biology were unknown must have amazed spectators. They surely felt a combination of fear, bafflement, and admiration when the lion performed his tricks all on his own—just like a trained circus cat, but with oddly stiff movements that would never be found in nature. The thought that only God can make animals that move, live, and procreate must have been swirling through their heads. Hadn't the builder of this mechanism tread suspiciously close to the realm of the Almighty? In any case, he seemed to have deciphered some of His secrets. People wondered whether the engineer had breathed a soul into his creation.

These feelings of shock and awe were exactly what Leonardo's employers were hoping to generate. Impressing people with marvels was proof positive of their power.[14] And Leonardo truly seemed to enjoy

shocking people—even his notes on painting had called artists "grandsons unto God" because artists could exercise power over the feelings
of others and "dismay folk by hellish fictions."[15] As Vasari tells us,
Leonardo's ability to "frighten the life" out of his friends delighted him
to no end.[16]

But Leonardo was not just trying to get a rise out of his audience.
His pleasure in bizarre games and his enthusiasm for automatons was
also fueled by his aversion to charlatans and superstitions of all kinds.
His notebooks inveighed against greedy "inveterate fools and magicians"
and scoffed at the "simple souls" who believed in pied pipers.[17]
Leonardo's spectacles cast the cold light of reason on white and black
magic, because they did not require the invocation of higher powers,
but instead relied solely on the laws and nature and the resourcefulness
of the human mind.

A LIFE FOR LEONARDO

The drawing of the wind-up car, the reconstruction of which I saw in
Minneapolis, is part of the Codex Atlanticus in Milan, the most extensive collection of Leonardo's technical sketches. Experts had known
about this sketch for quite some time, but no one had understood it
properly. Art historians and historians of technology interpreted the
jumble of ink as a plan for a nonfunctional, self-propelled vehicle. Carlo
Pedretti was the first to realize that Leonardo might have had an automaton rather than an automobile in mind.

In the world of research on Leonardo, Pedretti is a living legend.
He attained this status the first time he entered the public eye, just
after World War II. Pedretti, who had been fascinated by Leonardo
from the days of his childhood, distinguished himself by his enthusiasm, eloquence, and extraordinary visual facility. At the age of thirteen,

he could both read and write Leonardo's mirror writing; when he was sixteen, he published a newspaper article about Leonardo's friendship with Machiavelli. Soon afterward he was himself the subject of a news item. In 1951, *Corriere della Sera*, the most highly regarded daily newspaper in Italy, featured a portrait of the astonishing young scholar, with the heading: "At the age of twenty-three, he knows everything about Leonardo."

Pedretti later moved to Los Angeles and became a professor of art history at UCLA, to which a wealthy urologist had bequeathed a unique collection of Leonardo facsimiles. Pedretti, now over eighty and retired, has purchased an old villa in the hills over Vinci, where he gathers together scholars in the summer. The terrace affords a view of olive groves and the house where Leonardo was born.

A darkened upstairs room, nearly as large as a banquet hall and furnished with antiques, serves as his study. Behind the shutters at the back wall I was barely able to make out the June sun. Hefty tomes are piled up on an oak table in the middle of the room. Once my eyes had adjusted to the dim light, I saw that books, most of which were old, surrounded us on every wall. This was just a small part of his library, Pedretti explained to me while sitting down at his desk. Since he was still spending his winters in California, he had brought only his most important materials to Italy.

What fascinated Carlo Pedretti to the point of devoting his entire life to the pursuit of understanding Leonardo? "It is a heady experience to have a connection with one of the greatest minds of all time," Pedretti told me. "I quickly realized that there is a great deal more to be said about Leonardo." All the clichés about his genius, the flawed interpretations of his art, his character, and his ostensible views about sexuality and religion stemmed from the fact that we knew so little about what Leonardo actually wrote, drew, and thought.

Pedretti decided to begin right at the beginning and to understand Leonardo within the context of his era by focusing on what the manuscripts revealed. "Over the years, I learned how to recall every little detail of the many thousands of pages. My photographic memory was a big help. My brain was really like a computer scanning the pages for patterns and similarities to find out what might fit where."

He went to great lengths to introduce order into Leonardo's doubly muddled legacy. Although the looters and dealers who had torn apart his precious possession and scattered it throughout Europe were primarily to blame for the disarray, the notes were extremely jumbled even in their original condition, when Melzi received them from the hands of the dying Leonardo. Pedretti displayed a few pages of his facsimile volumes to show how much must have been buzzing around in Leonardo's head. Some pages have caricatures, technical plans, landscapes, studies of the flight of birds, and flow lines of water sketched adjacent to—or even on top of—one another.

To establish a basis for dating these pages, Pedretti and his colleagues examined how Leonardo's handwriting and drawing style evolved over the years. They compared paper qualities, watermarks, and the strokes made by various pens, inks, and even tears. This work took decades to complete, and by the end, the chronology of a large part of the drawings had been rearranged. Now it was finally possible to trace the path of Leonardo's thought from beginning to end.

In his search for evidence, Pedretti came across sheets that no one had ever studied because they were so difficult to interpret. Some of them show cable systems running over complicated pulleys and images of partial suits of armor and shoulder and elbow joints.[18] On one sketch, the structure of the cables suggests a man with outstretched arms, with pulleys where we might expect hands, elbows, and shoulders.

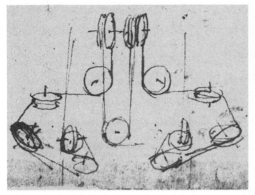

Cable system in the shape of outstretched arms

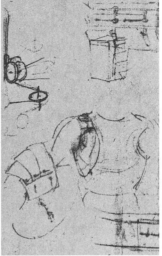

Knight and cable system

Did Leonardo have a mechanical man in mind? The contours of the armor suggest that he might have reconstructed a warrior in full uniform and made it appear to come alive with a system of cables. Pedretti does not know whether Leonardo ever built this robot, but the sketches prove how seriously he took the idea of automatons.

Pedretti concluded that the ominous wind-up car was also equipped with an automatic steering device, although as an art historian, he could not explain how it might function. The answer to this puzzle, Pedretti said, did not become apparent to him until the winter of 1994, when a young engineer, Mark Rosheim, appeared at his door in Los Angeles.

Rosheim had just finished writing a book about the history of robots, and since Leonardo's mechanical warrior was featured in it, the author hoped to interest Pedretti in his work. From the fragments in the notebooks, Rosheim had put together a rough blueprint for a robot, which meant that Leonardo really could have built an artificial knight—not that Rosheim could prove that he had had this exact machine in mind or that he might have actually built it. The fragmentary sketches fell short of providing this information.

The engineer had also studied the wind-up car that had consumed Pedretti's attention for so long. He surmised that this automaton was none other than the mechanism of the artificial lion that had pulled lilies from its breast to honor the French king. The artificial animal, he concluded, only appeared to walk, but actually rode, and the little car served as both steering device and propulsion. The figure of the lion was perched on the flat wooden car, which held the gearwheels, springs, and camshafts. Impressed by the young American's bold ideas, Pedretti arranged for Rosheim to give the keynote speech at a traditional ceremony commemorating Leonardo's birthday in Vinci. Never had this honor been bestowed on an individual without a doctorate. In this venue, exactly 547 years after the birth of Leonardo, Rosheim explained the mystery of the mechanical lion.

The Bell Ringer

Pedretti gave Rosheim another puzzle to work on. For years, Leonardo experts had been perplexed by a mysterious set of sketches in the possession of the Queen of England. Leonardo had made a series of about ten sketches showing a figure holding a hammer way above his head, poised to ring a bell. The figure resembles the two bronze statues on the clock town of Piazza San Marco in Venice that revolve every hour and strike the hour with mallets. Pedretti is convinced that Leonardo knew this mechanism.

However, Leonardo must have had something other than a standard clock in mind. An especially striking picture shows the bell ringer

Bell ringer and water cylinder to operate the device

bending his knee and resting his foot on the edge of a *bottino* (little barrel), with the bell hanging over the barrel on a pole. Under the sketch there are geometric diagrams and some text in mirror writing. According to Pedretti, this sheet was once joined to a second one on which the *bottino* is subdivided into twenty-four smaller containers. The fold lines on both sheets fit together perfectly.[19] The explanation is found on an additional sheet with a similar drawing, which shows that Leonardo was actually planning a timekeeper: "In 24 containers there are the 24 hours, and the one of these 24 containers that opens the first then opens all of them. Now you can make a drum-like well (*bottino*) that keeps all the 24 containers."[20] Leonardo was clearly working on a water clock. Whenever a container fills up at the top of the hour, the bell ringer is set in motion. After twenty-four hours, all the containers are emptied, and the process begins anew.

I had trouble imagining that such a sophisticated hydraulic operation could have been possible in the early sixteenth century, even if the engineer was Leonardo da Vinci, but Pedretti drew my attention to the astonishing machines in the Ancient Near East, in which the legacy of antiquity lives on. Later I came across *The Book of Knowledge of Ingenious Mechanical Devices* by Ibn al-Razzaz al-Jazari, a twelfth-century Mesopotamian engineer. It contains automata of the sort Leonardo might have planned. Al-Jazari's color drawings are so magnificent that they seem less like pages from a technical handbook than illuminations to accompany fables from the East. There are elephants with water clocks in their bellies playing with balls and beating drums at the top of the hour, jolly lads using a pump to measure out equal quantities of wine in a series of glasses, and a boat with mechanical dolls that play music when set in motion.[21]

Leonardo is likely to have known about these inventions; copies of Arabic manuscripts were in circulation. In any case, it is not all that far from al-Jazari's figures to Leonardo's own bell ringer and the mechanical lion. *The Book of Knowledge of Ingenious Mechanical Devices* started me thinking about what we hope to achieve with technical progress. Is human inventiveness truly impelled by a desire to lighten our workload and to wage war effectively? There is no trace of these motives in al-Jazari's brilliant constructions, which seem more playful than practical, as do Leonardo's designs for the bell ringer and the mechanical lion. Wouldn't the two most creative technicians of their respective eras have been better off spending their time on more useful pursuits? They were well aware that the reigning monarchs were more concerned with their palaces than with the houses of their subjects and were more inclined to invest in an intricate entertainment machine than a better loom. After all, part of the reason manufacturers today keep coming out with faster computers is to satisfy the desire of game players for better and better animation. But just as increasingly sophisticated computers spur on the development of office software, the technology of Leonardo's entertainment devices might have been used to enhance human productivity. If you can program a mechanical lion, you can also make machines to cut cloth. Leonardo was uniquely able to carry over solutions from one field to another.

LEONARDO'S COMPUTER

But what is so special about the strange bell ringer mechanism? "You are about to see the boldest invention that Leonardo ever came up with," Rosheim promised. For a minute I was hoping that I would finally get to peek into his workshop full of secret robots, but my host brought me to his kitchen instead. Then he disappeared into a storeroom and returned with a length of garden hose. I must have looked somewhat aghast; for the life of me, I could not make out anything remarkable about it. "There it is," Rosheim laughed. In the sink I saw a cylinder about as long as my arm, which looked like an oversized drain stopper. It had two parts: The upper half was black, and the lower half was made of clear Plexiglas, with a gray vertical tube and two red plastic rings inside. Copper tubing and three horizontal ports were attached to the area between the upper and lower halves. Rosheim stuck the garden hose into one of them, and attached the other end of the hose to the faucet with some insulating tape. When he turned on the faucet, the water sprayed in all directions, because, as might be expected, the insulating tape did not provide a tight seal. Rosheim had to hold his finger on the hose, and the hem of his shirt started dripping. The engineer did not seem to notice how wet he was. He kept his eyes trained

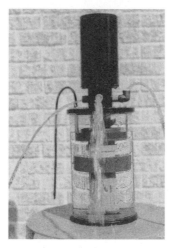

Rosheim's cylinder reconstruction

on his prized cylinder, where the water was splashing in the lower section. When the cylinder was nearly full, there was a sudden click, and a fountain gushed out of one of the other ports. This stream soon stopped and the water now poured out of the third port. "You are looking at man's oldest digital computer in action," Rosheim said.

I didn't know whether to question his sanity or mine, and I held my tongue. My host was unfazed. He leaned forward to suck at the siphon with his mouth. The cylinder emptied out. While the container was filling up again, Rosheim, who was soaked to the skin by this point, explained patiently how this spitting and spraying device could be used to measure time. The water supply just had to be set to make the containers fill in exactly sixty minutes. An array of twenty-four containers would yield a clock, with each cylinder representing an hour and serving as a timer for the bell ringer.

When an hour goes by and the cylinder is full, a rotary valve starts up in the gray vertical tube, blocking off the cylinder and diverting the water to the container for the next hour. At the same time, it opens

Rotary valve

up a reservoir in the black upper half—producing the fountain I had seen earlier. This surge, in turn, can be directed onto a waterwheel and set the bell ringer in motion. Since each cylinder has a larger reservoir than the one before, more water shoots out from one hour to the next. The amount in the first cylinder is just enough to make the figure strike the bell once, the water in the second reservoir generates two strikes, and so forth.

With this principle, which was clearly described in the notebooks, Leonardo had invented something altogether original. Although there were clock mechanisms and planetariums before him, notably the *astrarium* (astronomical clock) built by Giovanni de Dondi in Padua and hailed as a wonder of ingenuity, the passage of time was always marked by the gradual advancement of a hand, a cog, or a planet, using analogue technology. Leonardo may have learned how to use water for sensitive mechanisms from al-Jazari, but al-Jazari's clock repeated the same process hourly, as had earlier clocks, in contrast to Leonardo's design for a timepiece with an ability that no machine had ever had: It could count. If the water cylinders were connected in a different way, a calculator would result.

"Our computers today are made up of billions of identical electronic circuits," Rosheim said, "and each circuit operates with only two options: current or no current. Leonardo did the very same thing with his hydraulic clock." For the water cylinder, the only thing that matters is whether it is full or empty—it functions digitally. And by engaging a series of cylinders, Rosheim explained to me, Leonardo taught his machine how to count: "The only essential difference between this and the principle of a modern computer is that Leonardo worked with water and not with electric current."

How much of this hydraulic computer is Leonardo's work, and how much is Rosheim's? Most likely Leonardo never built a digital water clock. His sketches are too inexact, and too many details are left open. As was so often the case with Leonardo, who was busy with many projects at once, he appeared to lack interest in struggling with the countless tricky aspects that invariably arise in any attempt to translate a flight of fancy into practice. Rosheim tackled these difficulties, filling in the blanks in Leonardo's sketches with his own knowledge of engineering. The cylinder spouting water in his sink in Minneapolis is therefore just as much his creation as it is Leonardo's.

The fate of the digital water clock is quite typical for Leonardo's engineering ideas. His most remarkable projects generally came to a halt somewhere along the developmental stage and were not completed, apart from a few noteworthy exceptions, such as the spectacular performances by the mechanical lion. But often he saw no need to prove that his designs would actually work. So was he a daydreamer, and his inventions mere pie in the sky?

"Leonardo was a rebel," historian of science George Sarton once wrote. "He was anxious to obtain not money, or power, or comfort, but beauty and truth."[22] He was after not the pragmatic solution, but the ideal one. As an artist who often spent years on a painting, he chose to use experimental color mixtures, which resulted in two of his most important works disintegrating before they were complete. And as an engineer, he had to face the fact that he would never be able to realize many of his bold projects.

But perhaps it is wrong to judge inventors by how many of their ideas come to fruition. Ultimately, the implementation of an idea is only a minor element in intellectual achievement. The crucial part is what precedes it. Behind every significant milestone is a new perspective on a problem. Coming up with this concept—a digital clock, for example—is arguably the actual task of an inventor. Leonardo was brilliant at unearthing new approaches of this kind.

Anatomy of face, arm, and hand

VI

UNDER THE SKIN

ON A SHEET FILLED WITH writing in the British Library, which is located near the St. Pancras International train station, Leonardo recounts his exploration of a cavern. He does not reveal where this excursion might have taken place, but simply describes a horrific landscape: "[Not even] the tempestuous sea make[s] so loud a roaring when the northern blast beats it back in foaming waves between Scylla and Charybdis, nor Stromboli nor Mount Etna when the pent up, sulphurous fires, bursting open and rending asunder the mighty mountain by their force are hurling through the air rocks and earth mingled together in the issuing belching flames." But these horrors did not deter him from forging ahead:

> Drawn on by my eager desire, anxious to behold the great abundance of the varied and strange forms created by the artificer Nature, I came to the mouth of a huge cavern . . . my back bent to an arch, my left hand clutching my knee, while with the right I made a shade for my lowered and contracted eyebrows; and I was bending continually first one way and then another

in order to see whether I could discern anything inside, though this was
rendered impossible by the intense darkness within. And after remaining
there for a time, suddenly there were awakened within me two emotions,
fear and desire, fear of the dark threatening cavern, desire to see whether
there might be any marvelous thing therein.[1]

It is highly unlikely that Leonardo was recalling one of his solitary
hikes through the landscapes of Italy in this passage. When describing
his discoveries in nature, he tended to adopt a terse, sober tone, and
he nearly always named the setting. This big cavern, portrayed so haunt-
ingly with references to ancient legends, seems to have existed only in
his imagination. His venture into the underworld gives us a glimpse
into his own inner world. These few lines transport the reader into a
realm that Leonardo usually took pains to conceal: the realm of his
emotions.

The Russian historian of science V. P. Zubov called the cavern story
a literary self-portrait—the only one we have of Leonardo.[2] He succumbs to feelings that are not directed at another human being, as one
might expect, but at the exhilarating, yet unsettling conflict he faces
in his yearning to enter into uncharted territory while fearing the con-
sequences of pursuing this desire. Leonardo situates these wrenching
emotions at the fateful moment he first peers into the cavern. Exploring
terra incognita can be frightening, even if the pioneer does not have
to fear for life and limb. It is deeply disconcerting to come face-to-face
with something never seen before. Every new discovery entails the loss
of an old certainty, which is replaced by uncertainty, stumbling and
fumbling while attempting cautiously to resolve discrepancies between
old and new realities. The French geneticist François Jacob has called
this phase "night science." Announcing a revolutionary discovery is
sure to trigger attacks from contemporaries who defend the traditional

Raphael, portrait of Pope Leo X with two cardinals

view. Socrates paid for expounding his philosophy in public with a cup of hemlock, Galileo for his declaration "And yet it moves!" with years of house arrest. Conservatives are riled by Charles Darwin even today.

Research is about extending boundaries, and Leonardo was not willing to bow to the taboos of his day. He must have figured that one day his thirst for knowledge would land him in serious trouble. His long history of strong connections to the high and mighty allowed him to skirt such difficulties for decades. But in the final years of his life, luck turned against him. "The Pope has found out that I have skinned three corpses," he wrote anxiously in a draft of a letter to his patron Giuliano de' Medici in about 1515.[3] Now more than sixty years old,

Leonardo was trying to make yet another new start, this time in Rome. But the commissions he was hoping for did not materialize, because the new pope, Leo X, who was Giuliano's brother, did not appreciate Leonardo's art. He even made fun of Leonardo in public, claiming that the artist was spending his time distilling oils and plants to prepare the varnish instead of getting down to the work itself.[4] We also learn from Leonardo's letter that an employee in his own workshop was responsible for having maligned Leonardo to the Vatican as a desecrator of corpses, evidently as revenge for Leonardo's having accused this craftsman, whom he called Giovanni of the Mirrors, of divulging trade secrets. Leonardo wrote that Giovanni, who was originally from Germany, had spread this slander not only to the pope, but also to the hospital at which Leonardo was obtaining his cadavers.

If Leonardo's examinations of corpses had stopped short of full dissections, his actions would most likely have been overlooked. Clergymen were well aware why the artworks displayed in their churches were so astonishingly true-to-life. Many prominent artists of this era—from Domenico Veneziano to Luca Signorelli to Michelangelo—secretly studied the skeletons and the muscles of cadavers. But Leonardo went far beyond his colleagues. He was not content just to examine the visible surface of human limbs. He wanted to know how the body functioned deep inside, and he dissected hearts, brains, and reproductive organs. This invasive level violated the Church's time-honored view that the body was a microcosm of the universe as a whole, and its organs were ruled by the planets. And hadn't the blood of Christ been chosen to redeem the whole world? Anyone who undertook a voyage of discovery inside a human being was committing an offense against all of God's creation.

Not even doctors had the right to investigate the workings of the internal organs. Long gone was the enlightened era of the thirteenth century, when Friedrich Barbarossa required surgeons in his empire to have studied anatomy for at least one year before entering the medical profession. The Church ensured that dissections, even at universities, took place only under exceptional circumstances, and then solely on the bodies of people whom the clergy considered fallen individuals, namely executed criminals and executioners.[5] The resulting paucity of visual aids forced the medical students of Leonardo's day to rely on memorizing the writings of the ancient doctor Galen, who most likely never actually saw the internal organs of a human being. Disregarding the ban could result in the most severe punishment the Church could impose: excommunication. The unauthorized opening of cadavers thus held out the dismal prospect of ostracism on earth and rotting in hell for all eternity.

We do not know how Leonardo's conflict with the pope turned out, but he seems to have gotten off lightly. His letter to his patron, Giuliano de' Medici, the brother of the pope, states simply that he was "hampered" in his anatomical research. A few months later, Leonardo left Rome for good, and moved to France.

IN THE MORTUARIES OF SANTA MARIA NUOVA

He had been drawing interior views of the body for more than a quarter of a century before the big trouble began brewing in Rome. While in Milan, he had focused on the human skull, hoping to discover the location of the soul.[6] Like many artists of his time, Leonardo studied anatomy in order to hone his artistic skills. He sketched bones in the skeletal system, attempted to learn as much as he could from surface muscle movements, and pored through the imprecise (and generally inaccurate) depictions in medical books, but he did not dare to dissect bodies. In 1507 and 1508, during his second stay in Milan, he had to

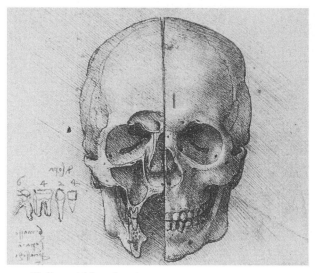

Skull, partial frontal section

spend several months in Florence to resolve a dispute over his uncle's inheritance. The major hospital here, Santa Maria Nuova, granted him access to cadavers.

Leonardo had been acquainted with some of the people whose bodies he opened in this facility. He was even at the side of one elderly man as he died: "And this old man, a few hours before his death, told me that he had lived a hundred years, and that he did not feel any bodily ailment other than weakness, and thus while sitting upon a bed in the hospital of Santa Maria Nuova without any movement or sign of anything amiss, he passed away from this life," Leonardo wrote. "And I made an autopsy in order to ascertain the cause of so peaceful a death."[7] This was one of his first autopsies.

The encounter with the old man must have taken place in the gigantic men's ward in Santa Maria Nuova, which is still used as a hospital today. The ward once encompassed a cruciform building, with corridors as long as the naves of a cathedral. It has been subdivided

Santa Maria Nuova, Florence

into a huge number of examination rooms, but a walk through the endless corridors that connect all the rooms now used for diagnoses, X rays, and various forms of therapy conveys a sense of how overwhelming this ward must once have felt. I was told by my guide, Esther Diana, an architectural historian who has been studying Santa Maria Nuova for many years, that in the nineteenth century there were still 450 beds here. Most of the patients lay head to toe, with two or even four to a bed. In the words of a late eighteenth-century visitor, "the odor of decomposition may be described as a mixture of the acidic, the sickly, and the fetid," which resulted in a nauseating stench, even though the ceiling in this ward was 40 feet high to promote better ventilation.[8]

By the time Leonardo began frequenting this building, Santa Maria Nuova had been in existence for over two centuries but was still considered the most modern hospital in Europe. In contrast to other hospitals, the physicians here tried not only to care for their patients, but to cure them. Over 80 percent of the men and women who were admitted to Santa Maria Nuova left alive, except during outbreaks of the plague. As the fame of the hospital spread, it prospered, and all around the central men's ward countless other buildings were constructed. A wall enclosed the entire site, and Santa Maria Nuova seemed like a small town within the city. Additional properties throughout Florence yielded such a large income that the hospital even opened its own bank and made funding available to Leonardo.

Santa Maria Nuova was a secular foundation, and its affluence gave the hospital an unusual degree of autonomy, even from the Church. Esther Diana explained to me that with this autonomy, the hospital could be more permissive about dissections than was the case elsewhere. Although the doctors were officially required to restrict their autopsies to the cadavers of criminals, and hospital regulations stipulated that these procedures could take place no more than once a year, pioneers such as Dr. Antonio Benivieni were able to conduct numerous autopsies on ordinary bodies as long as doctors kept quiet about these activities. Artists who were associated with the hospital were also permitted to work with the dead bodies. In many cases, they paid for this privilege with their artworks.

The cadavers were easily accessible anyway. After a brief chapel service, the dead were transported directly to the adjacent Chiostro delle Ossa (cloisters of the bones). Part of this area is now overgrown with ivy and rhododendrons, and another part has been turned into the hospital's entry wing. But back then, there were skeletons in the four corners to remind the visitor of the evanescence of earthly life. Of course, it is just as likely that the cemetery was named for the bones that washed out of the ground when it rained; even in Leonardo's day, the Chiostro delle Ossa was far too small to give a proper burial to the more than three hundred patients who died in this giant hospital every

Tub for washing corpses

year. People complained about the deplorable state of affairs here. On an area that measured no more than 30 by 30 feet, so many dead bodies were decaying "that there was no soil left to cover them."[9] New arrivals were often simply laid out on the ground, and if no family members claimed them, they were fair game for anyone who wanted to use them.

From the Chiostro delle Ossa, there is a walkway leading to a steep staircase and down into the vault under the hospital chapel. "This is where Leonardo is said to have washed his corpses," Esther Diana explained. Along the walls of the room, which had several bulky pillars, there were three stone tubs carved out of a single piece of rock and marked with Roman numerals. The tubs were large enough to hold horses, and my guide wondered whether they were really used to wash the dead. Perhaps they were actually granaries, as the Roman numerals would appear to indicate.

We walked past shelves full of dust-covered files into another vault, where in all likelihood the dissections once took place. Two bulbs were the only source of light in this low-ceilinged, windowless room. The light was so dim that I could picture Leonardo struggling to see as he labored by torchlight. This place was far from prying eyes. To make himself even less conspicuous, Leonardo worked after hours and wrote about his "fear of passing the night hours in the company of these cadavers, quartered and flayed and horrible to behold."[10]

Leonardo cautioned: "Though possessed of an interest in the subject, you may perhaps be deterred by natural repugnance."[11] Anyone who has ever witnessed an autopsy knows what he meant. At least cadavers are chilled these days, often preserved with chemicals, and opened up under a powerful ventilation hood. That observers are profoundly repulsed even under these conditions makes it disturbing to contemplate what an anatomist of the Renaissance must have experienced, with the decay of the body setting in after just a few hours in the abdominal cavity and spreading throughout the body. The cool temperature in the vault slowed down the decomposition process, but the putrefactive gases were surely overpowering in this windowless room.

Leonardo had no chance of winning the race against time and disintegration. Exposing the veins, nerves, and tendons in a manner that enables an artist to draw them is a laborious business, because they are embedded in fat and connective tissue, which the dissector has to scrape away slowly and carefully. The long fingernails of Leonardo's bare hands must have served as an important tool. It is not surprising that he needed access to many cadavers to get anything accomplished under these trying circumstances: "I have dissected more than ten human bodies [because] one single body did not suffice for so long a time [and] it was necessary to proceed by stages with so many bodies as would render my knowledge complete."[12] Working with decaying cadavers would have been difficult for anyone, but Leonardo's problematic relationship to physicality made the situation even worse, as is evident in his remarks about the genitalia: "The act of procreation and the members employed therein are so repulsive, that if it were not for the beauty of the faces and the adornments of the actors and the pent-up impulse, nature would lose the human species."[13]

Still, Leonardo was rewarded for his efforts with astonishing insights into the workings of the body. His autopsy of the old man whose death he had witnessed while sitting at the edge of his sickbed in Santa Maria Nouva was so thorough that he was able to establish that deterioration of the coronary vessels was the cause of death: "I found that it proceeded from weakness through failure of blood and of the artery that feeds the heart and the other lower members, which I found to be very parched and shrunk and withered. . . . Another autopsy was on a child of two years, and here I found everything the contrary to what it was in the case of the old man."[14] Leonardo had discovered arteriosclerosis—more than three centuries before this term was coined by Jean Lobstein, a surgeon in Strasbourg. He even correctly surmised why death ensues from what is often referred to as "hardening of the arteries," although he mistook these arteries for veins: "The old who enjoy good health die through lack of sustenance. And this is brought about by the passage to the mesaraic veins becoming continually restricted by the thickening of the skin of these veins; and the process continues until it affects the capillary veins, which are the first to close up altogether. . . . And this network of veins acts in man as in oranges, in which the peel becomes thicker . . . the more they become old."[15]

AN X-RAY VIEW OF SEX

Leonardo must have had more in mind than painterly ambition when he examined corpse after corpse over the following decade. He drew hundreds of views of human organs while living in Florence, Milan, and Rome. His knowledge of surface musculature and the skeleton was certainly valuable for his portraits, but the facts he amassed about the digestive system and the anatomy of heart valves were of no practical use in this regard. His initial desire to learn more about the human body in order to enhance his painting had long since become an end in itself. Leonardo conducted this research to enhance his understanding. He had peered into the cavern, and his burning desire to know won out over fear and revulsion.

At the same time, he could not escape the beliefs of his era. Like his contemporaries, Leonardo accepted the idea that the body was a microcosm of the world, but in contrast to his orthodox peers, Leonardo's acceptance of this idea did not impose any limits on his scientific inquiry. In fact, the idea of man as microcosm seemed to pique his interest in researching the body:

> So then we may say that the earth has a spirit of growth, and that its flesh
> is the soil; its bones are the successive strata of the rocks which form the
> mountains; its cartilage is the tufa stone; its blood the springs of its waters.
> The lake of blood that lies about the heart is the ocean. Its breathing is
> by the increase and decrease of the blood in its pulses, and even so in the
> earth is the ebb and flow of the sea.[16]

As abstruse as we may find these comparisons today, they made perfect sense to any educated person in the fifteenth century. Concepts of cause and effect were just beginning to take hold; people were far more accustomed to thinking in analogies. And Leonardo was the champion of the similarity game: If a mirror bounces back light according to the same laws that a wall bounces back a ball (he was correct on this point), if birds use the same principle to fly that fish use to swim (this was incorrect)—then why not regard the innermost layers of rock as the innards of the earth? To Leonardo, cutting open an ab-dominal wall and entering the darkness of a mountain cavern were one and the same thing.

His philosophy of nature, however, went well beyond the equation of "human body = planet earth" that prevailed in his day. In Leonardo's view, everything in the universe was part of a larger harmony that could be captured in simple geometric rules: "Proportion is found not only in numbers and measurements, but also in sounds, weights, times, positions, and in whatsoever power there may be."[17] Leonardo even saw harmonic laws at play in smells "just as in music."[18] He also believed that there was a single force (which he described in glowing terms) that set all things in motion and induced change. His most powerful portrayal of an all-encompassing mathematical order was his best-known drawing, the *Proportions of the Human Body According to Vitruvius*. The navel of the man with outstretched arms and legs appears at the exact center of a square, and the man's fingertips and the tips of his toes lie along the circumference of a circle. The length of each side of the square and the radius of the circle—and even the ratio of the in-dividual parts of the body to one another—correspond precisely to what is known as the "golden section."

But in his basic assumptions, Leonardo was too much a product of his era to make a complete break with traditional biases. He was also mistaken about certain anatomical features, particularly in regard to male genitalia, which seems odd in light of his attraction to men. He made a spectacular drawing of the act of sexual intercourse, with the united bodies of a man and a woman in a longitudinal section, as though using X-ray vision to see right through them. Still, he situated the base of the male sperm canal not in the testicles, but in the spinal column. This error can be explained in part by the early date of origin of this print. In 1492, Leonardo had yet to see the inside of a human

Coitus

body—which makes this depiction even more astonishing, since he needed to rely on ancient writings asserting that man's reproductive capacity was a function of his mental capacity, with the spine as the point of connection. The Church later embraced this notion because of its implication that too much sex sapped the lifeblood from the brain.[19]

Twenty years later, when Leonardo had long since opened up and studied internal organs, he continued to make errors of this magnitude. For example, he drew a septum of an ox heart perforated with pores and noted under it: "This is how it needs to be drawn." By then, Leonardo had already dissected dozens of hearts and certainly never saw perforations in the septum between the two ventricles of the heart—because there are none. The idea that the blood passes from the left ventricle to the right one through pores was nothing but a figment of the ancient Greek physician Galen's imagination.

Can we blame Leonardo, who normally paid such attention to detail, for his occasional tendency to attach more importance to the prejudices of others than to what lay before his own eyes? Scientists whose work results in revolutionary breakthroughs are famous for mistrusting what they see in front of them. Even the most self-assured spirits can hesitate to wage a solitary battle against the universally accepted dogmas promoted by the renowned scholars of their era. It is often easier to doubt one's own findings. And even those who come up with entirely new ideas rarely make a complete break with tradition. Leonardo's conservative bent put him in the best of company; some of the greatest innovators in science were conservative to a fault, in the view of their successors, who often wondered at their pigheadedness and sometimes even considered them downright insane. Galileo, who ought to have known better, rejected the notion of elliptical planetary orbits as described by Kepler with the argument that "God did not wish it so." In a respectable universe, celestial bodies would orbit on circular paths—just the way astronomers had been drawing them since antiquity. Einstein, whose ideas formed the basis of modern quantum physics, refused to accept the notion of randomness in the realm of atoms: "God does not play dice." Letting go of the errors of the past once and for all and completing an intellectual revolution is generally left to researchers of the following generation. In Leonardo's case it was a Flemish physician, Andreas Vesalius, whose 1543 edition of his anatomical textbook praised God for the wonderful creation of pores so small that the eye could not detect them, but amended his view in the revised edition and explained that no such pores existed.[20] Vesalius, who knew some of Leonardo's work, no longer regarded humans as a microcosm of the universe. For him, the body was just a body.

MAN IS A MACHINE

In 1509, the anatomist Marcantonio della Torre joined the faculty in Pavia. His presence gave new impetus to Leonardo's research on the human body. We know little about this young man, who enjoyed great fame as a medical researcher but who succumbed to the plague at Lake Garda in 1511, at the age of twenty-nine. Leonardo and he were definitely friends. When Leonardo, who was living in Milan at the time, visited della Torre in Pavia (only a day's journey away) to observe his dissections, both profited from the encounters: Leonardo soaked up medical knowledge, and della Torre came away with anatomical drawings of unparalleled quality.[21]

Spurred on by the young professor, Leonardo worked so feverishly on his anatomical studies that he now felt capable of completing a book on this subject, as he had been planning for more than two decades: "I hope to finish the whole of this anatomy in the winter of 1510."

Leonardo even developed special dissection methods for organs that are notoriously difficult to sketch, such as the eyes, which lose their shape when the gelatinous vitreous body is pierced. He came up with the idea of boiling eyes in the white of an egg to solidify them so that he would be able to cut them transversely after they cooled down

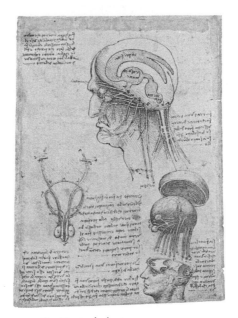

Cavities in the brain

and draw a sectional view.[22] He created air holes in the cavities of the brain and injected them with molten wax to make a cast, after inserting "narrow tubes into the holes so that the air in these ventricles can escape and make room for the wax entering the ventricles."[23]

Here, too, Leonardo derived great benefit from his powers of imagination. The soft tissues, the organs, the tendons, and the fibers under the skin, which we are used to seeing in clearly defined forms in anatomical illustrations, are in reality utterly shapeless. A heart without blood is nothing but a bulky lump of flesh, a dead man's lung is like a rag, and to the untrained eye, the various glands in the abdominal cavity are hard to tell apart. When medical students today take anatomy classes and dissect their first cadavers, they have a textbook and a mentor to guide them; Leonardo, by contrast, was in uncharted territory. Even so, he created vivid images of shapes he was never able to make

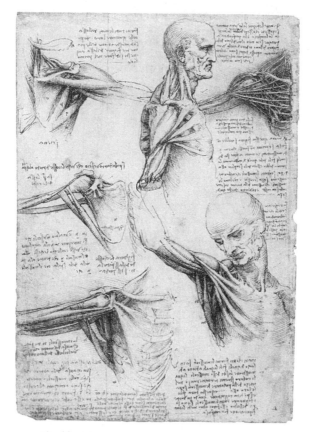

Shoulder joint

out clearly. He portrayed our soft tissue so graphically that it feels tempting to stick a finger into the aorta of the heart he drew.

Another impressive example of his anatomical artistry is found in his studies of the shoulder joint. The upper part of the body and the arm are juxtaposed in a series of perspectives, and subtle light and shadow effects highlight the interplay of the muscles.[24] In some places on the sketches the surface of the skin is included, and in others layers of the musculoskeletal system are exposed, so a single drawing takes the viewer from the familiar exterior to deeper and deeper interior realms of the body. Parts of a given drawing show lifelike tendons, and others nothing more than schematic lines to highlight a functional principle, with the humerus peeping out from between the muscle fibers.

On other pages he renders the organs translucent in spots, making them look somewhat like frosted glass, which keeps their shape visible while offering an unobstructed view of what lies behind them. And Leonardo's analysis of the blood vessels leads the viewer through all the stages of abstraction—from the amazingly lifelike pen-and-ink drawing of a body part with a network of tiny capillaries down to a mathematical scheme showing blood vessels branching off.

Leonardo was a consummate explainer, and he was convinced that pictures can offer a better overview than language. He noted on one illustration of the heart: "With what words O writer can you with a like perfection describe the whole arrangement of that of which the design is here? . . . I counsel you not to cumber yourself with words unless you are speaking to the blind."[25]

In an era ruled by laborious descriptions, with few explanatory images, Leonardo employed the very modern approach of emphasizing visual imagery. Even today, medical students learn from pictures, and it is no accident that Leonardo's anatomical drawings resemble visual aids of the kind found in today's magazines and the stylistic techniques we see on interactive computer images. His interior views of the body look as though they were drawn in the twenty-first century.

How had he developed this unusual way of depicting man? In the lower right corner of one sheet, we see only the bones of a foot. The long bones of the lower leg seem to fly up and away from the tarsus, and we recognize how perfectly the tibia, fibula, and anklebone combine to form the ankle joint. Leonardo had invented this technique, known as an exploded view, to explain his machines. In this illustration, the foot seems like part of a machine.

Leonardo employed many other optical strategies to bring out the complex dimensions of the body—light and shadow, transparency, views from various angles—that he had tried out on his earlier structural plans. And the idea of breaking something down to its component parts was not new to him, either. During the years he spent in Florence and Milan, he went to great lengths to understand the mechanics of machines by analyzing their elements piece by piece. Consequently, when he began to dissect cadavers in 1507, he merely had to switch the object of his investigations rather than devising a new approach. Instead of screws and gears, he now turned his attention to bones, muscles, and nerves.

The laws of mechanics had become second nature to him during his years as an engineer. He now scrutinized the human body with the eyes of a technician: Arms and legs, even the bite force of individual teeth, were consistent with the lever law. Tumescent muscles worked like gussets. Tendons, he wrote, hold thighs in joints the way shrouds hold up the mast of a ship. And hadn't he even designed a robot in human form, whose limbs moved by means of a complex system of ropes inside the body? Now he was drawing tendons as ropes.

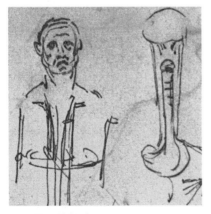

Engulfed valve

In one of the sketches for the bell ringer mechanism that Mark Rosheim reconstructed, man and machine actually merge: A man and the inner workings of the water cylinder to measure time are superimposed to make it look as though the man has engulfed the technology of the cylinder. His neck turns into a water pipe, and on the level of the diaphragm the rubber ring activates the striking of the hour. Next to it Leonardo drew two incisions through the stomach and esophagus. Evidently he was looking for analogies between his construction and the mechanics of swallowing—and wondering whether he could learn something from nature.[26]

Man is a machine. This view enabled Leonardo to break away little by little from traditional dogmas, although he never quite succeeded in liberating himself from superstitions. He recognized that the earth follows rules unlike those of the human body. The veins of the old man he autopsied in Florence had narrowed in old age, whereas the rivers, "the veins of the earth," "are enlarged by the prolonged and continuous passage of water."[27] Notions of the body as a mirror of the earth lost their persuasiveness and were replaced by the matter-of-fact laws of cause and effect, by verifiable rules of mechanics.

But although Leonardo described the body as a machine, he did not lose his sense of awe—quite the contrary. The longer he conducted his research, and the more cadavers he dissected, the more his amazement grew at the complexity and perfection of the human body. At an earlier point in his life, he had been optimistic that a clever engineer would be able to reconstruct nature and create an artificial bird or something of that sort. He now realized how presumptuous this wish had been. "[Humans] will never devise an invention more beautiful, more simple, or more direct than does nature," he wrote in reference to a drawing in which he tried to establish the origins of sounds in the movements of the lips and tongue.[28] An examination of the shoulder joint inspired him to praise nature for its "marvelous works."[29]

Precisely because he recognized the complexity of nature, Leonardo sought to fathom every single detail—and to render everything exactly, "as though the actual person were standing before you."[30] His goal was to understand every single mechanism in the body. It was here that medicine began to follow its current path. Only the focus has shifted; modern researchers are less interested in the rotations of the shoulder joint than in what occurs in the cell nucleus to cause cancer.

The years Leonardo spent at the dissection table transformed his view of the world. Up to the time Santa Maria Nuova opened its mortuaries to him, he was searching for a general principle behind the functioning of the cosmos. Once he had examined the body exhaustively, Leonardo abandoned his quest to find a totality of the world—and adopted the much humbler approach to nature on which modern science is based. To understand the world, you have to describe its phenomena one by one. There can be no shortcut. The leap of imagination that carries armchair scholars from the organism of man to that of the earth, from theology to physics, can lead them astray. The only way to advance a bold new theory is to make meticulous studies and conduct the requisite experiments. Truncating this laborious process "does injury to knowledge and to love, for love of anything is the offspring of knowledge, love being more fervent in proportion as knowledge is more certain."[31]

EXPEDITIONS INTO THE BEATING HEART

Leonardo's last major inquiry in Rome was also his most astonishing one. Just five years before his death, he explored the mysteries of the human heart. His discoveries are recorded in a series of ten bluish sheets now in the collection of the Queen of England. One of them contains his diatribe against "abbreviators."[32] The sketches are not easy to read, because they depict what no eye has ever seen: blood flowing through the ventricles of the heart.

Incisions through the aorta reveal the three crescent-shaped pockets of the aortic valve. This tripartite division is found again in an abstract

Interior views of the heart

sketch that bears a striking resemblance to the Mercedes logo. It looks as though Leonardo had wanted to explore the diversity of shapes in an artery. There are also helical swirls to indicate blood forced from the left ventricle into a protrusion of the aorta. Between the sketches, Leonardo squeezed in explanatory notes in mirror writing. When the heart muscle contracts and presses the blood out of the ventricle, swirls form in the aortic valve. As soon as the muscle relaxes at the end of the heartbeat, these swirls in some miraculous way press against the valve and shut it, thus blocking the blood from flowing back into the heart and sending it on its way through the body.

How could Leonardo know this? It is not possible to view blood flowing, because we cannot see into the beating heart. The sound of the valve shutting is all we can detect. Even centuries after Leonardo, scientists did not have a clear idea of how the human heart valve worked. In 1999, speculation came to an end when researchers in London, Boston, and California, using magnetic resonance velocity mapping, were finally able to obtain images of blood flow in the living heart. They found exactly what Leonardo had described.[33]

Morteza Gharib, a professor of bioengineering at Caltech, is one of the foremost specialists on heart function today. He holds more than a dozen patents for artificial hearts, improved heart valves, and other related devices. Gharib says that his own heart skipped a beat when he first saw Leonardo's drawings of the blood flow at the aortic valve. "Since I am an experimenter myself, I realized immediately that Leonardo must have conducted experiments. That is the only way he could have made these discoveries." Gharib scrutinized Leonardo's drawings for evidence to substantiate his assumption—and struck gold. Sure enough, Leonardo described a method of constructing an artificial heart. "Blow thin glass into a plaster mold and then break it. But first pour wax into this valve of a bull's heart so that you may see the true shape of this valve," he wrote on one of the blue pages.[34] Around these words, Leonardo drew the shape he had just described, which looks exactly like the curvatures of the aorta. His goal was "to see in the glass what the blood does in the heart when it closes the little doors of the heart."[35] Gharib interprets the odd Mercedes logos as plans for mechanical heart valves. Elsewhere Leonardo explains how flow patterns can be traced in the glass heart by adding particles to the fluid: "Do this test in the glass and stir in water and millet seeds."[36]

To prove that Leonardo really conducted these experiments, Gharib built a mechanical heart valve in his laboratory using Leonardo's sketches. A flask whose shape Leonardo had outlined with a few quick strokes of his pen on a blue sheet of paper sits atop a Plexiglas plate, with a pump pressing water from below into a container at regular intervals. With each pulse beat, a valve composed of three leaflets at the base of the flask opens like a swinging door. Its soft synthetic material makes the components seem like delicate flaps of skin. Whenever the supply of water from below stops, the opening shuts again, then the whole process begins anew, and the contents of the flask pulse to the beat of the pump.

Modern scientists observe flow patterns just as Leonardo had recommended—by placing particles in the liquid, except for the fact that Gharib did not pick up millet at the health food store, but instead used tiny, silver-coated glass spheres, in accordance with the now-standard practice. And instead of relying on the naked eye to follow their movements, he used a complex laser measuring device. But Gharib's computer screen showed him exactly the same flow lines that Leonardo had sketched more than five hundred years earlier. Gharib reports a feeling of profound humility while conducting these experiments: "Leonardo's eye was so sharp that he grasped connections using nothing more than his pencil that it took other scientists many generations later to formulate in equations."

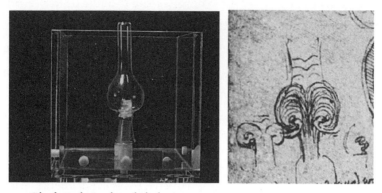

Blood circulation through the heart

But Leonardo's sharp eye would have been useless without his ability to synthesize knowledge from different arenas. Decades earlier, he had worked on flow patterns and lock gates. Now he understood what to look for in the heart, assuming that blood acted like water in a canal. After a constriction, a backwater builds up and eddies form, which can shut the lock gate from the outside. A hydraulic engineer had to prevent this from happening—but nature used this process to good effect in the heart.

But why does the aortic valve need to have three cusps? Here Leonardo benefited from his earlier obsession with squaring the circle. One could easily regard the countless pages he filled with similar geometric figures as the jottings of a madman, but they helped him understand the workings of the three triangular sections of the aortic valve.[37] If the valve had only two cusps, it would be harder to open, and with four it would be unstable.

Leonardo's glass heart proved that he was a true prophet. He anticipated scientific methods of the modern age. While his contemporaries continued to discuss how planets control the human heartbeat, Leonardo constructed a model based on nature to study it. The *Mona*

Lisa is the reconception of a face, and the artificial heart is the reconstruction of an internal organ according to the rules of nature.

"A PHILOSOPHER MORE THAN A CHRISTIAN . . ."

To announce his discoveries, Leonardo could have made use of the most significant invention of his era: Gutenberg's printing press. Why didn't he? Instead of going down in history as the creator of the first serious anatomical atlas, Leonardo never advanced his plan to publish an anatomy book beyond a set of loose manuscript pages. Quite a few biographers have puzzled over what made him falter, particularly because a note on those pages indicates that he had every intention of having his pictures of the insides of the body printed as a book: "I am marking how these drawings should be reprinted in order and I ask you, the successors, not to let stinginess cause you to print them in—"[38] Here the sentence breaks off.

The solution to this mystery is straightforward, and Leonardo himself provided it. This project, like so many others, was never realized because it would have required an endless amount of work to transform private jottings into a publishable text. At the close of a curious passage, in which Leonardo justifies himself to an imaginary reader of his unwritten books, he puts his finger on the problem: "Concerning which things, whether or no they have all been found in me, the hundred and twenty books which I have composed will give their verdict 'yes' or 'no.' In these I have not been hindered either by avarice or negligence, but only by want of time. Farewell."[39]

Leonardo was pursuing so many interests that he could rarely take full advantage of his chance to solve any particular problem; he simply lacked the time to do so. In cases where an additional experiment would have given him more precise information, he was already moving on to the next unknown territory. And because he was working for himself, rather than for others, he did not devote much time to the issue of publishing his findings. In contrast to modern researchers, Leonardo simply did not care whether others would be able to build on his work. Does a man who makes significant discoveries but keeps them to himself deserve the glory of a discoverer?

All the same, his reports about his expeditions inside of the body, unlike other manuscripts, were never forgotten altogether. When Leonardo left Italy, small bundles remained at the hospital in Santa Maria Nuova, where he had dissected his first cadavers. But the vast majority of the anatomical sketches were inherited by Melzi, who was happy to grant access to researchers and artists who had heard about this valuable collection.[40] They studied and copied Leonardo's pages, and some of his pictures of the human body were disseminated along strange byways. One depiction of the finger muscles, which is strikingly similar to a sketch by Leonardo, adorned the title page of the first anatomical atlas by Andreas Vesalius in 1543. Rembrandt, in turn, used this image as a model for the focal point of his *Anatomy Lesson of Dr. Nicolaes Tulp*, a painting of doctors observing the dissection of a forearm.[41]

Nevertheless, only a small group was aware of Leonardo's pioneering accomplishments, and it is fair to assume that no one in this select group fully grasped the breadth and depth of his research. Thus Leonardo's work, which could have marked the beginning of modern medicine, did not gain the recognition it deserved in the centuries to come. Today, Vesalius is considered the father of modern anatomy.

Judging by the merits of Leonardo's achievements, we would have to conclude that he would have been equally worthy of this honor. But apart from the muddled state of the manuscripts, it is, paradoxically, Leonardo's extraordinary talent as a draftsman that stood in the way of his fame as a scientist, because his anatomical depictions were regarded as the magnificent legacy of an artist. Drawing the mechanics of the shoulder, the muscle strands of the tongue, or the blood vessels of the forearm with such refinement represented an enormous artistic advance. Just as Columbus was discovering new territories beyond the ocean for the Spanish queen, Leonardo, at virtually the same time, was revealing a realm previously unknown to Western art. Until then, artists had portrayed the world as people were used to seeing it; even paintings of biblical miracles made the saints look pretty much like people on the street. Leonardo, by contrast, introduced objects beyond the realm of everyday experience. His anatomical drawings and his sketches of eddies and rock formations reveal the minutest details of the world in which we live, yet we do not really know.

Even so, Leonardo's anatomical drawings mark more than just the beginning of a new artistic era. They describe the path of a man who gradually cast off his own errors and the illusions of his era. Peeling away human skin altered far more than his vision of the human body; it shook the foundations of his view of life. Leonardo's fear of gazing into the unknown cavern proved all too justified. "In the course of philosophizing on nature . . . Leonardo formed such heretical ideas that no religion could be reconciled with them; evidently he wanted to be a philosopher more than a Christian," Vasari scolded in the first edition of his Leonardo biography. When the book was reprinted, Vasari deleted this passage.

The old man and the water

VII

FINAL QUESTIONS

AN OLD MAN IS SITTING on a rocky ledge, his back hunched, gazing into the distance.[1] He is resting his head on his left hand and knitting his brow as though deep in thought. A couple of wisps of hair stick up at the hairline, but otherwise his head is bald apart from a fringe of hair in the back. Only the full white beard, which comes down to his chest, conveys a sense of what a magnificent head of hair he must have had earlier in life. His right eye, which he turns to us in profile, is wide open and alert, but the crow's feet in the corner of his eye give his face a weary look. And his slumped posture makes him seem melancholy and even resigned. Who is this old man, and what is on his mind?

Several sketches on the reverse side of the page leave no doubt as to when and where Leonardo made this pen-and-ink drawing. They display details of Villa Melzi, the country residence of the family of Leonardo's favorite student, Francesco, where the master spent the better part of 1512. In Milan, a day's journey away, war was imminent: Troops sent by the deposed Sforza ruling family were advancing into the city to reconquer it. The end of French rule seemed to loom just

The old man and the water

a matter of weeks ahead. The French had paid Leonardo generously and given him every freedom as an artist; now the Sforzas would regard him as a collaborator. Here in the country, he was safe.

Leonardo must have sensed that he was running out of time—but he had no idea how he would spend the rest of his life. He did not yet know that he would soon travel to Rome to try his luck as a painter for the Vatican. And could he foresee that he would eventually undertake an odyssey to France and would die there, but that his art would return here, in Melzi's care?

It is revealing to compare the drawing of the old man with the portrait that Francesco Melzi had made of his master years earlier (facing first page of introduction). Leonardo had a luxuriant head of hair in the earlier picture, but the same pointed nose, the same forehead with the characteristic S-curve above the base of the nose, the same shape

Villa Melzi, Vaprio d'Adda

of the eyes as on the drawing of the old man. We can therefore assume that Leonardo's sad old man was a portrait of himself.

The elderly man's gaze is fixed on images of water. This page, which was once folded, consists of two halves. The man is on the left, and to the right of the fold—the direction he is facing—Leonardo made four drawings of the complex shapes that form when a current comes up against a barrier. With powerful strokes of his pen, he drew dams and eddies and waves interwoven like a woman's braid. He made many studies of this kind in those years, including the riveting picture of the torrent I have hanging over my desk.

Perhaps it was this setting that inspired him to return to the subject of water, the element he had begun investigating three decades earlier. The villa is perched on a hill overlooking the Adda River, which has its source in the Alps, crosses Lake Como, and eventually empties into the Po. At every turn, the visitor to this estate hears the gurgling of water. The imposing building is still in the possession of the family, but there is only a single remaining document here of Leonardo's once-rich legacy: his letter of appointment as chief engineer for Cesare Borgia. The rooms in the villa are now vacant. Most of them face east, along the length of the main facade, and the windows look out onto a terrace behind which the steep bank drops off. Down below is the Adda, originating in the mountains and cascading through a gorge into a wide valley. Leonardo drew this scenery repeatedly, and it is clear that he spent many hours on this terrace. Might he have drawn the picture of the old man here as well?

The windows facing north and south, which offer entirely different views, convey a sense of two worlds colliding. The view to the north is of the Alps; to the south is the Po Valley, which was once covered by the sea. On a clear day, the first hills of the Apennines can be made out on the horizon—a landmass that drifted up the unimaginably long time of 135 million years ago and impelled the Alps upwards and continues to move a few inches north every year.

Leonardo must have had a vague notion of the processes that took place here long before the advent of man, because it was in this landscape that he pondered the question of the origins of the world. The degree to which this question haunted him is recorded on the thirty-six pages of the Codex Leicester, which Leonardo probably bound himself and is in the private collection of Bill Gates today. In 1994,

Landscape on the Adda River

Gates bought the manuscript for thirty million dollars at an auction—the highest price ever paid for a book. Most of the Codex Leicester was composed while Leonardo was staying at Villa Melzi, and it recounts his version of the history of creation, based on his examinations of stones, watercourses, and landscapes. This was a scandalous undertaking, which shook at the foundations of biblical revelation.

Leonardo did not stop there. He contemplated not only the beginning of the world, but also its end. Would the mightiest mountain masses simply disappear one day? What is the future of our planet? Later, in Rome, he would try to provide an artistic answer to these questions. On a drawing of the Apocalypse he made at the Vatican, humans appear as tiny creatures at the mercy of an overpowering nature. Hurricanes and floods rage over them, and exploding mountains destroy every last shred of life.

Leonardo, who was now more than sixty years old, contemplated his own finiteness. He pondered the connection between body and soul. Is there really a substance within man that goes into another life after death? Perhaps the Church was right, and the mysteries of the origins of the world and those of immortality were indeed interconnected.

From the terrace of Villa Melzi, a staircase leads down to a wide canal flanked by stone walls, on which ships continued to sail as recently as the post–World War II period. Leonardo was commissioned by the French, who ruled in Lombardy, to design this waterway through the gorge to Lake Como,[2] but it was not built until three centuries after his death.

To work up a suitable design, Leonardo must have spent a good deal of time walking from the villa down to the gorge, just as he had walked along the canals of the plain in Lombardy decades earlier as an engineer in the service of Ludovico Sforza. At that time, he had devoted his attention to the fine points, such as the breaking of the waves in a current and the eddies at a closing lock gate. By studying flow patterns, he gained insights into the microcosm—the laws according to which water moves analogously to the flow of blood in the human heart. The Codex Leicester, by contrast, which he wrote much later in life, branched out to encompass the big picture, and comprised Leonardo's reflections on how water shaped the world. The topic was unchanged, but Leonardo now regarded it more expansively.

This shift in focus was reflected in his landscapes. In the austere plain in Lombardy, eye and ear are receptive to fine points that tend to be overlooked in spectacular surroundings; moreover, the flow lines of the water appear in their purest form along the very straight canal, almost as they would in a laboratory. For his studies of the development of mountain chains and entire continents, on the other hand, Leonardo could hardly have picked a better spot than the gorges of the Adda.

When glaciers still covered the Alps during the Ice Age, they accumulated an enormous amount of glacial debris known as end moraines through which the water flowing down from Lake Como had to carve a path to reach the alluvial land of the Po Valley, giving rise to rugged landscapes that suggest a sculptor at work even today. As we learn from his notes, Leonardo was also fascinated by the great variety of stones and cliffs that surrounded him.

After a good three hours of walking, the walls of the gorge loom so high and become so narrow that I was bathed in a mysterious light that I have never experienced anywhere else. The rays of light cannot take a direct path down onto the ground of the ravine, particularly since the sky is shielded by beech trees, which in some spots have grown almost horizontally out of the rock and span the gorge. The glint of light that fills the gorge is reflected back and forth dozens of times between the ocher, brown, gray, and reddish walls of conglomerate rock, and ultimately takes on these colors itself. Deep down there is neither white nor black, nor are there sharply defined shadows. Often the brightness seems to come from below as much as it does from above when the valley curves and the walls suddenly move apart. There the water turns calm and forms mirrors, bluish green pools with occasional reddish hues from the algae. The rock formations appear to be doubled, and the view of a submarine world opens out of the walls of the gorge descending into boundless depths.

When you come around the next rock ledge, the Adda again becomes a torrential river, although the canal and a power station have now depleted some of its water. In Leonardo's day, it must have been far more powerful. Not only does the water pour down on the bottom of the gorge; it also cascades from countless sources high up in the walls of rock and rushes toward the spume of the river. Waterfalls resembling veils mask the entrances to caves that the Adda has carved out of the stone, when its bed lay even higher. The history of the river over the course of many millennia is revealed in its slopes. Where the gorge widens out again, the ground is often strewn with pieces of rock that in the course of the ongoing metamorphoses have broken out of the solid compound.

The Adda gorge cuts a good 400 feet into the ground; crossing it made Leonardo feel as though he could dissect the earth. He thought of subterranean watercourses as planetary arteries that came to the surface in the depths of the gorge. He described mountain springs as "nosebleeds of the earth," producing liquid when a small blood vessel bursts, the way it does in man and in animals.[3]

SHELLS ON THE MOUNTAIN SLOPE

When Leonardo saw this scenery for the first time, it must have seemed as though his own imagination were coming to life before his very eyes. The background of *The Virgin of the Rocks* bears such a strong re-semblance to the Adda gorge, which the painter had not seen so soon after arriving in Milan. This painting, for the altar in the Franciscan church, which was the second-largest church in the city after the Milan Cathedral, was his first major commission in his new home, and he was asked to include rock formations in the background. Leonardo came up with a brilliant solution: In the cave, where Mary sits with the Christ child, John the Baptist, and an angel, there is faint yet color-ful light, which also illuminates the bottom of the Adda valley (Plate VII). A windowlike opening in the cave rock offers one a view onto a bluish green river that meanders out to the horizon between the mountains. The rocks are the same ocher color as those rising from the Adda and have a similar shape—a world molded by erosion and underground water.

This similarity is no coincidence. *The Virgin of the Rocks* displays the extent to which Leonardo regarded water as a force that shapes the earth. Some fifteen years later, he painted *The Virgin of the Rocks* a second time, and now the geological formations were even more detailed. He kept returning to this subject. In the view of art historians such as Martin Kemp, the *Mona Lisa* even draws a parallel between two mother figures: While the obviously pregnant Lisa Gherardini is creating a new human being, the water in the background is creating a new landscape. And *The Virgin and Child with St. Anne*, one of his last paintings, has an entire mountain chain rising from the ocean behind the heads of Mary and her mother, Anne.

Leonardo came up with odd theories about how continents might have arisen from the water. He reasoned that over the course of time the rivers washed so much debris into the sea that the bottom of the ocean was lowered and became unbalanced. To restore the balance, the bottom of the ocean rose elsewhere, like a scale, causing mountains to grow out of the water in those places.

These strange ideas notwithstanding, it is remarkable that Leonardo regarded creation in a totally new time perspective. As he saw it, continents did not originate on the day that God separated the water from the land, but were formed during immeasurably long periods of time. Thus he departed from the Christian Creation story and drew on the ancient idea of earth's gradual transformation. He was arguably the first man in the modern age to get a sense of what Stephen Jay Gould would later call "deep time," the billions of years of early history before man appeared on earth. In an age in which no one cast doubt on the story of Genesis, this was an enormous intellectual achievement: After all, Christian fundamentalists continue to dispute Darwin's theory of evolution and the theory of plate tectonics even today.

The Virgin and Child with St. Anne (*detail*)

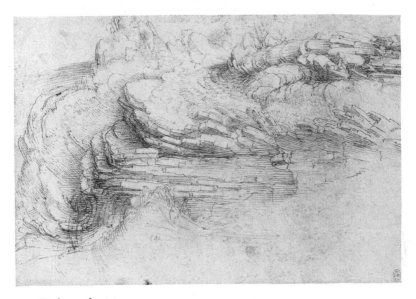

Rock stratifications

But Leonardo no longer believed that written texts—not even the Bible—could provide information about the events at the beginning of the world: "Since things are far more ancient than letters, it is not to be wondered at if in our days no record exists of how these seas covered so many countries."[4] But, he surmised, a researcher could learn to read the book of nature by studying fossils and the stratifications of stones.

And that is precisely what he did. The Codex Leicester recounts his studies of rocks as a young man during his first stay in Milan: "In the mountains of Parma and Piacenza multitudes of shells and corals filled with worm-holes may be seen still adhering to the rocks, and when I was making the great horse [the equestrian statue for Ludovico Sforza] in Milan, a large sack of those which had been found in these parts was brought to my workshop by some peasants, and among them were many which were still in their original condition."[5] Clearly his

Fossils

visitors were sensing a profitable business—every last mountain village knew about Leonardo's keen interest in fossils.

Nearly two thousand years earlier, the philosopher Xenophanes of Colophon, in Asia Minor, had realized that fossils contained the petrified remains of primeval beings, but after antiquity, interest in this evidence had faded.[6] Leonardo recognized the significance of fossils, so much so that while at Villa Melzi he planned to devote a whole book to them: "In this work of yours you have first to prove how the shells at the height of a thousand braccia were not carried there by the Deluge."[7] Feeling certain that this could not have happened, he reserved a combination of logic and scorn for the author of the biblical depiction and for those who considered it the sole truth:

If you should say that the shells which are visible at the present time within the borders of Italy, far away from the sea and at great heights, are due to the Flood having deposited them there, I reply that, granting this Flood to have risen seven cubits above the highest mountain, as he has written who measured it, these shells which always inhabit near the shores of the sea ought to be found lying on the mountain sides, and not at so short a distance above their bases, and all at the same level, layer upon layer.[8]

He explained in detail why the shellfish could not have descended from the shores on their own, nor could they have ended up as cadavers at the foot of the mountains when the sea ebbed. For one thing, it would have been impossible for the shells to have moved so far during the forty days the Deluge is said to have lasted, and for another, the animals had evidently been embedded alive inside the mud and later fossilized. The "set of ignoramuses" who did not wish to accept that, Leonardo wrote, were simply proving their "stupidity and ignorance."[9]

Leonardo contended that the entire continent was once an ocean floor. Gradually, the land rose out of the water, and the individual layers of shells simply marked the shorelines of various periods.[10] Leonardo regarded the human body as a machine, with fluid circulating throughout, and the planet earth as an enormous version of this same machine, with water ceaselessly winding its way "from the bottoms of the seas . . . to the summits of the mountains."[11]

"HOW ADMIRABLE THY JUSTICE, O THOU FIRST MOVER!"

Where was the Creator in this scheme of things? For Leonardo, nature was full of amazing wonders, but unlike traditional devout Christians, he did not think it held any unfathomable mysteries. When people did not understand a phenomenon, it was only because they had not conducted sufficient research. Everything in the cosmos adheres to invariable laws of nature—rules whose validity can be confirmed in experiments. Thus Leonardo transformed the metaphysical problem of how the world took shape into a matter of physics and did not mention a higher power intervening in the course of the world. If that were the case, a power of that kind would infringe on the unshakable laws of nature. God has to remain aloof from a world in which these rules apply and which man can explore.

The logical conclusion from these arguments is that the only moment for a higher power to have set the course for the cosmos was when the world originated, because the structure of the laws of nature had to come from somewhere. God could have set them in motion before leaving the universe to its own devices. Scientists cannot refute this view because events preceding nature are not their area of concern. Over the next few centuries, this idea proved to be the only way to reconcile faith and science. Today nearly all religious natural scientists envision God as the creator, but not as the guider of the world.[12]

Like most good ideas in philosophy, this one has quite a long history, dating back to Aristotle, who proceeded from the notion that all things change and move. Aristotle considered these two words synonymous, because every change is also a motion, and every motion a change. He saw the world as a giant billiard table with each ball moving the next one forward. Whenever one object changes, another one must have triggered the event. This purely physical explanation shows that all motion is caused by something else already in motion. Still, at some point there has to have been a beginning, a first cause of an altogether different nature. For Aristotle its origin lay outside this world and came from an "unmoved mover," the source of all change that does not take part in the cosmic activity and whose only connection to the world is having set it in motion. Thus the only thing that can be said about the unmoved mover is that this force exists. People cannot grasp this utterly otherworldly being with their senses or with their reason. The divine sphere is forever detached from the world of humans.

Leonardo knew about Aristotle's theories, and they certainly suited his own thinking. The harmonies of the world he was seeking accorded well with the idea of the unmoved mover as a starting place, and Leonardo experienced a rare sense of euphoria in hailing it: "How admirable Thy justice, O Thou First Mover! Thou has not willed that any power should lack the processes or qualities necessary for its results."[13] At the same time, Aristotle offered a view of life in which no higher power needed to—or even could—intervene in the harmonies of nature. Once created, the cosmos developed according to its own laws.

Mountains arise from the oceans, and streams wash their rocks back into the sea. Rivers reroute their beds and hollow out the subsoil; mountains collapse. Animal species die out, leaving behind only traces in rocks. New creatures appear. In this point, too, Leonardo had moved away from the biblical Creation story. According to Genesis, the world remains the way God created it; for Leonardo, however, everything is subject to constant change.

Leonardo was not out to refute (or to substantiate) Church doctrine. He regarded his research task as providing solutions to solvable problems, in contrast to the humanists who demanded that science be of noble rather than of practical use. Jurisprudence was loftier than medicine, they explained, because it can be derived directly from God's wisdom. Medicine, by contrast, concerned itself only with mortal, filthy creatures.[14] Philosophy and theology were considered the noblest of all scholarly pursuits in the view of this intellectual movement. For Leonardo, what mattered was not which subject was under investigation, but only whether it was assessed accurately. The sketch of a non-descript heart valve seemed to him far more valuable—assuming it was accurate—than any learned debate about the Trinity: "Falsehood is so utterly vile that though it should praise the great works of God it offends against His divinity. Truth is of such excellence that if it praises the meanest things they become ennobled."[15] Accordingly, the noblest questions are those that can be answered clearly.

Leonardo railed against all metaphysical speculation. He considered it fruitless to bother with phenomena that "the human mind is incapable of comprehending and that cannot be demonstrated by any natural instance."[16] All philosophical efforts by the ancients to grapple with questions of that kind were a waste of time: "What trust can we place in the ancients who have set out to define the nature of the soul and of life—things incapable of proof—whilst those things which by experience may always be clearly known and proved have for so many centuries either remained unknown or have been wrongly interpreted."[17]

Of course there are problems that do not lend themselves to empirical solutions, and Leonardo saw no reason to speculate about them: "The rest of the definition of the soul I leave to the wisdom of the friars, those fathers of the people who by inspiration know all mysteries." Leonardo wrote these words at the conclusion of a series of remarks about the soul of the fetus in the mother's body.[18] This remark might be seen as an ironic sideswipe at the arrogance of the clergy, but he added: "I speak not against the sacred books, for they are supreme truth." Leonardo knew that research was fundamentally incapable of finding the answers to certain questions, which remained a matter of faith. He thus drew a dividing line between science and religion and concluded that they could coexist as long as their adherents respected the boundaries that separate logic and experiment on the one side, and faith and tradition on the other. The stage was set for future conflicts, and the Church would spend centuries resisting the idea that it was no longer in sole possession of the truth.

THE SOUL OF THE FETUS

If Leonardo had followed his own principles, he would not have had to grapple with the question of the nature of the soul at all. But his curiosity was too great to leave it alone. Even he had difficulty keeping apart the spheres of knowledge and faith.

A drawing housed at the Royal Library in Windsor, in ink and red chalk, shows a tiny human—who is hard to make out at first—crouched inside a capsule. Its face is concealed, its head on its knees, the backs of its hands covering the spot where we might assume its eyes to be. What would it look like if it raised its head? The creature seems so unfinished—and slippery—that we almost shudder at the sight of it. The head is little more than an orb with a tiny ear sprouting from it. Maybe it is a good thing that the front of the creature is hidden from sight.

The right arm is bent and fits right into the space between the upper body and thigh like a puzzle piece. You can almost feel how cramped it is. The little creature has its legs crossed, and holds the sole of its left foot out to the viewer. The umbilical cord is coiled under its heel.[19]

The capsule, which provides a tight fit for the fetus, has a thick three-layered shell and is opened up like the cupule of a chestnut. Huge veins branch out on the exterior, making the skin of the unborn child look even more delicate. Leonardo may well have had a fruit breaking open in mind. Three smaller sketches, containing the word "Afterbirth," show an indefinable something emerging from its spherical shell. Farther down there is a reminder to give "Marco Antonio the book about water."

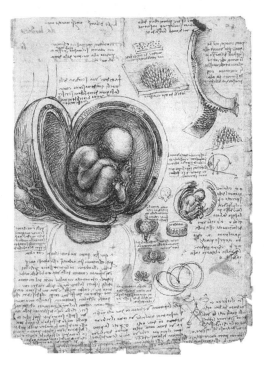

The fetus in the womb

This sheet is part of a series Leonardo drew while studying reproduction in Milan and Pavia with the anatomist Marcantonio della Torre. In this case he did not have the cadaver of a pregnant woman to work from, but a cow, as details of the placenta reveal. He drew a human fetus into the womb of a cow, presumably basing the shape of the fetus on specimens he had viewed. Thus the unborn baby and its surroundings are more Leonardo's invention than reality. Even so, the viewer feels oddly moved, perhaps because the artist's drawings convey, in Martin Kemp's words, "an extraordinary sense of the wonder and mystery of the generative process."[20]

Years later, in Rome, Leonardo pulled out the sketch of the crouching fetus again and added extensive commentary about the symbiosis of mother and child. He noted that the unborn child is dependent on its mother for life and food,[21] and remarked, "A single soul governs these two bodies, and the desires and fears and pains are common to this creature [and] the mother."[22] In Leonardo's view, the soul is so inextricably linked to the body that two connected bodies share a soul.

This was heresy, pure and simple. The Church held that a human is imbued with a soul at the moment of conception, and although the soul is linked to the body, it is not dependent on it, because the soul is immortal. This topic was a matter of such concern to Leo X that in his very first year as pope he issued a bull condemning the "despicable heretics" who dared to cast doubt on Church doctrine regarding the immortality of the soul.

But Leonardo had seen too much to continue believing in dogmas. In the world as he understood it, every object had its purpose. Nature did not allow for luxuries. What aim would a soul without a body serve? It would be powerless, because without a link to the sense organs it would not be able to perceive anything, and without a body it could not accomplish anything. Aristotle had already advanced this argument. "Every part is designed to unite with its whole, that it may escape from its imperfections. The soul desires to dwell in the body because without the body it can neither act nor feel," Leonardo commented.[23]

He disagreed with the Church's view that the "soul" was a nonmaterial essence in man. He thought it was more along the lines of a cerebral hub where all sensations merge and are transformed into thoughts and feelings. In this respect the soul bore some resemblance to an organ; he imagined that it was located in the ventricles, the four cavities of the brain filled with bodily fluids. Today we know that there is no such single location. What we perceive, think, and feel originates in the interaction of many brain centers with the rest of the body, and so it makes no sense to speak of a seat of personality.

Of course Leonardo's reflections on the soul were pure speculation. And he knew quite well that as a researcher he really had nothing to say on the subject. In a note that extols the amazing nature of the human body and denounces the destruction of life, he confessed his ignorance on matters pertaining to the soul: "Thou shouldst be mindful that though what is thus compounded seem to thee of marvelous subtlety, it is as nothing compared with the soul that dwells within this structure; and in truth, whatever this may be, it is a divine thing."[24]

Here Leonardo was contradicting his own notion of a disembodied soul, and was evidently quite aware of his own ambivalence. But he could not go back to the traditional Church view. Vasari was probably right in claiming that Leonardo's mind, honed by scientific inquiry, had serious doubts from early on about the "highest truth" of Church dogma. In one of the first notebooks he kept in Milan, he wrote a lengthy passage poking fun at the supposed capabilities of spirits who are unable to speak: "There can be no voice where there is no motion or percussion of the air; there can be no percussion of the air where there is no instrument; there can be no instrument without a body; this being so a spirit can have neither voice, nor form, nor force; and if it were to assume a body it could not penetrate nor enter where the doors are closed."[25] Leonardo may have had the twentieth chapter of The Gospel of John in mind, where Jesus speaks to disciples cowering in fear behind their doors.

The metaphysical question of whether death could be surmounted ought to have been of no concern to him as a researcher, but he pondered the issue of mortality. He was evidently not holding out much hope for himself. While not entirely discounting the idea that another world would await him after death, he thought it unlikely: "Every evil leaves a sorrow in the memory except the supreme evil, death, and this destroys memory itself together with life."[26]

In 1515, he joined the order of St. John of the Florentines, evidently to provide for his old age rather than as an expression of religious faith. The men in the Brotherhood of Good Death—this was the actual name of the congregation—had to pledge to take care of one another when they were ill and to arrange for a dignified burial of their deceased fellow members. For Leonardo, who had no living relatives, this arrangement made good sense. But these benefits, like a health insurance plan today, continued only as long as members stayed up-to-date on their premiums. When Leonardo repeatedly fell behind, the Brotherhood ousted him.[27]

While the body perishes, a person can triumph over death by leaving traces in the generation to come. Parents imagine that they can live on in their children, but Leonardo had no heirs. As far as we know, he was not especially interested in sex, and if he was, he seems to have been more partial to men than to women. The only remaining option in triumphing over his own mortality was his fame. And although a dead man has nothing to gain from living on in the minds of others, the prospect of doing so was enough of an incentive for Leonardo and many of his contemporaries to make good use of their time on earth: "O thou that sleepest, what is sleep? Sleep is an image of death, Oh, why not let your work be such that after death you become an image of immortality; as in life you become when sleeping like unto the hapless dead."[28]

In the Middle Ages, life was considered a mere prelude to eternity. Those who, like Leonardo, had a hard time believing in the hereafter in the new age of the Renaissance had to adopt a different perspective on how best to spend their remaining time on earth. Every day, every hour was precious. Leonardo's productivity, which seems immense to us, and his desire for utter perfection, which made him devote years to a single painting in the face of considerable opposition, also signified his rebellion against death.

Religion no longer offered him consolation. His notes include laments about war and ephemerality, as well as gloomy prophecies about creatures whose monstrosity knows no bounds and who are perpetually at war. But there is no mention of redemption, higher justice, or a future Kingdom of God—ideas that had prevailed in Europe for over a millennium. Leonardo was one of the pioneers who used his own body to put the possibility of a successful life in a secular world to the test. He did not reject Church doctrine, but it did not weigh on his mind. He felt that a thirst for knowledge was more commensurate with man than faith, freedom more desirable than humility, and he valued responsibility over obedience. He considered his attempts to shape the world into a better and more beautiful place by his own creative power more promising than hoping for life after death.

Did he believe in a reality beyond what can be perceived by the senses? Clearly he had no intention of invoking God to alter the course of his own destiny. If Leonardo recognized a higher reality, it was in the order of the cosmos rather than in his own individual life.

Visions of the End of the World

By the end of the fifteenth century, it no longer seemed plausible, as it had in the Middle Ages, that the world had been created and then remained just as it was. People had had to cope with too many upheavals. Leonardo lived in a world of turmoil and sweeping change, of war and catastrophe. He saw in nature the same brutality he had observed in society, and commented while contemplating a fossil: "O Time, swift despoiler of created things! How many kings, how many peoples hast thou brought low! How many changes of state and circumstance have followed since the wondrous form of this fish died here in this hollow winding recess? Now, destroyed by Time, patiently it lies."[29]

Deluge (detail)

Leonardo considered water the perfect symbol of the maelstrom of time: "In rivers, the water that you touch is the last of what has passed and the first of that which comes: so with time present."[30] This element, which was so familiar to him, also dominated Leonardo's visions of an unstable world during the final years of his life. In Rome he now explored the artistic implications of a subject he had tackled years earlier as a researcher: the Deluge. All his predecessors depicted man and animal struggling to save themselves from the slowly rising floods; Leonardo's archrival, Michelangelo, portrayed the end of the world in similar terms in the Sistine Chapel. Leonardo, by contrast, no longer referred to the stories in the Bible in his old age. He painted neither a kindhearted Noah nor a vengeful God. Only a single earlier version of the ten drawings of the Flood that are housed in Windsor Castle today has any people on it—and they are tiny.[31]

Instead, Leonardo shows the pure force of the elements. On one of the most impressive sheets, a giant tidal wave is striking the earth (Plate X).[32] Its first offshoots are racing toward a range of hills in the foreground. Evidently they are bringing a wave of pressure, because the first trees are already bowing. The viewer gets the feeling that the whole landscape will have disappeared in a tenth of a second, washed away by the water and demolished. The scenery appears in an eerily pale light; Leonardo later painted over the chalk drawing with ink to add even more detail to the forces of destruction. Every wave is a deadly missile. High in the sky, clouds are brewing. Rain is beating down from them, but the rain never reaches the ground. The center of the wave of pressure between heaven and earth pushes the rain back into the clouds.

We do not learn what unleashed the catastrophe. At the spot where the turbulence seems fiercest, a cliff side collapses, and giant blocks of basalt whirl through the air. Perhaps a hollow space has caved in deep in the earth and has created an explosive shock in the atmosphere. But the collapse might be the effect rather than the cause of the disaster, because the stone blocks whirling through space do not appear to be coming from the earth. It looks as though they originated in the turbulent air itself, in a concentration of enormous energy. A viewer born in the twentieth century cannot help but think of Einstein's $E = mc^2$, a formula in which energy is converted to mass.

For all its drama, the apocalyptic drawing calls to mind Leonardo's scientific studies of hydrodynamics. The eddies in the waterfall drawing, for example, reappear in similar form in the Deluge drawing, albeit on a different scale. The lettering that extends across the clouds demonstrates that Leonardo also had his earlier studies in mind: "Take into consideration the density of the falling rain at various distances and differing degrees of darkness." Even the end of the world had to adhere strictly to the laws of nature and be drawn accordingly.

The idea that nature spun out of control, rather than divine judg-ment, would bring about the end of all civilization seems plausible to us in the age of climate change. But regarding Leonardo as a cautionary ecologist would mean ascribing prophetic gifts to him that he did not possess. Even though his notebooks repeatedly referred to the destruc-tion of nature by man, his aim in sketching the end of the world was more likely to display the power of natural forces on a grand scale. This explains why humans are virtually absent from these drawings: In a truly cosmic catastrophe, these small creatures are beside the point. Leonardo was moving away from an anthropocentric worldview and looking at man as one creation of nature among many others.

He did not pass judgment on the destruction of the world; he simply portrayed it as a natural process. But he realized that he himself was subject to the same law of creation and destruction that reigned throughout the cosmos. Thus he found the answer to the question of what comes after death by recognizing that man is a part of nature. When the individual dies, his ultimate destination is a simple return to a greater whole.

> Behold now the hope and the desire of going back to one's own country
> or returning to primal chaos, like that of the moth to the light, of the man
> who with perpetual longing always looks forward with joy to each new
> spring and each new summer, and to the new months and the new years,
> deeming that the things he longs for are too slow in coming; and who
> does not perceive that he is longing for his own destruction. But this long-
> ing is in its quintessence, the spirit of the elements, which finding itself
> imprisoned within the life of the human body desires continually to return
> to its source. And I would have you to know that this same longing is in
> its quintessence inherent in nature, and that man is a type of the world.[33]

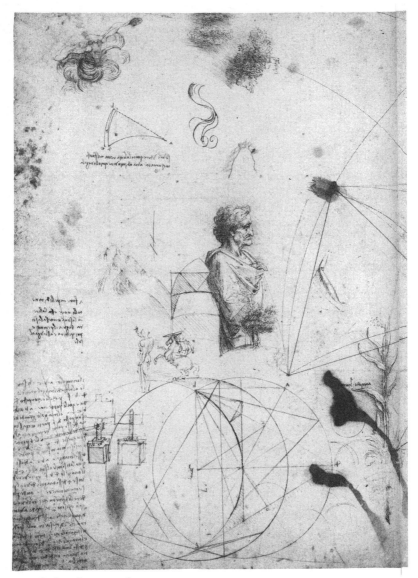

Studies of geometric figures

EPILOGUE:
The Legacy

IN THE SUMMER OF 1516, Leonardo decided to leave Italy for good. He evidently spent months wrestling with the decision whether to accept an offer from the twenty-one-year-old king of France, François I, after meeting the young monarch the previous December. Leonardo's final journey was also his longest, and since he sensed that he was unlikely ever to see his homeland again, he brought his entire oeuvre with him when he headed out over the Alps just before the onset of winter. The ever-loyal Francesco Melzi, his assistant Salai, and the servant Battista came with him.

Leonardo had apparently suffered a stroke in Rome, as we know from a visitor's remark that Leonardo's right hand was paralyzed. The artist himself complained about his maladies in letters without going into details.[1]

The next dated sign of life was a sheet with geometric studies dividing the circle, marked May 21, 1517, which was Ascension Day. A note indicates that the sketches were drawn at Amboise on the Loire,

*Clos-Lucé, where Leonardo spent the final years
of his life*

in the little castle of Cloux, which the king had made available for the
exclusive use of Leonardo and his staff.

The manor house is a few minutes downstream from the royal
palace, which then served as the main residence of the rulers of France.
The palace was later converted into a state prison and ultimately most
of it was destroyed, but the manor house seems to have changed little
since Leonardo's stay there apart from being renamed Clos-Lucé by
later owners. It is the only one of Leonardo's many places of residence
that still exists today. The property is on a hill overlooking the Loire,
and gables and an octagonal tower top the brick and tufa construction.
The battlement parapet and watchtower are reminiscent of the medieval
castle that once stood on this spot.

Just inside the entranceway is a hall with a large open hearth adjacent
to a tiled kitchen. Above this hall are the rooms Leonardo seems to
have used as a studio and bedroom. A canopy bed decorated with elab-
orate carvings may be the one in which he died. A tablet on the wall
bears a remark Leonardo made during the turbulent years following
his first flight from Milan: "While I thought I was learning how to
live, I was really learning how to die."[2] In the basement of the house,
at the entrance to a 6-foot-high tunnel, the current owners have put

up a cardboard figure with Leonardo's features. This underground connecting passage once led to the palace and allowed the artist and king to visit each other without being seen by others.

Evidently the ruler made ample use of this setup: "King François, being extremely taken with [Leonardo's] great *virtù*, took so much pleasure in hearing him reason that he was apart from him but a few days a year. . . . He believed there had never been another man born in the world who knew as much as Leonardo [and] that he was a very great philosopher."[3] These words were written by the Florentine sculptor Benvenuto Cellini, who was also employed at the French court and had obtained this information directly from François I. At the manor house in Cloux Leonardo finally had the freedom he had sought. His only duty was to be visible at court. The monarch assured him that he could pursue his interests wholly unconstrained by other obligations, and he paid Leonardo an annual salary of 1,000 ecus—an enormous sum of money. The governor, who received one of the top salaries, earned only 100 ecus. This money enabled Leonardo to devote himself exclusively to the matters that captured his interest.

Leonardo subscribed to the logic that "iron rusts from disuse, stagnant water loses its purity and in cold weather becomes frozen; even so does inaction sap the vigor of the mind."[4] He remained active to the very end of his life. Leonardo traveled fifty miles to the town of Romorantin, where the king was planning to have a new palace built, and furnished designs for a palace with parks, plotting out an extensive system to drain the marshes and render the tributaries of the Loire navigable. He also organized several splendid pageants for which he sketched the costumes. And his mechanical lion took the stage again on October 1, 1517.

Leonardo began sorting out his scattered notes to compile the volumes he had been planning for decades. Melzi transcribed Leonardo's notes, which were nearly impossible for any outsider to decipher, and took dictation for missing passages. The eventual result of Melzi's continued work on these notes was the *Treatise on Painting*, one of the hundreds of volumes Leonardo dreamed of publishing someday. This volume would be Leonardo's only treatise to reach publication in a thematically organized form.

On Midsummer Day, June 24, 1518, Leonardo was in his manor house, puzzling over geometry problems as he had for so much of his life. Then he evidently heard a voice—probably the voice of his housekeeper Maturine—calling him for dinner, and he wrote these words at the bottom of a page filled with triangular diagrams: "etcetera. Because the soup is getting cold."[5] It is Leonardo's last written note to have been preserved.

But it was not until April 23 of the following year that he sent for the notary to dictate his will in the presence of Melzi and other witnesses. The young Francesco would get all his books, writings, and paintings; Salai and the servant Battista were each bequeathed one-half of Leonardo's garden outside Milan. To his half brothers who lived in Florence, he left a sum of money with the treasurer of the hospital of Santa Maria Nuova, where he had once begun his research on cadavers, and he left his housekeeper Maturine a fur-trimmed coat. Leonardo also ordered three high masses and thirty low masses to be celebrated in his memory, in accordance with his status as the king's painter. For the funeral he stipulated that sixty poor men bear sixty candles and "receive money for this." And he commended his soul to God.

Leonardo da Vinci died on May 2, 1519. Melzi remained in Amboise for another year so that he and his father, Girolamo, who came in from Milan to help his son, could sort through the papers. Then he left, Leonardo's legacy in hand.

Melzi lamented in a letter to Leonardo's family, "nature will never have the power to create another like him." He was right in speculating that no one else would create an even remotely comparable oeuvre. But was it really nature's doing? According to the Law of Large Numbers, many similarly gifted children ought to have come into the world by now. More than twenty-five billion people have been born since Leonardo's death, and a good 6½ billion of them are alive today.[6] There should have been men and women with the talents of a Leonardo many times over—and there ought to be more than ever today.

So what was so special about Leonardo? No one can be understood completely, and most certainly not someone as multifaceted and contradictory as Leonardo. The best way of gaining insights into Leonardo is not to focus on the anecdotes and legends that others have circulated about him, but rather to study his own writings.

One sheet of his notes provides a dazzling illustration of the special quality of Leonardo's thought process. It is a large piece of paper, almost the size of a newspaper, which at first glance resembles a puzzle, with nearly two dozen sketches, adjacent to and on top of each other. No two are the same.[7] An exquisitely detailed plant grows into a geometric diagram of circular arcs. An elderly Roman gazes sternly out into the distance, his belly enmeshed with two trees, and his back to a mountain range, making him appear gigantic. Near the bottom, we can make out the axonometrics of a machine, and up top there are curlicues—or are they eddies? Light breaks through the clouds and falls on a church tower. And at the edge of the sheet are instructions in mirror writing for dying hair with nuts boiled in lye.

The sheet, sketched in 1488, shows that Leonardo must have been pondering all these subjects at the same time. The viewer marvels at Leonardo's versatility, then starts to recognize a well-ordered whole in this apparent diversity of themes. Leonardo was juggling shapes, identifying their similarities, and transforming one into another, high-lighting their unexpected connections. Things that seem randomly scribbled at first are actually well thought-out. The hatched arc segments, for example, are equal in size and facing each other. In the plant that juts into this design, nature is transformed into geometry. The curve of a leaf continues in two parallel circles and reappears in abstract crescent-shaped figures. But the little drawing of the Roman is a showpiece of Leonardo's ability to think in images rather than words. The diagram behind the Roman takes up the drapery of his toga, and the mountain chain reflects this geometry as well. And it is no coincidence that the man overlaps with the two trees. As though one could see right through the toga of the old man, the one bare tree seems to merge into the arteries of his body. Was Leonardo exploring the idea that branches and blood vessels open out in the same pattern? Clearly he envisioned the peculiar arrangement even before he began to draw. Leonardo did not even have to put pen to paper to tinker with highly complex shapes. This un-imposing sketch reveals his extraordinary visual talent. Cognitive psy-chologists now associate this aptitude with spatial thinking.[8]

Although his mastery and wealth of ideas in more than a dozen areas gave Leonardo the reputation of a universal genius, he was not universally talented. For example, he tackled mathematics for years without ever getting the hang of long division—not that failings of this kind stood in the way of his enormous productivity. Leonardo de-rived the greatest possible benefit from his extraordinary powers of imagination. A mathematician would describe the similarity between the ramifications of branches and veins using formulas and numbers. Leonardo instead compared the two patterns in an image, and devel-oped a kind of thinking that suited his talent.

The analogies he kept finding everywhere he looked not only helped him to explain the world, but also gave wing to his creative genius. His world was like a set of building blocks, which he used to make ever-new combinations. He let his thoughts roam and alight on ideas. His manuscripts explained "a way to stimulate and arouse the mind to various inventions" by staring at random patterns, such as those found on a discolored rock, and discovering new shapes.[9] Leonardo used this method to hone his creativity.

Anyone can adopt strategies of this kind, and at least some people today ought to be blessed with a gift for spatial thinking on a par with Leonardo's. Perhaps we are not aware of any such amazingly creative individuals because modern Leonardos tend to be invisible: They may be out there, but they work in highly specialized niches in a world that has been thoroughly investigated. It is incomparably more difficult now to delve into every conceivable discipline the way Leonardo did and to make a discovery that would make people sit up and take note.

But how likely is it that young people today would learn to use their talents as Leonardo did? What would become of Leonardo if he went to school today? He would have to pass the standard courses, and the teachers would educate him in a methodology based on language and mathematics. But this system is not designed for aptitudes that deviate from the norm. Leonardo's great visual talents would be of little benefit to a young Leonardo today, as must be the case for countless children with unusual abilities. They do not have much of an opportunity to employ their special gifts to learn about the world in their own way and avoid conforming to a rigid curriculum.

It was probably a good thing that Leonardo's formal schooling was limited and that he entrusted his development to an extraordinary mentor.[10] Andrea del Verrocchio had a remarkable ability to turn talented youngsters into successful artists,[11] and his wide-ranging expertise helped lay the foundation for Leonardo's achievements in a great many fields. Verrocchio was a painter, sculptor, restorer of artworks, goldsmith,

Andrea del Verrocchio

metallurgist, curator of the Medicis' collection of antiques, and mechanical engineer. When he was commissioned to fashion a large gold ball for the dome of the cathedral in Florence, he worked with Paolo dal Pozzo Toscanelli, one of the leading scientists in his city.[12] Verrocchio also used cadavers to teach his apprentices human anatomy.

The versatility of Verrocchio and his pupil Leonardo typified the era in which artists had to master not just their craft, but also a wide range of knowledge. The famous Florentine sculptor Ghiberti compiled an entire catalogue of fields that his colleagues were expected to study, from philosophy and medicine to astrology. When could the "learned artist" have found the time to paint and sculpt in Ghiberti's plan? But Leonardo had the ambition, the stamina, and the intelligence to try his hand at achieving what Ghiberti had outlined—and went well beyond it. Ghiberti thought it necessary to read widely to understand the world, but Leonardo set out to research matters for himself.

His devotion was extraordinary. He could spend decades circling in on the same problem, even if it seemed hopeless. If despite his best efforts he could not arrive at a solution, he blamed his failure on his inability to sharpen his mind sufficiently. In a fable, he compared the mind to a flint that had to "endure its martyrdom" while being struck by a steel so that it could "give birth to the marvelous element of fire."[13] Where does what Leonardo once called the "determined steeliness of will,"[14] a willingness to suffer for a self-assigned task, originate? Most renowned artists and scientists cite a mentor as having played a decisive role in their early years. The key element that a teacher communicates to a student is neither experience nor knowledge—it is enthusiasm. That is where Verrocchio excelled.

Where would the young Leonardo get an incentive of that kind today? What teacher would impress on him that effort is its own reward? In fifteenth-century Florence, being an outsider presented an opportunity. As an illegitimate child, Leonardo da Vinci had no family tradition to pin him down, and he was spurred on by a strong desire to rise above the milieu into which he was born. Would this boy, born on the margins of society today, have the opportunity and the aspiration to rise above his circumstances?

After graduating from high school, he would have to find his way in a highly regulated world. Professors, bosses, and coworkers would reward him for specializing in one field and penalize him for branching out beyond the narrow confines of this field. The intelligent Leonardo would soon learn how to solve problems easily on paths that others had paved long before him. But could he figure out how to define his own tasks, how to pose new questions, how to find answers to questions using unconventional means?

In all probability, the young man would be trained in a working method diametrically opposed to the methods of the historical Leonardo. Today we are guided by our knowledge; Leonardo was open to seeing issues with the eyes of a child even in his old age. We divide up our knowledge according to disciplines and demand logic from them; he regarded the world as a single entity and sought similarities between the most dissimilar phenomena. We try to solve problems as systematically as possible; he did so by employing creative combinations. We want answers; he posed questions. But there is nothing to stop us from learning from Leonardo's approach—not to replace the modern way of thinking, but to supplement it.

Above all, however, Leonardo demonstrated how far a person can take research that has no set goal. Driven by curiosity, he worked for the sheer pleasure of understanding the world. His very lack of objective enabled him to advance to more horizons than anyone before or since and left him free to opt for the most interesting rather than the quickest route. Leonardo da Vinci showed us what man is capable of when liberated from the constraints and apparent certainties of the world. This is his true legacy.

PLATE I: *Portrait of Lisa del Giocondo (Mona Lisa), 1503–1506 and later*

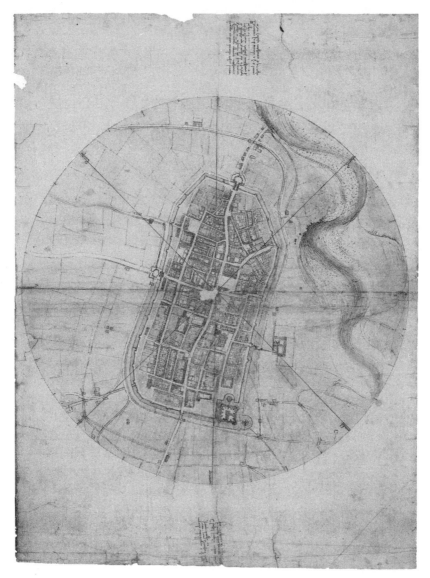

PLATE II: *Map of Imola, 1502*

PLATE III: *Baptism of Christ (together with Andrea del Verrocchio), 1476*

PLATE IV: *John the Baptist, ca. 1508*

PLATE V: *Peter Paul Rubens, Copy based on Leonardo's Battle of Anghiari*

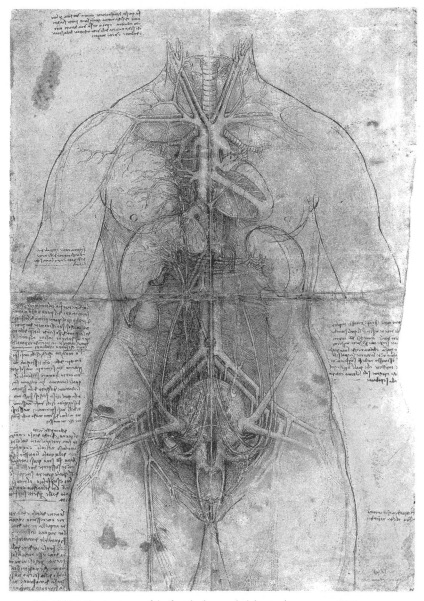

PLATE VI: *Anatomy of the female chest and abdominal organs, ca. 1508*

PLATE VII: *Virgin of the Rocks* ("London version"), ca. 1495

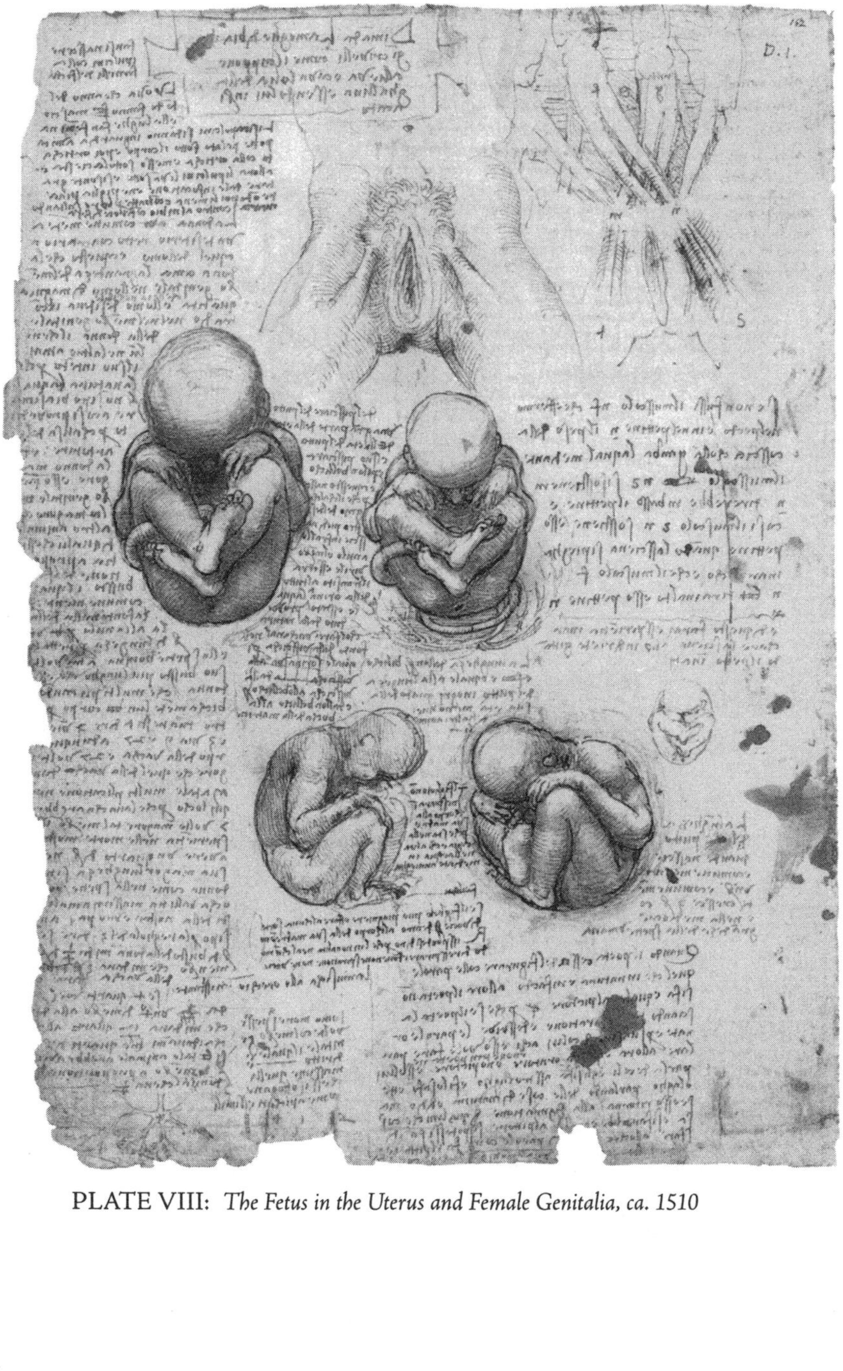

PLATE VIII: *The Fetus in the Uterus and Female Genitalia, ca. 1510*

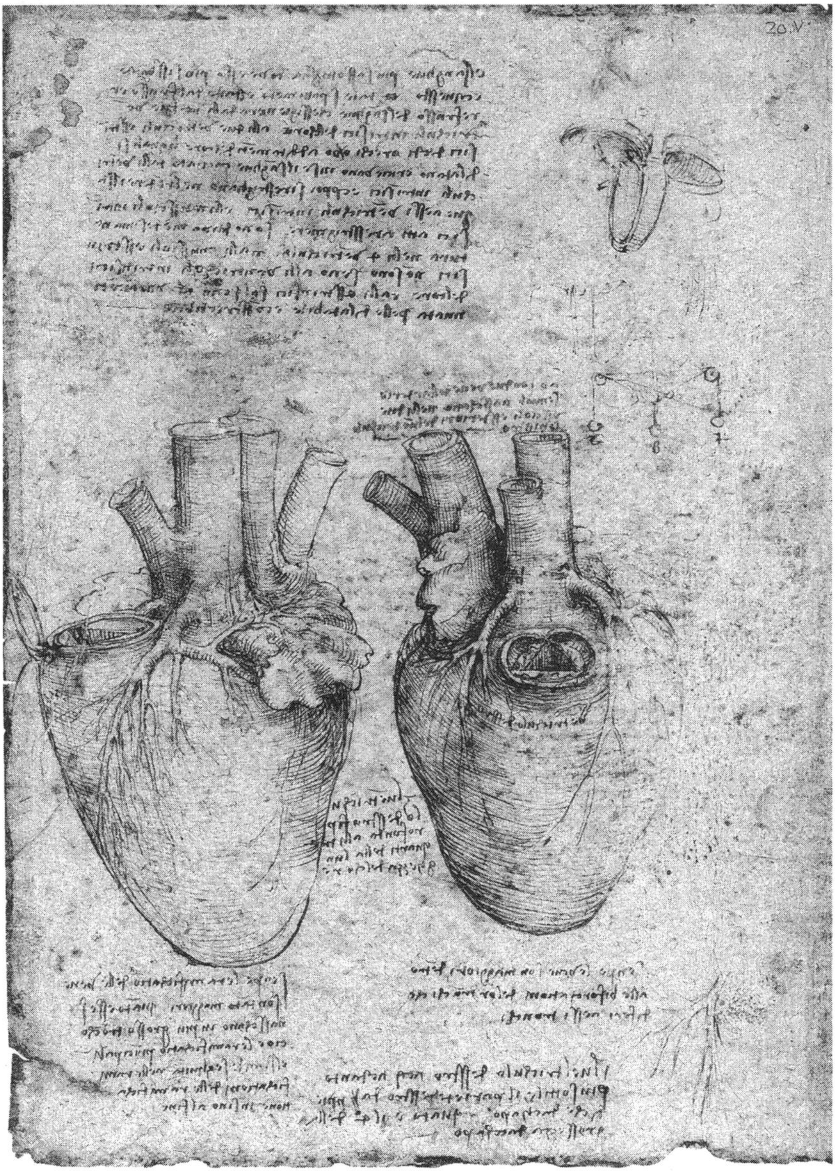

PLATE IX: *Heart and Its Blood Vessels, ca. 1513*

PLATE X: *Deluge, ca. 1515*

CHRONOLOGY

VINCI (1452 TO CA. 1482)

1452

On April 15, Leonardo is born at about 10:30 P.M. in Vinci as the illegitimate child of Ser Piero da Vinci, a notary, and Caterina, a farmer's daughter. Neither his mother nor his father attends his baptism. A few months later, Leonardo's father marries Albiera di Giovanni Amadori, the sixteen-year-old daughter of a rich notary in Florence.

Johannes Gutenberg begins printing the Bible. His printing method using movable metal letters quickly spreads throughout Europe; books become mass-produced goods.

1453

Leonardo's mother, Caterina, marries Accattabriga di Piero del Vacca, a farmer.

Sultan Mehmed II conquers Constantinople. Many intellectuals flee the Byzantine Empire, which has now collapsed, and move to Italy. They bring previously unknown manuscripts by ancient scholars to

Leonardo's birthplace

the West, which reawakens interest in the cultural achievements of antiquity.

1457
According to tax files in the town of Vinci, Leonardo lives with his grandfather Antonio.

FIRST PERIOD IN FLORENCE (CA. 1469 TO 1482)
1469
Tax files reveal that Leonardo is living with his father in Florence. His father is employed as a notary at the chief public prosecutor's office in what is today the Palazzo del Bargello. Leonardo has probably begun his apprenticeship with Andrea del Verrocchio.

After the death of his father, Piero, Lorenzo I. de' Medici assumes a leading role in the Republic of Florence. He promotes the fine arts and philosophy. Under his rule, Florence becomes the intellectual center of Italy.

1472

Leonardo joins the painters' Guild of St. Luke.

1473

Leonardo completes his first dated pen-and-ink drawing, a view over the Arno Valley, on August 5 (*Our Lady of the Snows*). This is the first pure landscape picture in Western art. (See the section "Water Music" in chapter 2.)

The Portuguese explorer Lopes Gonçalves is the first European to cross the Equator.

1474

Leonardo paints his earliest known painting, *The Annunciation* (Florence, Uffizi Gallery). The commission originally went to Verrocchio.

The Republic of Venice enacts the world's first patent law.

Annunciation, ca. 1473–1475

1476

Leonardo works with his mentor Verrocchio on the *Baptism of Christ* (Florence, Uffizi Gallery). The kneeling angel and the landscape in the background are by Leonardo.

Leonardo is accused of sodomy. He and other pupils of Verrocchio are said to have assaulted a seventeen-year-old apprentice in a goldsmith's workshop. The complaint is dropped for lack of evidence.

After the murder of his brother, Galeazzo, the rightful heir, Ludovico Sforza, denies power to the underage Gian Galeazzo and ascends the throne of Milan himself.

1476–1478

Leonardo, who is still working in Verrocchio's workshop, paints the *Madonna of the Carnation* (Munich, Alte Pinakothek) and the *Portrait of Ginevra de' Benci* (Washington, D.C., National Gallery).

Leonardo drafts his first technical sketches, including a design for a spring-driven car (see page 130). He experiments with optical devices.

Hanging of Bernardo Di Bandino Baroncelli, 1479

1478

The municipal authorities in Florence give Leonardo his first public commission: to create an altarpiece to display in the Capelli di San Bernardo, the chapel of the Palazzo della Signoria. The work is later completed by Filippino Lippi, possibly as a result of political turmoil.

On April 26, Lorenzo de' Medici and his brother Giuliano are stabbed during a high Mass in the cathedral in Florence. Only Lorenzo survives. The assassins are associated with the so-called Pazzi Conspiracy, in which Florentine patrician families try to overthrow the Medicis. The conspirators are hanged. Leonardo draws a hanged man.

1480

Leonardo works on a painting commonly referred to as the *Madonna Benois* (St. Petersburg, Hermitage) and on two others that are never completed: *Adoration of the Magi* (Florence, Uffizi Gallery) and *St. Jerome in the Wilderness* (Vatican).

He evidently moves into his own apartment, as he is no longer mentioned in his father's tax returns.

FIRST PERIOD IN MILAN (1482 TO 1499)

1482

Leonardo arrives in Milan with his assistants Atalante Migliorotti and Tommaso Masini, known as Zoroastro. He submits a written application at the court of Ludovico Sforza.

1483

On April 25, Leonardo signs a contract to paint the *Virgin of the Rocks* (Paris, Louvre) for a high altar in the Franciscan church in Milan.

1484

Sandro Botticelli paints *The Birth of Venus*.

1485

Leonardo witnesses the plague epidemic in Milan and draws sketches for a hygienic "ideal city" (see page 43). He paints *Portrait of a Musician* (Milan, Ambrosiana), which he never completes. Ludovico Sforza commissions him to paint the birth of Christ

Portrait of a Musician, ca. 1485

for the king of Hungary, Matthias Corvinius. On March 16, Leonardo
watches a total eclipse of the sun.

1486

Leon Battista Alberti's influential book about architecture is published.
It includes a description of then-standard hydraulic engineering designs.

1487

Leonardo draws the grotesque heads (see page 23) and develops his
first plans for flying machines. Leonardo designs a model for parts of
the dome of the cathedral in Milan.

1489

Leonardo dates a study of the human skull "April 2, 1489" (see page
162). Ludovico Sforza offers him a written commission to make a
colossal bronze equestrian statue.

In ca. 1489, Leonardo paints *Lady with an Ermine*, a portrait of Ludovico's mistress, Cecilia Gallerani (Krakow, Czartoryski Museum;
see page 154).

1490

Leonardo organizes a "Paradise Festival" for the wedding of the de-
throned Gian Galeazzo Sforza to Isabella of Aragon and designs a
mechanical stage set.

He accompanies Francesco di Giorgio Martini, one of the preeminent engineers of his day, to Pavia, to redesign the dome there. He
draws the first complex automatons and begins the codex on the flight
of birds.

On July 22, the ten-year-old Gian Giacomo Caprotti di Oreno joins
his workshop as an assistant and remains with him until Leonardo's

death. Leonardo calls him Salai ("little devil"). On September 7, Salai steals a silver pen from one of Leonardo's assistants.

Prince Francisco Tasso sets up the first ongoing postal service between the Innsbruck court of the Habsburg king, Maximilian I, and his son Philipp I in the Netherlands.

1491

Leonardo organizes the spectacle for the wedding reception of Ludovico Sforza and Beatrice d'Este. Salai steals another silver pen.

The conquest of Granada by Spanish troops brings an end to seven hundred years of rule by the Moors on the Iberian Peninsula.

1492

Leonardo travels through Lombardy.

He draws the *Vitruvian Man.*

In an undated letter written in 1492, he complains to Ludovico Sforza about insufficient payment for the *Virgin of the Rocks.*

Pope Alexander VI, the father of Cesare Borgia, takes office.

In Florence, Lorenzo I de' Medici dies. His successor as the head of the city-state is his son Piero II the Unfortunate.

Columbus lands in America.

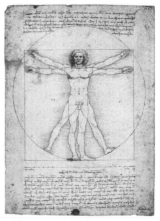

1493

Leonardo has completed the fireclay model for the casting of the equestrian statue. The model is displayed on the occasion of the wedding of Ludovico Sforza's niece Bianca Maria to Maximilian I of Habsburg, who is appointed head of the Holy Roman Empire in the same year.

Drawing of proportions
according to Vitruvivus

Leonardo begins the Codex Madrid I, an encyclopedic volume on machine parts.

The poet Bernardo Bellincioni praises Leonardo's portrait of Cecilia Gallerani in his ode *Rime* (rhymes).

Pope Alexander VI divides the Americas between Spain and Portugal.

Albrecht Dürer's self-portrait documents a new sense of artistic pride.

1494

Leonardo spends the beginning of the year in La Sforzesca, Ludovico Sforza's model farm in Lombardy.

On November 17, Ludovico sends the bronze that had been selected for Leonardo's equestrian statue to his father-in-law, Ercole d'Este, the Duke of Ferrara, to have a cannon made from it.

In September, the French troops invited by Ludovico to Italy occupy Milan. On October 22, the rightful heir to the throne, Gian Galeazzo Sforza, deprived of power by his uncle Ludovico, is murdered. Ludovico Sforza has himself crowned Duke of Lombardy.

Study for the Sforza monument,
ca. 1488–1489

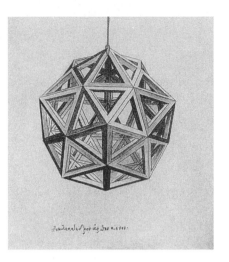

Illustration for Pacioli's De divina
proportione

Piero the Unfortunate is driven from Florence; the Dominican
monk and mathematician Luca Pacioli, a pupil of the painter Piero
della Francesca, publishes his work *Summa de arithmetica*, which explains
the principle of double-entry bookkeeping that is still used today.

1495
Leonardo travels to Florence, where he is enlisted as an adviser for the
construction of the assembly room in the Palazzo Vecchio.

In this year he apparently begins work on the *Last Supper* fresco in
the monastery of Santa Maria delle Grazie in Milan and paints rooms
in Sforza's palace in Milan and a second version of the *Virgin of the
Rocks* (London, National Gallery; Plate VII).

Charles VIII, king of France, occupies Naples on February 22. His
ally Ludovico Sforza switches sides; the bloody Battle of Fornovo on
July 6 ends with the French driven out of Italy.

1496

Leonardo paints a portrait of Lucrezia Crivelli, one of the other lovers of Ludovico (*La Belle Ferronnière*; Paris, Louvre).

The project to paint the rooms in the Milan palace is put on hold for the time being. The mathematician Luca Pacioli arrives at the court of the Sforzas and strikes up a friendship with Leonardo, who draws the illustrations for Pacioli's book *De divina proportione* over the next few years.

1497

Ludovico Sforza has his secretary pressure Leonardo to complete the *Last Supper* fresco.

Savonarola has books, paintings, and other "luxury items" collected in Florence and burned in a public "bonfire of the vanities" on February 7. On May 13, Savonarola is excommunicated.

Vasco da Gama rounds the Cape of Good Hope.

1498

On February 9, Leonardo and Pacioli take part in an "honorable and scientific debate" with theologians, philosophers, and physicists, under the auspices of Ludovico Sforza.

On March 17, Leonardo travels to Genoa to examine the harbor, which has been damaged by a storm.

He now works on murals in the so-called Sala delle Asse in the northeast tower of the Sforza palace.

On February 17, Savonarola again orders a painting and book burning in Florence. On May 23, he is hanged and his body burned.

The French king Charles VIII dies; his successor is Louis XII.

1499

On April 26, Ludovico Sforza gives Leonardo a vineyard near Milan.

On September 9 and 10, French troops storm the city, and on October 6, the new king, Louis XII, makes a formal entrance in Milan. Ludovico Sforza flees.

Leonardo meets the French courtier Ligny and plans to accompany him to Rome and Naples; he probably also meets Cesare Borgia.

Switzerland gains independence from the German Empire.

*SECOND PERIOD IN FLORENCE (**1500 TO 1505**)*

1500

Leonardo and Pacioli flee to Mantua in February. In March, Leonardo arrives in Venice. Commissioned by the city government to design a defense system against a Turkish invasion, he travels through Friuli. On April 24, Leonardo arrives in Florence. He is evidently provided rooms in Santissima Annunziata, the mother church of the Servite order, where he makes preliminary sketches for his later painting of *The Virgin and Child with St. Anne.*

*The Virgin and Child with St. Anne
and St. John the Baptist, 1499–1500*

On January 5, Ludovico Sforza reconquers Milan with the help of troops sent by the Holy Roman Empire, but he is soon repelled again by the French and on April 10 is defeated once and for all at Novara. He is captured by the French.

The Turkish fleet defeats Venice in the naval battle of Lepanto in the eastern Mediterranean.

Cesare Borgia, leader of the Vatican troops, conquers the greater part of central Italy for his father, Pope Alexander VI.

1501

At the beginning of the year, Leonardo takes a brief trip to Rome to study ancient art. Back in Florence, he continues working on the cartoon of *The Virgin and Child with St. Anne* and on the *Madonna of the Yarn-winder* (today in the private collection of the Scottish duke Buccleuch). He devotes himself to studies of geometry and mathematics.

The Signoria (municipal government) of Florence awards Michelangelo the official commission to carve a marble statue of David. Cesare Borgia becomes Duke of Romagna. Louis XII of France conquers Naples. The first slaves are sent by ship to America from Africa.

1502

Leonardo is in the service of Cesare Borgia. In April, he travels to the port of Piombino, whose ruler has been deposed by Borgia, and then returns to Florence. After the rebellion of Arezzo against Florence (June 4) he again travels to the other side of the front and on Borgia's behalf inspects Urbino, Cesena, Porto Cesenatico, Rimini, and Imola. A document dated August 18 appoints him Borgia's "architect and general engineer." Most likely in the fall he draws the map of Imola as well as plans for the reconstruction of the fortification there. Leonardo meets Niccolò Machiavelli, who serves as the Florentine envoy for the Borgia court.

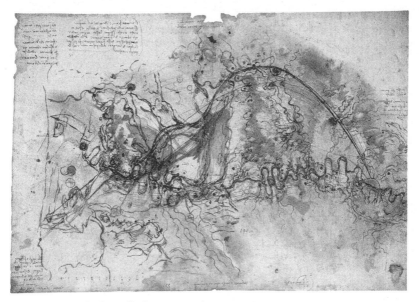

Map with the design for the Arno canal, ca. 1503–1504

Conspiracy of Borgia's officers against their commander. On New Year's Eve, 1502/03, Borgia has his adversaries arrested and murdered in Senigallia. The victims include Vitellozzo Vitelli, with whom Leonardo had a good relationship.

All Jews and unconverted Moors are expelled from Spain.

1503

Leonardo parts company with Borgia, most likely in February, and returns to Florence.

In a letter, he offers to build Sultan Bayezid II a bridge over the Bosporus.

In July, the Signoria of Florence has him draw up plans to divert the Arno River to block enemy Pisa's access to the sea. (The project is later dropped.) In October, the Signoria also commissions him to paint a colossal fresco of the *Battle of Anghiari* in the council hall (Plate V).

Leonardo begins his work on the *Mona Lisa* at about this time (Paris, Louvre; Plate I).

Pope Alexander VI dies on August 18. After just five weeks, his successor, Pius III, succumbs to complications of gout. The next pope, Julius II, dismisses Cesare Borgia from all the offices he holds, and Borgia flees to Spain.

1504

On January 25, Leonardo attends a committee meeting to decide on the best location for Michelangelo's *David*. He receives a regular salary for the preparatory work for the fresco of the *Battle of Anghiari*.

On July 9, his father, Ser Piero, dies; his will leaves nothing to Leonardo.

On November 1, he travels to Piombino, which has reverted to its previous ruler after Borgia's flight, and draws up plans to reinforce the docks.

On November 30, Leonardo notes that he has solved the problem of squaring the circle.

Naples becomes Spanish. The Inquisition begins in Spain.

The painter Raphael Santi relocates to Florence from Perugia and begins producing his *Madonna* paintings. He sees a preliminary sketch of the *Mona Lisa* in Leonardo's workshop.

The painter Matthias Grünewald begins his greatest work, the Isenheim Altarpiece, in the Vosges.

1505

On June 6, Leonardo begins his preparations to apply paint to the fresco of the *Battle of Anghiari* and recounts this inauspicious course of events: "The cartoon tore, the water spilled . . . and just then the weather turned bad, and it started to pour."

He devotes himself to the subject of the flight of birds and the development of flying devices. On Monte Ceceri, he probably conducts a test flight.

Martin Luther is nearly struck by lightning, then joins the Order of St. Augustine. Albrecht Dürer travels to Venice, where he most likely sees Leonardo's anatomical sketches.

SECOND PERIOD IN MILAN (1506 TO 1516)
1506
On April 27, a court of arbitration rules that Leonardo has to finish painting the *Virgin of the Rocks*, which is still incomplete after twenty-three years. In a contract with the Signoria, dated May 30, he agrees to return to Florence after three months in Milan to complete his work on the *Battle of Anghiari*. In August, however, Milan's French governor Charles d'Amboise negotiates with the Signoria to let Leonardo give up the project without financial penalty.

In September, Leonardo sets off to Milan, where he designs a villa and garden for Charles d'Amboise.

The construction of St. Peter's Basilica begins in Rome.

1507
Leonardo travels to Florence in March.

On June 14, he organizes a gala in Milan for Louis XII, the king of France. The French governor insists that the Florentines release Leonardo once and for all from his contract for the *Battle of Anghiari* because "he has to paint a picture for Louis XII."

In Vinci, Leonardo's uncle Francesco dies. To settle an inheritance dispute between Leonardo and his half brothers, he arrives in Florence on September 18 and presumably stays there. In the hospital of Santa Maria Nuova, he performs an autopsy of a man said to be one hundred years old.

Pope Julius II begins selling indulgences to finance St. Peter's Basilica.

Cesare Borgia is caught in an ambush during a battle in Spain and is killed.

A map of the New World signed by the Freiburg cartographer Martin Waldseemüller is the first to use the word "America."

1508

In the spring, Leonardo returns to Milan. He works on the painting *Leda and the Swan* (now lost) and evidently begins work on the paintings *The Virgin and Child with St. Anne* and *John the Baptist* (both Paris, Louvre; see page 243 and Plate IV).

Maximilian I of Habsburg accepts the title of Holy Roman Emperor and starts a war against Venice.

Ludovico Sforza dies in French captivity.

Michelangelo begins painting the Sistine Chapel.

Study for the Kneeling Leda with Swan,
ca. 1505–1510

1509

In Pavia, the twenty-seven-year-old Marcantonio della Torre is appointed professor of anatomy and begins an intensive collaboration with Leonardo.

Copernicus submits his *De hypothesibus motuum caelestium*, which presents his theory of planetary orbits and situates the sun in the center. In Venice, Luca Pacioli's *De divina proportione* is published with illustrations by Leonardo.

1510

Peter Henlein, a locksmith from Nuremberg, makes one of the first portable watches.

1511

Leonardo's patron Charles d'Amboise and the anatomist Marcantonio della Torre die. When rumors circulate that an attack by troops of the Holy League (Vatican, Habsburg, Venice, the Swiss Confederation) is imminent in Milan, Leonardo flees to the family estate of his pupil Francesco Melzi in Vaprio d'Adda and settles there for the time being. On December 10, he witnesses the fires started by Swiss soldiers in the town of Desio in Lombardy.

1512

Leonardo spends the year in Vaprio d'Adda primarily on studies of anatomy and water. In the Codex Leicester he brings together his theories of geology, cosmology, and the origins of the earth. He explains that moonlight is a reflection of solar radiation and that the radiance on the dark portions of the waxing and waning moon comes from the light the earth casts on the moon.

The origin of moonlight

Hurricane over horsemen and trees

The French are defeated in the Battle of Novara; Massimilano Sforza, Ludovico's son, takes the throne in Milan.

The Fifth Council of the Lateran affirms the immortality of the soul as Church dogma.

1513

In October, Leonardo and his pupils and employees leave Lombardy and arrive in Rome on December 1, where Leonardo moves into the Palais Belvedere in the Vatican. His patron is Giuliano II de' Medici, the brother of Leo X, the new pope.

Leonardo completes his final anatomical studies, especially his studies of the heart.

On March 8, Leo X becomes the successor of the deceased pope, Julian II.

Niccolò Machiavelli writes *The Prince*. The model for the main figure is Cesare Borgia.

A woman standing in a landscape,
ca. 1513–1516

1514

Leonardo works on the Deluge drawings and again on the *Mona Lisa*. In September, he makes a brief trip to Parma. In Civitavecchia he explores the harbor and the ancient ruins. He devises a plan to drain the Pontinian swamps south of Rome.

Albrecht Dürer produces his master engraving *Melencolia I*.

1515

Louis XII, king of France, dies on January 1.

On July 12, at a banquet in Lyons to honor his successor to the throne, François I, Leonardo's mechanical lion is presented. The lion is a gift from the Duke of Urbino, Lorenzo di Piero de' Medici.

The new king invades Italy and reconquers Milan. In November Leonardo accompanies the pope to Florence and Bologna, where he probably meets François I.

Leonardo joins the Brotherhood of Good Death. The Curia forbids him to dissect cadavers.

1516

Leonardo's patron Giuliano de' Medici dies on March 17. In August, Leonardo measures the early Christian basilica San Paolo fuori le Mura in Rome.

In the late fall, he goes to France as "painter of the king" François I. Melzi and Salai accompany him.

FRENCH PERIOD (*1517* TO *1519*)

1517

Leonardo moves into the manor house in Cloux near the royal residence in Amboise on the Loire. In his final drawings, the figures seem to merge with the light that surrounds them.

On October 1, the mechanical lion is again presented in honor of François I in Argentan.

On October 10, Cardinal Louis d'Aragon visits Leonardo. The cardinal's secretary, Antonio de Beatis, writes in his diary that he has viewed manuscripts and three paintings by Leonardo, including the *Mona Lisa*, and notes that the artist is paralyzed on the right side of his body, "apparently as the result of a stroke."

The humanist Erasmus of Rotterdam publishes his book *The Complaint of Peace*, which condemns war as an instrument of politics.

1518

At the beginning of the year, Leonardo spends time with François I at his castle in Romorantin, where he designs a new royal palace and a drainage system.

The stage set from the 1490 "Paradise Festival" in Milan is rebuilt for the wedding reception of the king's niece.

On June 24, Leonardo writes his final dated notebook entry.

Luther appears before the papal legate in Augsburg.

Adam Ries (now called Riese) publishes his first mathematics book.

1519

On April 23, Leonardo dictates his will.

Leonardo dies on May 2. On June 1, Melzi sends a letter informing Leonardo's family of his death.

Magellan sets sail for the first circumnavigation of the globe.

NOTES

INTRODUCTION
1. Jean Paul Richter, vol. 2, p. 235.
2. CA 76 r-a (ex 280 r-a); MacCurdy, p. 1067.
3. Vasari, p. 255.
4. Quoted in Goldscheider, p. 30.

CHAPTER I
1. Pater, p. 103. The versification of this text is by W. B. Yeats.
2. Vecce 1990.
3. Vecce 1998.
4. Schwartz 1995; Schwartz 1988.
5. See Sassoon.
6. Leonardo may have been inspired by Flemish painting. The subjects portrayed by Jan van Eyck (ca. 1390–1441) faced the viewer in three-quarter turns, but they lacked background landscape and the display of the subjects' hands, which are key elements of the *Mona Lisa*. It is likely that Leonardo knew the Flemish style: The art collection in the court of Mantua included paintings by Rogier van der Weyden and others, and prints were also in circulation.
7. Kemp 1981, p. 266.
8. MacCurdy, pp. 853–854.
9. TP 68 and B N 2038 20 r; see also Kemp 1971. A passage in Alberti's book about the art of painting expresses the same idea: "We painters ... wish to represent emotions through the movement of limbs," Alberti, p. 78.

10. TP 61 v.

11. The neurons first discovered in monkeys by the Italian neurophysiologist Giacomo Rizzolatti and his team in the early 1990s have a double function: First, they control the musculature of the body. Some give impulses to raise an arm, others to curl the corners of the mouth upward to form a smile, and still others produce looks of sorrow. Second, however, the mirror neurons send out the exact same signals when we merely watch *other* people raising an arm or looking happy or sad—and they prepare us to do the same. In this latter case, the movement of our own muscles is delayed for a later phase of response to signals in the brain, but the signal is retained for the corresponding emotion. Rizzolatti, Fogassi, and Gallese.

12. Zeki, pp. 2–3.

13. TP 289, TP 290.

14. B 29 r, B 38 v, B 42 v; see MacCurdy, p. 144f., p. 156f., and p. 158f.

15. See Nicholls et al.

16. See Ekman and Hager.

17. Even if we were able to keep our eye trained on a particular part of the woman's face, we would still be unable to discern the expression of the *Mona Lisa* with any certainty, because the areas around the eyes and the corners of the mouth—the areas we use to draw the key information about a person's mood—are hard to make out. Shadows over these areas make it impossible to read Mona Lisa's expression. This painting seems perfectly lifelike precisely because Leonardo deliberately kept it so unclear.

18. Kontsevich and Tyler.

19. Quoted in Zubov, p. 190.

20. CA 1002 r-1004 r (ex 360 r).

21. CA 527 v (ex 195 v).

22. Leonardo's contemporaries were aware of optical illusions, and libraries had copies of a seven-volume *Book of Optics* by Abu Ali al-Hasan Ibn al-Haitham, a vizier at the court in Cairo in the eleventh century who was known in the West as Alhazen. But apparently Leonardo was one of the very few to be taken with Alhazen's ideas. The only extensive writings on the foundations of optics in the fifteenth century of which we are aware are his. Alhazen was interested in understanding the laws of light propagation and perception; Leonardo sought to apply them to create a perfect work of art. On Leonardo's reception of Alhazen, see Arasse; Ackerman.

23. CA 207 r (ex 76 r); Irma Richter, p. 225.

24. CA 34 r-b (ex 9 v-b) 1480–1482, CA 17 v (ex 4 v-a) 1478–80, CA 5 r (ex 1 to r-a). According to Keele, these sketches date from the years 1480–1482.

25. A 8 v (1492); Veltman, p. 91f.

26. Leic 10 v.

27. Leonardo invented neither color perspective (distant objects appear bluish) nor aerial perspective (these objects appear blurry), but he was the first to understand the reasons for these phenomena and apply them to his artworks with unparalleled virtuosity.

28. TP 262.

29. BN 2038 18 r.
30. RL 12604 r.
31. D 3 v.
32. F 25 v; MacCurdy, p. 280.

33. It took Leonardo quite a few missteps to make his way to a realistic notion of the act of seeing. As a young man, he embraced the ancient belief that rays of light did not strike the eye from without, but actually emanated from within the eye as it scanned its surroundings. After years of doubt, he was finally persuaded by Alhazen's argument that rays of light take a period of time to travel from the eye to the objects, but if you open your eyes under the night sky, you see the stars right away, so the light must come from outside the eye, and the eye merely registers it. On the sketch Leonardo made in 1508, the candle is the source of the rays (CA 545 r [ex 204 r]; see also Ackerman).

His contemporaries also clung to the medieval image of the lens of the eye as a mirror. From each thing we see, exactly one ray returns to the lens, and images are composed. (In this construal, all parts of the eye behind the lens serve only to pass along a fully realized image to the brain.) But Leonardo devised an ingenious experiment, which anyone can reenact at home, to prove that the matter was not quite this simple. He closed one eye, held a needle close to his face, and fixed on a point in the distance. A mirror would now show the needle, which covers up one part of the background. The eye, by contrast, sees the complete background, while the needle appears pale and hazy, nearly transparent.

Leonardo contended that there could be only one explanation. Many rays—not just a single one—strike the eye from each object. If the needle masks just a few of these rays, it makes no difference, because the remaining rays allow the background to be made out. So the lens is more than just a mirror. This is how Leonardo later came upon the idea of comparing the lens of the eye to the side of a glass bowl.

Just after making this discovery, however, he faced the next puzzle: Why don't we see things as bigger when the pupil dilates? (In his early writings, however, Leonardo uses the word *popilla* for the lens of the eye; only later does he use it in its current meaning.) Leonardo, who was now forty years old, had grasped the fact that the lens of the eye is not a mirror, but he still thought that the image somehow originated on it. If this were the case, the image would be able to occupy a larger surface when the iris constricts and opens up a greater part of the lens (F 32 v). Wouldn't the object being viewed have to appear larger as well?

It took Leonardo until 1495 to realize the true function of the pupil: "At night . . . the diameter of the pupil of the horned owl or the long-eared owl is increased to ten times what it is by day, which amounts to saying that the pupil is a hundred times as large as it is by day" (CA 704 c [ex 262 r-d]; MacCurdy, p. 222). Thus, the pupil does not regulate the size of the image, but rather the amount of light in the eye.

34. D 10 v.

35. This is why the man holding his face inside the bowl is not looking directly at the water at the base, but instead at a glass ball suspended from ropes at the edge of the bowl, in which the light rays refract yet again, making the image revert. Leonardo was

of course unable to locate an organ of this kind during his dissections of animal and human eyes, because it does not exist.

CHAPTER II

1. See Gombrich 1999.
2. Kemp 1981, p. 100.
3. CA 656 r-a (ex 240 r-c), CA 80 r (ex 28 r-b).
4. Lombardini 1872.
5. Beltrame 1987.
6. William Barclay Parsons (1976), a renowned American hydraulic engineer and historian of technology, was one of those who advanced this argument. Dozens of other sketches verify how intensely Leonardo worked on the technology of locks.
7. CA 656 r-a (ex 240 r-c).
8. Lücke, p. 610.
9. CA 127 (ex 46 v-b); Lücke, p. 610.
10. Maschat, p. 25.
11. Later in his life, Leonardo's own income depended on water, when the French ruler in Milan allowed him to sell water to farmers.
12. See Della Peruta.
13. CA 1082 r-a (ex 391 r-a); MacCurdy, p. 1153.
14. Quoted in Garin, p. 201.
15. MacCurdy, p. 779.
16. Leic 32 a; MacCurdy, p. 1051.
17. Leic 9 v. See also Vaccari, Solmi, and Panazza, p. 70.
18. Irma Richter, pp. 330–331.
19. I 71 v, 72 r.
20. CA 327 v (ex 119 v-a); Irma Richter, p. 2.
21. He pictured a temple of Venus, the goddess of love, as an idyll surrounded by water: "You should make steps on four sides by which to ascend to a plateau formed by nature on the summit of a rock; and let this rock be hollowed out, and supported with pillars in front, and pierced beneath by a great portico, wherein water should be falling into various basins of granite and porphyry and serpentine, within recesses shaped like a half-circle; and let the water in these be continually flowing over; and facing this portico towards the north let there be a lake with a small island in the center, and on this have a thick and shady wood." RL 12591 r; MacCurdy, p. 370.
22. CA 302 r (ex 108 v-b); quoted in Marinoni, p. 115.
23. Quoted in Arasse, p. 107.
24. CA 468 r (ex 171 r-a); Irma Richter, p. 47.
25. CA 417 r (ex 154 r).
26. See Oberhummer.
27. See Alberti de Mazzeri.
28. See Pedretti 2003.

29. See Büttner.

30. See Kecks, p. 297.

31. See Perrig, p. 52.

32. New studies, so-called infrared reflectography, prove that this part of the landscape is definitely by Leonardo (and not by Verrocchio). The picture was painted over in this spot. An earlier version featured a more conventional landscape. See Zöllner, p. 215; Galluzzi 2006, p. 66.

33. See Galluzzi 1996, p. 65.

34. F 62 v, MacCurdy, p. 786.

35. I 73 r, MacCurdy, p. 788.

36. One of Leonardo's predecessors was Roger Bacon, a thirteenth-century British Franciscan monk who experimented with the refraction of light and the production of gunpowder. Paolo dal Pozzo Toscanelli, an Italian doctor and mathematician who had also predicted the possibility of a sea route to India, succeeded in determining that the obliquity of the ecliptic was 23°30'. ("Ecliptic" refers to the angle between the plane of the earth's equator and the plane in which the earth orbits the sun. The obliquity of the ecliptic is responsible for the change of seasons.) He was only 14 angular minutes off the correct value. Toscanelli accomplished this with an astronomical instrument that he had attached to the dome of the cathedral in Florence. But these men were exceptional figures. (For an overview, see Walzer.)

37. See Clagett, p. 13.

38. CA 160 a/160 b (ex 57 v-a/57 v-b); see also Macagno.

39. CA 812 (ex 296 v); see also Clagett, p. 13.

40. CA 407 r (ex 151 r-a).

41. F 2.

CHAPTER III

1. Vasari, p. 257.

2. Jean Paul Richter, vol. 2, p. 104.

3. MacCurdy, p. 80.

4. This sketch is preserved in the École Nationale des Beaux-Arts in Paris (Zöllner, no. 578); the statement is found in Manuscript B, and quoted in Dibner, p. 122.

5. Turin, Biblioteca Reale, Inv. 15583 r.

6. MacCurdy, p. 846.

7. BN 2037 100 r; MacCurdy, p. 806.

8. CA 158 r (ex 56 v-b), CA 518 v (ex 217 v-a), CA 979 ii (ex 353 r-c). It is unclear, however, whether the first wheel lock was developed by Leonardo or by clockmakers in Nuremberg. See Dibner, pp. 110–112.

9. CA 1070 r/1071 r (ex 387 r-a/b) and CA 498 r (ex 182 r-b) / CA 182 v-b (ex 64 v-b).

10. See Gille, p. 144.

11. VU 13 r.; MacCurdy, p. 413.

12. C 7 r; quoted in Dibner, p. 109.

13. See also Ma I 147 r. Both sheets were drawn in ca. 1490.

14. RL 12275 r.

15. See Keele, pp. 27–28.

16. TP 177; MacCurdy, p. 22.

17. Leic 22 v; MacCurdy, p. 746.

18. CA 669 r (ex 247).

19. CA 608 v (ex 224 v-b). For the interpretation of the coded note, called the Promemoria Ligny, see Vecce 1998 and the literature cited there.

20. MacCurdy, p. 1123.

21. CA 638 ii (ex CA 234 r-b); MacCurdy, p. 1154.

22. Vecce 1998.

23. Paolo Capello; quoted in Burckhardt, p. 89.

24. MacCurdy, p. 1170.

25. See Masters.

26. CA 628 e (ex 230 v-c); RL 12277.

27. Vecce 1998.

28. See Cloulas.

29. See Montanari, p. 22.

30. See Pedretti 1985.

31. Kemp 1981, p. 221.

32. CA 1 br (ex 1 r-b); see also Pinto, p. 393.

33. Kemp 1981, p. 230.

34. L 80 v.

35. These are their plan to divert the course of the Arno River, the fresco of the Battle of Anghiari, and the mission in Piombino.

36. It is likely that Leonardo was staying in Imola at this time. His personal contact with Borgia cannot be substantiated after October 1502, but there are no documents to confirm his stay in Florence until March 1503. See Kemp 1981.

37. Machiavelli, p. 29.

38. L 43 v; see also Marani.

39. Vasari, pp. 267–268.

40. MacCurdy, p. 1112.

41. CA 1033 v (ex 370 v-a); MacCurdy, p. 1113.

CHAPTER IV

1. See Boffito.

2. Quoted in Keele, p. 34.

3. Quoted in Vallentin, p. 368.

4. See Solmi; cited in Boffito.

5. Cardano, p. 816.

6. Galluzzi 1996.

7. Oppenheimer, p. 26.

8. Simon Magus is considered the first heretic in Christianity. The apocryphal Acts of Peter report how he rose into the air to prove his divinity. See Behringer and Ott-Koptschalijski.

9. For a good overview of the Neoplatonic Renaissance, see Kristeller.

10. CA 186 (ex 66 v-b); MacCurdy, p. 1122.

11. Burke, p. 194.

12. Luigi Tansillo (1510–1568) lived one generation after Leonardo, primarily in Naples. Quoted in Cirigliano, 383.

13. Canto XXIV, lines 49–51. In Leonardo, CA 43 v (ex 12 v-a).

14. Laurenza 2007, pp. 52–53.

15. CA 747 r (ex 276 r-b).

16. CA 201 r (ex 074 r-a).

17. CA 844 r (ex 308 r-a).

18. RL 19115 r.; MacCurdy, p. 179.

19. F 53 v.; MacCurdy, p. 472.

20. Quoted in Kemp 1981; see Manuscript K.

21. See, for example, VU 15 (14) v.

22. CA 434 r (ex 161 r-a).

23. CA 1006 v (ex 361 v-b); MacCurdy, p. 496.

24. B 74 v.

25. VU 17; MacCurdy, p. 418.

26. Ma 64 r.

27. E 23, 45, 46, CA 1098 r-b (ex 395 r-b).

28. Giacomelli, p. 181f.

29. G 8 r; MacCurdy, p. 910.

30. However, the reason is not that the air has to move more quickly above the wing because it has farther to travel. Wind tunnels reveal that this common misperception is incorrect. In reality, circulation arises when the air current under the wing stops at its back end, resulting in a self-contained eddy current around the wing profile. This current moves over the wing in the direction of flight. Its speed is added to the speed of flight, making the air over the wing flow more rapidly than the speed of flight. Underneath the wing, by contrast, the circulation flows against the direction of flight, which is why the total speed of the air is lower here.

31. CA 195 r (ex 71 r). It is not clear whether this line was written by Leonardo himself (see Pedretti 1977, p. 386), but the same page contains a melancholy remark by Leonardo about the passage of time and the futility of his efforts.

32. Vasari, p. 268.

CHAPTER V

1. Olschki 1949, pp. 308–309.

2. CA 1105 r (ex 397 r-a).

3. Gille, p. 166.

4. CA 875 r (ex 318 r).

5. Pedretti 1957.

6. Lomazzo 1973.

7. Reti, p. 135.

8. Dibner, p. 86.

9. Galluzzi 1996.

10. For II 92 v; MacCurdy, p. 803.

11. CA 812 r (ex 296 v), CA 878 v (ex 320 v), GDS 4085 A r, GDS 446 r, CA 926 r (ex 339 r a), CA 656 r (ex 347 r b).

12. See Arasse.

13. Similar though far less sophisticated entertainment machines had been displayed in the courts of Europe on occasion. The Duke of Burgundy's account books, which were recorded in the thirteenth century, make reference to a group of mechanical monkeys and a hydraulic stag. See Daston and Park, p. 95.

14. Daston and Park, esp. pp. 100–108.

15. MacCurdy, p. 854.

16. Vasari, p. 269.

17. RL 19070 v, TP 222 r.

18. CA 579 r (ex 216 v-b).

19. RL 12716 and RL 12688. See also Pedretti 1985.

20. CA 943 r (ex 343 v-a); quoted in Rosheim, pp. 124–125.

21. The fourteenth-century Burgundian court owned much simpler reproductions of hydraulic machines from the East. See Daston and Park.

22. Sarton, p. 233.

Chapter VI

1. Ar 155 r; MacCurdy, pp. 1127–1128.

2. Zubov, p. 278.

3. CA 500 (ex 182 v-c); quoted in Keele, p. 38.

4. Vasari, p. 269.

5. See Turner and the literature cited there; also see Sarton; Roberts 1990.

6. By "soul," Leonardo meant not a metaphysical entity, but an organ in which all sensory impressions converge and are assessed. See the next chapter, "Final Questions."

7. RL 19027 v, RL 19028 v; MacCurdy, p. 116.

8. Henderson 2006, p. 158.

9. Diana, p. 16.

10. MacCurdy, p. 166.

11. RL 19070 v; MacCurdy, p. 166.

12. RL 19070 v.; MacCurdy, p. 166.

13. RL 19009 r.; MacCurdy, p. 97.

14. RL 19028; MacCurdy, p. 116.

15. RL 19027 v.; MacCurdy, p. 116.

16. Leic 34 r; MacCurdy, p. 86.

17. K 49 r.; MacCurdy, p. 622.

18. Ma II, 67r.

19. This theory originated with Hippocrates and Plato.

20. See Zwijnenberg.

21. It is likely that della Torre was the one to acquaint Leonardo with Galen's original writings. Until then, Leonardo, who had never attended college and barely understood Latin, must have known about Galen's theories only from others' interpretations. Under della Torre's guidance, he was finally able to gain inspiration from the findings of this ancient anatomist unhampered by secondhand or thirdhand errors.

22. K 119 r.

23. RL 19127 r.

24. RL 19003 v and RL 19011 v.

25. RL 19071 r; MacCurdy, p. 166–167.

26. RL 12282 v.

27. F 1 r.

28. RL 19115 r; MacCurdy, p. 179.

29. RL 19001 r; MacCurdy, p. 80.

30. RL 19061 r.

31. RL 19084 r; MacCurdy 83.

32. RL 19073 r, RL 19074 v, RL 19076 v, RL 19079 v, RL 19082 r, RL 19083 r, RL 19084 r, RL 19087 r, RL 19088 r. Thematically related (though evidently written earlier) are RL 19116 r, RL 19117 v. The dating is from Kemp 2006.

33. See Kilner et al.

34. RL 19082 r.

35. RL 19076 v.

36. RL 19116–19117 v.

37. Kemp 1981, p. 294.

38. RL 19007; Zubov, p. 71.

39. RL 19070 v; MacCurdy, p. 166.

40. See Roberts 1999.

41. Heydenreich, p. 147.

Chapter VII

1. RL 12579.

2. CA 335 r-a; CA 141 v-b.

3. Leic 21 v.

4. Leic 31 r; Irma Richter, p. 27.

5. Leic 9 v.; MacCurdy, p. 337.

6. For a history of paleontology, see Rudwick.

7. Leic 3 r.; MacCurdy, p. 330.

8. Leic 8 v.; MacCurdy, pp. 330–331.

9. Leic 10 r; MacCurdy, p. 338. Leonardo was not claiming that the Old Testament was in error. He did not dare to pass judgment on whether an enormous flood actually occurred. He merely stated that it did not account for the fossils he found.

10. E 4 v and Leic 8 v.

11. Ar 58 v; MacCurdy, p. 345.

12. Leonardo changed his mind on this issue in the course of his life, as he did on so many others. As a young man, he still believed in a God who shaped history: "I obey thee, O Lord, first because of the love which I ought reasonably to bear thee; secondly, because thou knowest how to shorten or prolong the lives of men." (For III 29 r; MacCurdy, p. 80). He wrote this in the oldest extant notebook, during his first years in Milan.

13. A 24 r; MacCurdy, p. 519.

14. It is not that humanists thought of science as a purely theoretical pursuit. They certainly considered the practical implications, but they regarded it primarily as intellectual enrichment. The argumentation above is from Coluccio Salutati (1330–1406), who held the key political office of chancellor of Florence for three decades. Cited in Zubov, p. 92.

15. VU 12 r; MacCurdy, p. 87.

16. RL 19084; MacCurdy, p. 83.

17. CA 327 v (ex 119 v); MacCurdy, p. 232.

18. RL 19115 r; MacCurdy, p. 179.

19. RL 19102 r.

20. Kemp 1999, p. 263. On the back of RL 19102 v, he drew an embryo four to six weeks after conception. He distinguished the yolk ("lemon-yellow") from the "crystal clear" liquid of the amniotic fluid and the embryonic sac, known as the allantois. He also wondered why the liver is located in the center of the body of the unborn child at this stage, but later moves to the right side of the body. He was thus describing the development of the embryo in the earliest phase after conception.

On RL 19101 v, he contemplated the act of procreation at its inception: "The woman commonly has a desire quite the opposite of that of man. This is, that the woman likes the size of the genital member of the man to be as large as possible, and the man desires the opposite in the genital member of the woman, so that neither one nor the other ever attains his interest because Nature, who cannot be blamed, has so provided because of parturition." Quoted in O'Malley and Saunders, p. 480.

21. See Laurenza 2004.

22. RL 19102 r; MacCurdy, p. 173.

23. CA 166 r (ex 59 r-b); quoted in Nuland, p. 100.

24. RL 19001 r.; MacCurdy, p. 80.

25. B 4 v.; Irma Richter, p. 51.

26. H 33 v; MacCurdy, p. 71.

27. Frommel 1964.

28. CA 207 v (ex 76 v a); MacCurdy, p. 63.

29. Ar 158 r; MacCurdy, p. 1128.

30. Triv 34 v, p. 68; Irma Richter, p. 274.

31. Clark counts RL 12377 to RL 12386 as the Deluge series. RL 12376, a picture of scattered horsemen, apparently belongs just before it.

32. RL 12380 r.

33. Ar 156 v.; MacCurdy, p. 75.

EPILOGUE

1. CA 671 r (ex 247 v-b); MacCurdy, pp. 1141–1142.

2. CA 680 r (ex 252 r-a); Pedretti 1975.

3. Cellini, pp. 858–860; quoted in Turner, p. 52.

4. CA 785 b-v (ex 289 v-c); MacCurdy, p. 88.

5. The dated sheet is CA 673 r (ex 249 r-a-b). "Etcetera" is on Ar 245 r, but this quite obviously belongs with CA 673 r. The two sheets have the identical black markings, and Leonardo's handwriting, pen strokes, and triangular diagrams are unvarying. We may therefore assume that Leonardo worked on CA 673 r and Ar 245 r on the same day (Pedretti 1975).

6. These data are from the Population Reference Bureau, Washington, D.C.

7. RL 12283 r, which Carlo Pedretti has aptly called a "Theme Sheet."

8. Juggling images and shapes in the mind places high demands on the perceptive faculty. Neuropsychological research has shown that mental imagery and perception are essentially based on the same brain functions. They are almost like two sides of the same coin. Careful perception sharpens the ability to think in images, and vice versa. Experiments by Roger Shepard and Jacqueline Metzler provided the first substantiation for spatial thinking. These two cognitive psychologists showed subjects illustrations of several contraptions that looked like a cross between a Rubik's cube and an IKEA wrench. Some of these shapes were dissimilar, others were identical but in different orientations. The more twisted the shapes, the longer it took the test subjects to figure this out. Evidently the rotation in their mind's eye functioned exactly as though the subjects were actually holding the objects in their hands and watching them rotate. Since then, many experiments have confirmed an extremely close link between perception and mental imagery in other arenas. When it comes to colors, shapes, sounds, or faces, the brain uses the same regions when processing sensations as it does when indulging in flights of fancy. See Shepard and Metzler. For an extensive current overview of the connection between visual perception and visual mental imagery, see Bartolomeo and the literature cited there.

9. "If you look at any walls spotted with various stains or with a mixture of different kinds of stones . . . you will be able to see in it a resemblance to a variety of landscapes adorned with mountains, rivers, rocks, trees, plains, wide valleys and various groups of hills. You will also be able to see diverse combats and figures in quick movement, and strange expressions of faces, and outlandish costumes, and an infinite number of things which you can then reduce into separate and well-conceived forms." BN 2037 22 v;

MacCurdy, p. 873–874. My book *Alles Zufall* (All a Matter of Chance) contains a long discussion on the foundation of this method.

10. Modern longitudinal studies substantiate the importance of an early teacher-student relationship in the lives of people who have made significant contributions to their disciplines. Cognitive psychologist Benjamin Bloom made an exhaustive analysis of this issue in 1985 when interviewing the 120 top young American pianists, sculptors, mathematicians, and brain researchers. There was little in their early childhood to indicate their spectacular gifts and likelihood of future success apart from their dogged determination—and the degree of support they had from adults. Their parents were typically willing to make great sacrifices of time and money for their children's careers; sometimes they even moved to a new town so that their children could have better teachers. Strikingly often, the young people who achieved fame in their fields reported that they had a strong bond with their mentors. Great achievements thrive in a climate of emotional closeness. Bloom summarized his findings with the statement that he had sought out extraordinary *children*, but had found extraordinary *circumstances*.

In any case, great accomplishments cannot be explained solely on the basis of a high degree of giftedness. Longitudinal studies have also shown that the vast majority of the highly gifted do not demonstrate unusual achievements at any point in their lives. (See Terman; also Subotnik et al. The Marburg Giftedness Project in Germany has conducted one of Europe's largest longitudinal studies of the development of the highly gifted and of high achievers; see Rost 2000.)

By the same token, extraordinary success in life does not necessarily imply extraordinary intelligence. The majority of those who stand out in the sciences, as artists, or as chess grandmasters have above-average IQs ranging between 115 and 130 (see Dobbs; Ross), but that is not a very high bar, because 14% of the population falls in that range. In Germany alone, that adds up to more than eleven million men and women.

Surveys of the most gifted artists and scientists and of top-ranked athletes consistently show that they worked much harder to foster their talents from an early age than their less accomplished peers. They consistently take on challenges that lie beyond their current capabilities, and do not give up until they have surmounted any hurdles. Their success ultimately depends on this tenacity. No matter what the field of endeavor, people nearly always overestimate the role of talent and underestimate the extents to which training determines success. Without tireless effort, the best talents never amount to anything. (A 2006 study by Ericsson et al. offers extensive data on this subject. In Ericsson's extreme, but influential and well-founded view, the quantity and quality of practice are the sole crucial factors in determining the standard of performance that people achieve. See Ericsson and Lehman.)

11. Perugino, Lorenzo di Credi, and several others who were able to make names for themselves on the competitive Florentine market did their training in his workshop.

12. Vecce 1998.

13. CA 692 r (ex CA 257 r-b).

14. RL 12701.

BIBLIOGRAPHY

Leonardo's Manuscripts
A-M, BN 2037, BN 2038 Paris Manuscripts, Institut de France (Mss 2172–2185)
Facsimile edition: I manuscritti dell'Institut de France, ed. Augusto Marinoni. 12 vols.
    Florence, 1986–1990.

Ar Codex Arundel, British Museum, London (Arundel MS 263). 283 sheets in a typical
    format of 210 x 50 mm.
Facsimile edition: Il Codice Arundel, 263, ed. Carlo Pedretti and Carlo Vecce, Florence,
    1998, with a chronological rearrangement of the sheets.

CA Codex Atlanticus, Biblioteca Ambrosiana, Milan. Collection of diverse drawings
    and writings that earlier consisted of 401 large-format (645 x 435 mm) sheets com-
    piled by Pompeo Leoni in the sixteenth century and made into an edition of 12
    volumes with a total of 1,119 pages between 1962 and 1970. The marked difference
    in length came about because many pages of the old compilation had smaller pieces
    affixed to them, and these were detached in the new one. Because the old numbering
    system is still often used in the secondary literature, I have provided it alongside
    the new numbering. Thus, CA 52r (ex 191 r-a) refers to the front side (recto) of
    the new page 52, which was formerly designated as part "a" on the front side of
    Sheet 191.
Facsimile edition: Il Codice Atlantico, ed. Augusto Marinoni. 24 vols. Florence, 1973–
    1980.

For Codices Forster, Victoria & Albert Museum, London. 3 vols. with 5 diaries: Fors 1¹, 40 sheets; Fors 1², 14 sheets, 135 x 103 mm; Fors 2¹, 63 sheets; Fors 2², 96 sheets, 95 x 70 mm; Fors 3, 88 sheets, 94 x 65 mm.
Facsimile edition: I Codici Forster, ed. Augusto Marinoni. 3 vols. Florence, 1992.

GDS Gabinetto dei Disegni e delle Stampe, Uffizi, Florence.

Leic Codex Leicester, Bill Gates Collection, Seattle, 88 sheets, 94 x 65 mm. Formerly known as Codex Hammer.
Facsimile edition: The Codex Hammer, ed. Carlo Pedretti, Florence, 1987.

Ma Codices Madrid, Biblioteca Nacional, Madrid (MSS 8936/8937). Ma I, 184 sheets, 149 x 212 mm; Ma II, 157 sheets, mostly 148 x 212 mm.
Facsimile edition: The Madrid Codices, ed. Ladislao Reti. New York, 1974.

RL Royal Library, Windsor. Collection of 655 drawings and manuscripts, designated sheet by sheet as nos. 12275–12727 (general) and nos. 19000–19152 (anatomical). The anatomical sheets were previously compiled in three volumes: Anatomical mss. A (RL 19000–19017), B (RL 19018–19059), and C, which was divided into six anatomical diaries "Quaderni di anatomia I-VI" (RL 19060–19152).
Facsimile editions: The Drawings of Leonardo da Vinci in the Collection of Her Majesty the Queen, ed. Kenneth Clark and Carlo Pedretti. 3 vols. London: Phaidon, 1968.

TP Biblioteca Vaticana, Codex Urbinas Latinus 1270. Selection of diverse diaries and manuscripts compiled by Francesco Melzi ca. 1530; an abridged version was published as Trattato della pittura. Paris 1651.

Triv Codex Trivulziano, Castello Sforzesca, Milan, Biblioteca Trivulziana MS N2162, 55 sheets, 195 x 135 mm.
Facsimile edition: Il codice nella Biblioteca Trivulziana, ed. A. Brizio. Florence, 1980.

VU Manuscript about the flight of birds, Biblioteca Reale, Turin, 13 sheets, 213 x 153 mm.
Facsimile edition: Il Codice sul volo degli uccelli, ed. Augusto Marinoni. Florence, 1976.

Anthologies and Commentaries
Chastel, André, ed. *Leonardo da Vinci: Sämtliche Gemälde und die Schriften zur Malerei.* Trans. Marianne Schneider. Munich: Schirmer-Mosel, 1990.
Lücke, Theodor, ed. *Leonardo da Vinci: Tagebücher und Aufzeichnungen.* Leipzig: List Verlag, 1952.
MacCurdy, Edward, ed. *The Notebooks of Leonardo da Vinci.* New York: George Braziller, 1958.

McMahon, A. Philip. *The Treatise on Painting by Leonardo da Vinci*. 2 vols. Princeton, NJ: Princeton University Press, 1956.

Richter, Irma A., ed. *The Notebooks of Leonardo da Vinci*. New York: Oxford University Press, 1952.

Richter, Jean Paul, ed. *The Literary Works of Leonardo da Vinci*. 2 vols. London: Oxford, 1939.

SECONDARY LITERATURE

Ackerman, James S. "Leonardo's Eye." *Journal of the Warburg and Courtauld Institutes* 41 (1978): 108–146.

Alberti, Leon Battista. *On Painting*. Trans. Cecil Grayson. London: Penguin, 1991.

Alberti de Mazzeri, Silvia. *Leonardo: Die moderne Deutung eines Universalgenies*. Munich: Heyne, 1995.

Andenna, Giancarlo, et al. *Storia d'Italia*. Vol. 6: *La Lombardia*. Turin: Einaudi, 1998.

Arasse, Daniel. *Leonardo da Vinci*. Old Saybrook, CT: William S. Konecky Associates, 1998.

Bartolomeo, Paolo. "The Relationship between Visual Perception and Visual Mental Imagery: A Reappraisal of the Neuropsychological Evidence." *Cortex* 38 (2002): 357–378.

Bauer, Joachim. *Warum ich fühle, was du fühlst: Intuitive Kommunikation und das Geheimnis der Spiegelneurone*. Hamburg: Hoffmann & Campe, 2005.

Behringer, Wolfgang, and Constance Ott-Koptschalijski. *Der Traum vom Fliegen*. Frankfurt: S. Fischer, 1991.

Beltrame, Giovanni. "Leonardo, I navigli milanesi e I disegni Windsor RL 12399 e MS H f 80 r." *Raccolta Vinciana* 22 (1987): 271–289.

Beltrami, Luca. *Documenti e memorie riguardanti la vita e le opere di Leonardo da Vinci in ordine cronologico*. Milan: Fratelli Treves, 1919.

Benivieni, Antonio. *De abditis nonnullis ac mirandis morborum et sanationum causis* [1507]. Rpt. Florence: Olschki, 1994.

Bloom, Benjamin. *Developing Talent in Young People*. New York: Ballantine, 1985.

Boffito, Giuseppe. *Il volo in Italia*. Florence: Barbera, 1921.

Brown, David Alan. *Leonardo da Vinci: Origins of a Genius*. New Haven, CT: Yale University Press, 1998.

Burckhardt, Jacob. *The Civilization of the Renaissance in Italy*. Trans. S. G. C. Middlemore. New York: Penguin, 1990.

Burke, Peter. *The Italian Renaissance: Culture and Society in Italy*. Princeton, NJ: Princeton University Press, 1999.

Büttner, Nils. *Geschichte der Landschaftsmalerei*. Munich: Hirmer, 2006.

Calvi, Gerolamo. *I manoscritti di Leonardo da Vinci*. Bologna: Zanichelli, 1925.

Capra, Fritjof. *The Science of Leonardo*. New York: Doubleday, 2007.

Cardano, Girolamo. *De subtilitate libri XXI*. Basel 1554, 1611.

Cellini, Benvenuto. *Opere*. Ed. Bruno Maier. Milan: Rizzoli, 1968.

Chastel, André. *Leonardo da Vinci: Studi e ricerche*. Turin: Einaudi, 1995.

Cirigliano, Marc A. *Melancolia Poetica*. Leicester: Troubador Publishing, 2007.

Clagett, Marshall. "Mechanics, an Excerpt from the Leonardo da Vinci Entry." In Claire Farago, ed. *Leonardo's Science and Technology*. New York: Routledge, 1999, pp. 1–20.

Clark, Kenneth. "Mona Lisa." *The Burlington Magazine* 115, no. 840 (1973): 144–151.

Cloulas, Ivan. *César Borgia: Fils du Pape, Prince et Aventurier*. Paris: Tallendier, 2005.

Daston, Lorraine, and Katharine Park. *Wonders and the Order of Nature, 1150–1750*. New York: Zone Books, 1998.

Della Peruta, Franco, ed. *Storia di Milano*. Milan: Elio Sellino, 1993.

Diana, Esther. "Società 'Corpo Morto,' Anatomia: I luoghi e I personaggi." In Enrico Ghidetti, ed. *Anatomia e storia dell'anatomia a Firenze*. Florence: Edizioni Medicea, 1996, pp. 9–41.

Dibner, Bern. "Machines and Weaponry." In Ludwig Heydenreich, Bern Dibner, and Ladislao Reti. *Leonardo the Inventor*. London: Hutchinson, 1981, pp. 72–123.

Dobbs, David. "How to Be a Genius." *New Scientist*, September 15, 2006, 40–43.

Ekman, Paul, and J. C. Hager. "The Inner and Outer Meanings of Facial Expressions." In John T. Cacioppo and Richard E. Petty, eds. *Social Psychophysiology*. New York: Guilford Press, 1983, pp. 287–306.

Ericsson, K. Anders, and A. C. Lehman. "Expert and Exceptional Performance: Evidence on Maximal Adaptations on Task Constraints." *Annual Review of Psychology* 47 (1996): 273–305.

Ericsson, K. Anders, et al., eds. *The Cambridge Handbook of Expertise and Expert Performance*. Cambridge: Cambridge University Press, 2006.

Fiocca, Alessandra, ed. *Arte e scienza delle acque nel Rinascimento*. Venice: Marsilio, 2003.

Frommel, Christoph Luitpold. "Leonardo fratello della Confraternità della Pietà dei Fiorentini a Roma." *Raccolta Vinciana* 20 (1964): 369–373.

Galluzzi, Paolo. *Renaissance Engineers*. Florence: Giunti Editore, 1996.

Galluzzi, Paolo, ed. *The Mind of Leonardo: The Universal Genius at Work*. Trans. Catherine Frost and Joan M. Reifsnyder. Florence: Giunti Editore, 2006.

Gardner, Howard. *Creating Minds*. New York: Basic Books, 1993.

Garin, Eugenio. "La cultura a Milano alla fine del Quattrocento." In Eugenio Garin, *Umanisti, artisti, scienziati. Studi sul Rinascimento italiano*. Rome: Riuniti, 1989, pp. 189–204.

Ghidetti, Enrico, and Esther Diana, eds. *La bellezza come terapia*. Florence: Edizioni Polistampa, 2005.

Giacomelli, Raffaele. *Gli scritti di Leonardo da Vinci sul volo*. Rome: Dott. G. Bardi, 1936.

Gille, Bertrand. *The Engineers of the Renaissance*. Cambridge, MA: MIT Press, 1966.

Goldscheider, Ludwig. *Leonardo da Vinci*. London: Phaidon, 1948.

Gombrich, Ernst. "Leonardo and the Magicians: Polemics and Rivalry." In Ernst Gombrich, *New Light on Old Masters. Studies in the Art of the Renaissance, no. IV*. Chicago: University of Chicago Press, 1986, pp. 61–88.

———. *The Story of Art*. Englewood Cliffs, NJ: Prentice Hall, 1998.

———. "The Form of Movement in Water and Air." In Claire Farago, ed. *Leonardo's Science and Technology*. New York: Routledge, 1999, pp. 311–344.

Grafton, Anthony. *Leon Battista Alberti: Master Builder of the Italian Renaissance*. Cambridge, MA: Harvard University Press, 2002.

Henderson, John. *The Renaissance Hospital*. New Haven, CT: Yale University Press, 2006.

Henderson, John, and K. P. Park. "'The First Hospital Among Christians': The Ospedale di Santa Maria Nuova in Early Sixteenth-Century Florence." *Medical History* 35 (1991): 164–188.

Heydenreich, Ludwig. *Leonardo da Vinci*. New York: Macmillan, 1954.

Howe, Michael, et al. "Innate Talents: Reality or Myth?" *Behavioral and Brain Sciences* 21 (1998): 399–442.

Kecks, Ronald. "Naturstudium und ikonographische Bildtradition." In Wolfram Prinz and Andreas Beyer, eds. *Die Kunst und das Studium der Natur vom 14 zum 16. Jahrhundert*. Weinheim: Wiley-VCH, 1987, pp. 289–305.

Keele, Kenneth David. *Leonardo da Vinci. Elements of the Science of Man*. New York: Academic Press, 1983.

Kemp, Martin. "'Il Concerto dell'Anima' in Leonardo's Early Skull Studies." *Journal of the Warburg and Courtauld Institutes* 34 (1971): 115–134.

———. *Leonardo da Vinci: The Marvellous Works of Nature and Man*. London: Oxford University Press, 1981.

———. "Dissection and Divinity in Leonardo's Late Anatomies." In Claire Farago, ed. *Leonardo's Science and Technology*. New York: Routledge, 1999, pp. 230–264.

———. *Leonardo da Vinci: Experience, Experiment, and Design*. Princeton, NJ: Princeton University Press, 2006.

Kilner, Philip J., et al. "Asymmetric Redirection of Flow Through the Heart." *Nature* 404 (2000): 759–761.

Klein, Stefan. *Alles Zufall*. Reinbek: Rowohlt, 2004.

———. *The Science of Happiness*. Trans. Stephen Lehmann. New York: Da Capo Press, 2006.

Kontsevich, Leonid L., and Christopher W. Tyler. "What Makes Mona Lisa Smile?" *Vision Research* 44 (2004): 1493–1498.

Kristeller, Paul. *Renaissance Concepts of Man and Other Essays*. New York: Harper & Row, 1972.

Laurenza, Domenico. *Künstler, Forscher, Ingenieur: Leonardo da Vinci*. Heidelberg: Spektrum der Wissenschaft Biografie, 2000.

———. *Leonardo nella Roma di Leone X*. XLIII Lettura Vinciana. Florence: Giunti Editore, 2004.

———. *Leonardo on Flight*. Baltimore: The Johns Hopkins University Press, 2007.

Lomazzo, Gian Paolo. *Idea del tempio della pittura*. Milan: P. G. Ponzio, 1590.

———. *Scritte sulle arti*. Ed. R. P. Ciardi. Florence: Marchi & Bertolli, 1973.

Lombardini, Elia. *Dell'origine e del progresso della scienza idraulica*. Milan: Saldini, 1872.

Losano, Mario G. *Automi d'Oriente*. Milan: Medusa Edizioni, 2003.

Lüdecke, Heinz. *Leonardo da Vinci im Spiegel seiner Zeit*. Berlin: Rütten & Loening, 1952.

Luporini, Cesare. *La mente di Leonardo*. Florence: Le Lettere, 1953.

Lykken, David. "The Genetics of Genius." In Andrew Steptoe, ed. *Genius and the Mind: Studies of Creativity and Temperament in the Historical Record*. New York: Oxford University Press, 1998, pp.15–37.

Macagno, Emmanuel. "Lagrangian and Eulerian Descriptions in the Flow Studies of Leonardo da Vinci." *Raccoalta Vinciana* 24 (1992): 251–276.

Machiavelli, Niccolò. *The Essential Writings of Machiavelli*. Ed. and trans. Peter Constantine. New York: Modern Library, 2007.

Marani, Pietro. *L'architettura fortificata negli studi di Leonardo da Vinci*. Florence: Olschki, 1984.

Marinoni, Augusto. "Leonardo's Writings." In Carlo Zammattio, Augusto Marinoni, and Anna Maria Brazio, *Leonardo the Scientist*. London: Hutchinson, 1981, pp. 68–123.

Marx, Karl Friedrich Heinrich. "Über Marc'Antonio della Torre und Leonardo da Vinci: Die Begründer der bildlichen Anatomie." *Abhandlungen der K. Gesellschaft der Wissenschaften zu Göttingen* 4 (1847): 131–148.

Maschat, Herbert. *Leonardo da Vinci und die Technik der Renaissance*. Munich: Profil, 1989.

Masters, Roger D. *Machiavelli, Leonardo, and the Science of Power*. South Bend, IN: University of Notre Dame Press, 1996.

Mazenta, Ambrogio. *Le memories su Leonardo da Vinci*. Rpt. with illustrations by Don Luigi Gramatica. Milan: Alfieri & Lacroix, 1919.

Montanari, Massimo. *La storia di Imola dai primi insediamenti all'ancien régime*. Imola: La Mandragora Editrice, 2000.

Nicholls, Michael, et al. "Detecting Hemifacial Asymmetries in Emotional Expression with Three-Dimensional Computerized Image Analysis." *Proceedings of the Royal Society*, London, B 271 (2004): 663–668.

Nuland, Sherwin. *Leonardo da Vinci*. New York: Penguin, 2000.

Oberhummer, Eugen. "Leonardo da Vinci and the Art of the Renaissance in Its Relations to Geography." *The Geographical Journal* 33, no. 5 (May 1909): 540–569.

Olschki, Leonardo. *Geschichte der neusprachlichen wissenschaftlichen Literatur*. 3 vols. Heidelberg: Carl Winter, 1919–1927.

———. *The Genius of Italy*. New York: Oxford University Press, 1949.

O'Malley, Charles D., and J. B. de C. M. Saunders. *Leonardo da Vinci on the Human Body: The Anatomical, Physiological, and Embryological Drawings of Leonardo da Vinci*. New York: H. Schuman, 1952.

Oppenheimer, Paul. *Till Eulenspiegel: His Adventures*. Oxford: Routledge, 2001.

Pacioli, Luca. *De divina proportione*. Venice, 1509.

Panksepp, Jaak. *Affective Neuroscience. The Foundations of Human and Animal Emotions*. New York: Oxford University Press, 1998.

Park, Katharine. *Doctors and Medicine in Early Renaissance Florence*. Princeton, NJ: Princeton University Press, 1985.

Park, Katharine, and Lorraine Daston, eds. *The Cambridge History of Science*. Vol. 3: *Early Modern Science*. New York: Cambridge University Press, 2006.

Parsons, William Barclay. *Engineers and Engineering in the Renaissance*. Cambridge, MA: MIT Press, 1976.

Pater, Walter. "Leonardo da Vinci." In Walter Pater, *The Renaissance: Studies in Art and Literature*. Ed. Donald L. Hill. Berkeley: University of California Press, 1980, pp. 77–101.

Pedretti, Carlo. "Il codice di Benvenuto di Lorenzo della Golpaja." In *Studi vinciani: documenti, analisi e inediti leonardeschi*. Geneva: E Droz, 1957, pp. 23–33.

———. *Eccetera: perché la minestra si fredda*. Florence: Biblioteca Leonardiana, 1975.

———. *The Literary Works of Leonardo Da Vinci, Compiled and Edited from the Original Manuscripts by Jean Paul Richter: Commentary by Carlo Pedretti*. 2 vols. Oxford: Phaidon, 1977.

———. *Leonardo, Architect*. Trans. Sue Brill. New York: Rizzoli, 1985.

Pedretti, Carlo, ed. *Leonardo, Machiavelli, Cesare Borgia: arte storia e scienza in Romagna*. Rome: De Luca editori d'arte, 2003.

Perrig, Alexander. "Die theoretischen Landschaftsformen in der italienischen Malerei des 14. und 15. Jahrhunderts." In Wolfram Prinz and Andreas Beyer, eds. *Die Kunst und das Studium der Natur vom 14 zum 16. Jahrhundert*. Weinheim: Wiley-VCH, 1987, pp. 41–53.

Pidcock, M. "The Hang Glider." *Achademia Leonardi Vinci* 6 (1994): 222–225.

Pinto, John A. "Origins and Development of the Ichnographic City Plan." In Claire Farago, ed. *Leonardo's Science and Technology*. New York: Routledge, 1999, pp. 387–394.

Reti, Ladislao. "The Engineer." In Ludwig Heydenreich, Bern Dibner, and Ladislao Reti. *Leonardo the Inventor*. London: Hutchinson, 1981, pp. 124–185.

Rizzolatti, Giacomo, Leonardo Fogassi, and Vittorio Gallese. "Mirrors in the Mind." *Scientific American* 295, no. 5 (November 2006): 30–37.

Roberts, Jane. "The Early History of the Collecting of Drawings by Leonardo da Vinci." In Claire Farago, *An Overview of Leonardo's Career and Projects Until c. 1500*. New York: Taylor & Francis, 1999.

———. "An Introduction to Leonardo's Anatomical Drawings." In Frances Ames-Lewis, ed. *Nine Lectures on Leonardo da Vinci*. London: Birkbeck College, 1990.

Rosheim, Mark. *Leonardo's Lost Robots*. Berlin: Springer, 2006.

Ross, Philip E. "The Expert Mind." *Scientific American* 295, no. 2 (August 2006): 64–71.

Rost, Detlef, ed. *Hochbegabte und hochleistende Jugendliche: Neue Ergebnisse aus dem Marburger Hochbegabtenprojekt*. Münster: Waxmann, 2000.

Rudwick, Martin. *The Meaning of Fossils: Episodes in the History of Palaeontology*. Chicago: University of Chicago Press, 1972.

Sarton, George. *Six Wings: Men of Science in the Renaissance*. Bloomington: Indiana University Press, 1957.

Sassoon, Donald. *Mona Lisa: The History of the World's Most Famous Painting*. London: Harper Collins, 2001.

Schneider, Marianne. *Leonardo da Vinci. Eine Biografie in Zeugnissen, Selbstzeugnissen, Dokumenten und Bildern.* Munich: Schirmer/Mosel, 2002.

Schwartz, Lillian F. "The Mona Lisa Identification: Evidence from a Computer Analysis." *The Visual Computer* 4 (1988): 40–48.

———. "The Art Historian's Computer." *Scientific American* 293, no. 3 (April 1995): 80–85.

Shepard, Roger, and Jacqueline Metzler. "Mental Rotation of Three-Dimensional Objects." *Science* 171 (Feb. 17, 1971): 701–703.

Starnazzi, Carlo. *Leonardo: Water and Lands.* Florence: Grantour, 2002.

———. *Leonardo cartografo.* Florence: IGM, 2003.

Subotnik, Rena, et al. *Genius Revisited: High IQ Children Grown Up.* New York: Ablex Publishing, 1993.

Terman, Lewis, and Melita Oden. *The Gifted Group at Mid-Life: 35 Years' Follow-Up of the Superior Child.* Stanford, CA: Stanford University Press, 1959.

Turner, A. Richard. *Inventing Leonardo.* Berkeley: University of California Press, 1992.

Vaccari, Pietro, Edmondo Solmi, and Gaetano Panazza. *Leonardo da Vinci e Pavia.* Pavia: top. Ticinese di C. Busca, 1952.

Vallentin, Antonina. *Leonardo da Vinci: The Tragic Pursuit of Perfection.* Trans. E. W. Dickes. New York: Viking, 1938.

Vasari, Giorgio. *The Lives of the Artists.* Trans. George Bull. New York: Penguin, 1965.

Vecce, Carlo. "La Guarlanda." *Achademia Leonardi Vinci* 3 (1990): 51–72.

———. *Leonardo da Vinci.* Rome: Salerno Editrice, 1998.

Veltman, Kim. *Linear Perspective and the Visual Dimensions of Science and Art.* Munich: Deutscher Kunstverlag, 1986.

Walzer, W. "Kunst und Wissenschaft komplementär." In Wolfram Prinz and Andreas Beyer, eds. *Die Kunst und das Studium der Natur vom 14 zum 16. Jahrhundert.* Weinheim: Wiley-VCH, 1987, pp. 197–219.

Zeki, Semir. *Inner Vision: An Exploration of Art and the Brain.* New York: Oxford University Press, 2000.

Zöllner, Frank. *Leonardo da Vinci: The Complete Paintings and Drawings.* Cologne: Taschen, 2003.

Zubov, V. P. *Leonardo da Vinci.* Cambridge, MA: Harvard University Press, 1968.

Zwijnenberg, R. "Poren im Septum—Leonardo und die Anatomie." In Frank Fehrenbach, ed. *Leonardo da Vinci: Natur im Übergang.* Munich: Fink, 2002, pp. 57–80.

LIST OF ILLUSTRATIONS

ILLUSTRATIONS PLATES

ACKNOWLEDGMENTS

Several of the people who know Leonardo's work best generously allowed me to pick their brains while I was writing this book: Fabio Frosini, Paolo Galluzzi, Claudio Giorgione, Morteza Gharib, Martin Kemp, Pietro Marani, Carlo Pedretti, Mark Rosheim, and Francis Wells. This book would not have been possible without their extensive research and without their patience in answering my questions.

I owe an equal debt of gratitude to the people who familiarized me with the settings where Leonardo worked. Luisella Cerri guided me through the Mill of Mora Bassa, Giuseppe Petruzzo through the gorges of the Adda River, and Esther Diana through the vaults of the Ospedale Santa Maria Nuova. Steve Roberts and Judy Leden filled me in on their attempts to build and operate a flying machine using Leonardo's designs. Manfred Dietl and Andreas Winkelmann of the Charité Hospital in Berlin gave me a vivid introduction to anatomy.

I am greatly indebted to the obliging staff at the manuscript division of the Berlin State Library, the art library of the National Museums of Berlin, and the Biblioteca Leonardiana in Vinci. Giuseppe Garavaglia made available to me numerous documents in the Ente Raccolta Vinciana at the castle in Milan. Martin Clayton and Jean Cozens kindly granted me access to the private collections of Queen Elizabeth in Windsor Castle. My thanks go to all of them.

The historian Jörg Deventer gave me valuable pointers on the social history of the early modern age and went to the effort of checking through the entire manuscript to ensure its historical accuracy. Any remaining errors in the text are of course mine.

Monika Klein provided invaluable help with the source material. I would like to thank Ingrid and Felix Klein for their hospitality in Milan on several occasions.

Franz Stefan Bauer, Thomas de Padova, Volker Foertsch, and Florian Glässing (who also did an outstanding job in placing the book abroad) read earlier versions of the manuscript, and their thoughtful comments helped me improve the text. Hermann Hülsenberg guided my selection of the artwork.

I have had the pleasure and privilege of working with S. Fischer Verlag in the past, and this new project was equally delightful. I would like to thank everyone who transformed my words into a book, in particular my very dedicated editor, Peter Sillem; Katrin Bury, whose resourceful detective work brought together the book's set of illustrations; and, last but not least, Heidi Borhau, who devoted great energy to the book's publicity. Matthias Landwehr was, as always, the best agent there is.

I am deeply grateful to Shelley Frisch. Once again, it was a pleasure to work with her on this book, and once again, her flair for language and scholarly attention to detail so magnificently transformed my words into an English-language book that I cannot imagine how any author could wish for a better translator.

I am at a loss for words to convey my thanks to my beloved wife, Alexandra Rigos. Her unerring instinct for what makes a book good vastly improves my texts, in ways too numerous to mention. The neuroscientist Antonio Damasio once called his wife a "colleague, worst critic, best critic, and day-to-day source of inspiration and reason." I could not have put it better.

INDEX